Uncover 4

Ben Goldstein • Ceri Jones
with Kathryn O'Dell

Student's Book

CAMBRIDGE
UNIVERSITY PRESS

University Printing House, Cambridge CB2 8BS, United Kingdom

One Liberty Plaza, 20th Floor, New York, NY 10006, USA

477 Williamstown Road, Port Melbourne, VIC 3207, Australia

314–321, 3rd Floor, Plot 3, Splendor Forum, Jasola District Centre, New Delhi – 110025, India

103 Penang Road, #05-06/07, Visioncrest Commercial, Singapore 238467

Cambridge University Press is part of the University of Cambridge.

It furthers the University's mission by disseminating knowledge in the pursuit of education, learning and research at the highest international levels of excellence.

www.cambridge.org
Information on this title: www.cambridge.org/9781316643679

© Cambridge University Press 2017

This publication is in copyright. Subject to statutory exception and to the provisions of relevant collective licensing agreements, no reproduction of any part may take place without the written permission of Cambridge University Press.

First published 2017

20 19 18 17 16 15 14 13 12

Printed in Great Britain by CPI Group (UK) Ltd, Croydon CR0 4YY

A catalog record for this publication is available from the British Library

ISBN 978-1-107-49353-7 Student's Book 4
ISBN 978-1-107-49357-5 Student's Book with Online Workbook and Online Practice 4
ISBN 978-1-107-49367-4 Teacher's Book 4
ISBN 978-1-107-49364-3 Workbook with Online Practice 4
ISBN 978-1-107-49392-6 Presentation Plus Disc 4
ISBN 978-1-107-49386-5 Class Audio CDs 4
ISBN 978-1-107-49391-9 DVD 4

Additional resources for this publication at www.cambridge.org/uncover

Cambridge University Press has no responsibility for the persistence or accuracy of URLs for external or third-party Internet Web sites referred to in this publication and does not guarantee that any content on such Web sites is, or will remain, accurate or appropriate. Information regarding prices, travel timetables, and other factual information given in this work is correct at the time of first printing but Cambridge University Press does not guarantee the accuracy of such information thereafter.

Art direction, book design, layout services, and photo research: QBS Learning
Audio production: John Marshall Media

Acknowledgments

Many teachers, coordinators, and educators shared their opinions, their ideas, and their experience to help create *Uncover*. The authors and publisher would like to thank the following people and their schools for their help in shaping the series.

In Mexico:

María Nieves Maldonado Ortiz (Colegio Enrique Rébsamen); Héctor Guzmán Pineda (Liceo Europeo); Alfredo Salas López (Campus Universitario Siglo XXI); Rosalba Millán Martínez (IIPAC [Instituto Torres Quintero A.C.]); Alejandra Rubí Reyes Badillo (ISAS [Instituto San Angel del Sur]); José Enrique Gutiérrez Escalante (Centro Escolar Zama); Gabriela Juárez Hernández (Instituto de Estudios Básicos Amado Nervo); Patricia Morelos Alonso (Instituto Cultural Ingles, S.C.); Martha Patricia Arzate Fernández, (Colegio Valladolid); Teresa González, Eva Marina Sánchez Vega (Colegio Salesiano); María Dolores León Ramírez de Arellano, (Liceo Emperadores Aztecas); Esperanza Medina Cruz (Centro Educativo Francisco Larroyo); Nubia Nelly Martínez García (Salesiano Domingo Savio); Diana Gabriela González Benítez (Colegio Ghandi); Juan Carlos Luna Olmedo (Centro Escolar Zama); Dulce María Pascual Granados (Esc. Juan Palomo Martínez); Roberto González, Fernanda Audirac (Real Life English Center); Rocio Licea (Escuela Fundación Mier y Pesado); Diana Pombo (Great Union Institute); Jacobo Cortés Vázquez (Instituto María P. de Alvarado); Michael John Pryor (Colegio Salesiano Anáhuac Chapalita)

In Brazil:

Renata Condi de Souza (Colégio Rio Branco); Sônia Maria Bernal Leites (Colégio Rio Branco); Élcio Souza (Centro Universitário Anhaguera de São Paulo); Patricia Helena Nero (Private teacher); Célia Elisa Alves de Magalhães (Colégio Cruzeiro-Jacarepaguá); Lilia Beatriz Freitas Gussem (Escola Parque-Gávea); Sandra Maki Kuchiki (Easy Way Idiomas); Lucia Maria Abrão Pereira Lima (Colégio Santa Cruz-São Paulo); Deborah de Castro Ferroz de Lima Pinto (Mundinho Segmento); Clara Vianna Prado (Private teacher); Ligia Maria Fernandes Diniz (Escola Internacional de Alphaville); Penha Aparecida Gaspar Rodrigues (Colégio Salesiano Santa Teresinha); Silvia Castelan (Colégio Santa Catarina de Sena); Marcelo D'Elia (The Kids Club Guarulhos); Malyina Kazue Ono Leal (Colégio Bandeirantes); Nelma de Mattos Santana Alves (Private teacher); Mariana Martins Machado (Britannia Cultural); Lilian Bluvol Vaisman (Curso Oxford); Marcelle Belfort Duarte (Cultura Inglesa-Duque de Caxias); Paulo Dantas (Britannia International English); Anauã Carmo Vilhena (York Language Institute); Michele Amorim Estellita (Lemec – Lassance Modern English Course); Aida Setton (Colégio Uirapuru); Maria Lucia Zaorob (CEL-LEP); Marisa Veiga Lobato (Interlíngua Idiomas); Maria Virgínia Lebrón (Independent consultant); Maria Luiza Carmo (Colégio Guilherme Dumont Villares/CEL-LEP); Lucia Lima (Independent consultant); Malyina Kazue Ono Leal (Colégio Bandeirantes); Debora Schisler (Seven Idiomas); Helena Nagano (Cultura Inglesa); Alessandra de Campos (Alumni); Maria Lúcia Sciamarelli (Colégio Divina Providência); Catarina Kruppa (Cultura Inglesa); Roberto Costa (Freelance teacher/consultant); Patricia McKay Aronis (CEL-LEP); Claudia Beatriz Cavalieri (By the World Idiomas); Sérgio Lima (Vermont English School); Rita Miranda (IBI – [Instituto Batista de Idiomas]); Maria de Fátima Galery (Britain English School); Marlene Almeida (Teacher Trainer Consultant); Flávia Samarane (Colégio Logosófico); Maria Tereza Vianna (Greenwich Schools); Daniele Brauer (Cultura Inglesa/AMS Idiomas); Allessandra Cierno (Colégio Santa Dorotira); Helga Silva Nelken (Greenwich Schools/Colégio Edna Roriz); Regina Marta Bazzoni (Britain English School); Adriano Reis (Greenwich Schools); Vanessa Silva Freire de Andrade (Private teacher); Nilvane Guimarães (Colégio Santo Agostinho)

In Ecuador:

Santiago Proaño (Independent teacher trainer); Tania Abad (UDLA [Universidad de Las Americas]); Rosario Llerena (Colegio Isaac Newton); Paúl Viteri (Colegio Andino); Diego Maldonado (Central University); Verónica Vera (Colegio Tomás Moro); Mónica Sarauz (Colegio San Gabriel); Carolina Flores (Colegio APCH); Boris Cadena, Vinicio Reyes (Colegio Benalcázar); Deigo Ponce (Colegio Gonzaga); Byron Freire (Colegio Nuestra Señora del Rosario)

The authors and publisher would also like to thank the following contributors, script writers, and collaborators for their inspired work in creating *Uncover*:
Anna Whitcher, Janet Gokay, Kathryn O'Dell, Lynne Robertson and Dana Henricks

Unit	Vocabulary	Grammar	Listening	Conversation (Useful language)
1 Tell Me About It! pp. 2–11	■ Media ■ Time expressions	■ Past tense review ■ *used to* and *would* Grammar reference p. 106	■ Cell phones were huge!	■ Expressing interest and disinterest
2 Best Foot Forward pp. 12–21	■ Personal qualities ■ Phrasal verbs related to making progress	■ Present perfect with present perfect continuous ■ Past perfect with past perfect continuous Grammar reference p. 107	■ It's turned into so much more!	■ Showing concern
3 Planning for the Future pp. 22–31	■ Verbs of the future ■ Achievements	■ Future review ■ Future continuous and future perfect Grammar reference p. 108	■ The waters around you	■ Expressing cause and effect
4 What's Cooking? pp. 32–41	■ Cooking verbs ■ Adjectives describing foods	■ First conditional review ■ Zero conditional ■ Second conditional review Grammar reference p. 109	■ A taste test	■ Cooking instructions
5 Fame and Fortune pp. 42–51	■ Verbs expressing opinions ■ Adverbs of degree	■ Defining and non-defining relative clauses ■ Tag questions Grammar reference p. 110	■ I see your point, but. . .	■ Making a point

Unit 1–5 Review Game pp. 52–53

Writing	Reading	Video	Accuracy and fluency	Speaking outcomes
- A blog post about an event	- *Finding the Facts* - Reading to Write: *Crazy About Comics* - Culture: *Cinderella's Closet*	- *Real or Fake?* - *What music and fashion were your parents into?* - *Milan's Fashion Week*	- Not using *would* or *used to* for one-time events - Pronunciation of *used to*	I can . . . - talk about my news-watching habits. - talk about experiences in the past. - talk about habits in the past. - talk about a special event.
- A thank-you email for support	- *A Natural Born Climber* - Reading to Write: *Thanks for your help!* - Culture: *Leaving Home to Help*	- *Born to Dive* - *How have you helped a friend?* - *Shanghai Heights* - *The House of the Future* (CLIL Project p. 116)	- Separable and not separable phrasal verbs - Syllable stress	I can . . . - talk about a person's qualities. - talk about recent events. - talk about personal experiences. - talk about someone who has helped his/her family.
- An opinion essay	- *A Career in Space* - Reading to Write: *Leaving School Early* - Culture: *School in the Cloud*	- *What a Waste!* - *Are you saving up for something?* - *Mission: Possible?*	- Word order for future perfect - Elisions with silent *h* - Spelling the *-ing* forms	I can . . . - talk about people's plans for the future. - talk about plans for the near and distant future. - make predictions about the future. - discuss what schools will be like in the future.
- An article about a family dish	- *Food for Thought* - Reading to Write: *A Traditional Dish* - Culture: *Pots and Pans of the Past*	- *The Origin of Argan Oil* - *What would you make if you had to cook for your family?* - *Fruits of the Sea* - *You Are What You Eat* (CLIL Project p. 117)	- Using simple present with *if*, *when*, and *unless* to talk about the future - Word stress with conditionals	I can . . . - talk about how to prepare a simple dish. - talk about party preferences. - discuss imaginary situations in the future. - talk about traditional ways of cooking.
- A comparison/contrast essay	- *Celebrity Causes* - Reading to Write: *The Book Is Better!* - Culture: *Getting Paid for Your Opinions*	- *A Cool Experiment* - *How do you prepare for a sports event?* - *Trendsetters*	- Not repeating subjects in relative clauses - Intonation with tag questions	I can . . . - express opinions about different topics. - give reasons why I'd support a cause. - ask questions to confirm and find out information. - give my opinion about a movie, book, or fashion trend.

Unit	Vocabulary	Grammar	Listening	Conversation (Useful language)
6 It's the Little Things pp. 54–63	■ Everyday objects ■ Modifiers	■ Passive infinitive ■ Review of causative *have/get* Grammar reference p. 111	■ All kinds of unusual things	■ Buying a gadget
7 Have a Ball! pp. 64–73	■ Celebration phrases ■ Descriptive adjectives	■ verb + *-ing* form (gerund) or infinitive ■ *-ing* form (gerund) as subject ■ *by/for* + *-ing* form Grammar reference p. 112	■ Weird and wonderful celebrations	■ Making exclamations
8 Mysteries and Secrets pp. 74–83	■ Adjectives with *un-* ■ Reporting verbs	■ Time clauses ■ Present participle clauses ■ Reported speech ■ Indirect questions Grammar reference p. 113	■ A mysterious act of kindness	■ Confirming and denying
9 Weird and Wonderful pp. 84–93	■ Story elements ■ Linking phrases	■ Third conditional ■ *wish* + past perfect ■ Past modals of speculation Grammar reference p. 114	■ Who or what is a hoodoo?	■ Asking for more information
10 I Have To! I Can! pp. 94–103	■ Training and qualifications ■ Jobs	■ Past ability ■ Modal expressions for past and future ■ *make* and *let* Grammar reference p. 115	■ Job talk	■ Making decisions

Unit 6–10 Review Game pp. 104–105

Writing	Reading	Video	Accuracy and fluency	Speaking outcomes
A product review for a gadget	*Light in a Bottle* Reading to Write: *Let's Hear It For Headphones!* Culture: *Before There Was Texting*	*Survival Obects* *What's your favorite gadget?* *The Start of the Web* *Inside the Guitar* (CLIL Project p. 118)	*get/have* for actions done for someone else dropping consonant sounds with *kind of*	I can . . . talk about everyday objects and why they're important. talk about new uses for everyday objects. talk about inventions. talk about how inventions have changed the world.
A description of a celebration	*How to Plan a Party* Reading to Write: *A Great Family Party!* Culture: *Korea: Coming of Age*	*Let's Celebrate* *What's the worst party you've ever been to?* *Like Father, Like Daughter*	Using *so* and *too* Word stress with verb + infinitive	I can . . . talk about party preparations and activities. plan an end-of-school party. describe events and festivals. talk about coming-of-age celebrations.
A story about a secret	*A Secret Under the Street* Reading to Write: *The Secret Room* Culture: *An Unbelievable Book*	*A Lost Civilization* *What's the biggest lie you've ever been told?* *Mysteries of the Brain* *Reliving History* (CLIL Project p. 119)	Time clauses in present tense with future Intonation with indirect questions	I can . . . describe unusual events. talk about an imaginary discovery. solve a mystery by using reported speech and questions. discuss world mysteries.
A story about an event	*Lucky's Luck* Reading to Write: *Bicycle Accident!* Culture: *Mesa Verde: Homes Up High*	*On the Run* *What's the biggest mistake you've ever made?* *Insectmobile*	*so that* and *in order to* Shortening *had* and *would* with third conditional	I can . . . talk about the story elements in a story. talk about imaginary situations in the past. discuss possible explanations for past events. talk about what my life might have been like in the past.
A biography about a musician	*Building a Dream* Reading to Write: *A Singing Star* Culture: *Young and Talented Australians*	*Future Directions* *What do you see yourself doing ten years from now?* *The Young and the Brave* *Lions in Danger* (CLIL Project p. 120)	Not using *could* for ability in certain cases Eliding words ending in vowels with words beginning with vowels	I can . . . talk about my plans after graduation. discuss careers and abilities. talk about my abilities and obligations in the past. compare someone's abilities and obligations to mine.

Irregular verbs p. 121

1 Tell Me About It!

Discovery EDUCATION

BE CURIOUS

Real or Fake?

What music and fashion were your parents into?

Milan's Fashion Week

1. How much information can you see in this photo? How does it make you feel?

2. How do you get information about local or world events?

3. What important things are happening in your area right now?

UNIT CONTENTS

Vocabulary Media; Time expressions
Grammar Past tense review; Review of *used to* + infinitive and *would*
Listening Cell phones were huge!

2 | Unit 1

Vocabulary: Media

1. Complete the sentences.

article	interview	report
blogger	✓ news / the news	reporter
headline	paper	review

Zoo-mania
A tiger escaped from the zoo yesterday.

Escape to Wonder Mountain
★★★★
Escape to Wonder Mountain is an exciting action film that takes place in Canada.

1. I watch __the news__ on TV every night. My brother gets his __news__ online.
2. Did you see the big _____ in today's _____? The _____ is about a tiger escaping from the zoo.
3. The _____ did an _____ with a local teen about a neighborhood fire.
4. I'm going to read the _____ before I go see that movie.
5. The _____ wrote about common trends in teen fashion on her website. She included a _____ about the most popular places to shop.

2. Listen, check, and repeat.

3. Work with a partner. Put the words from Exercise 1 in the correct categories. Some words can go in more than one category.

Things you read	Things you watch	Things you listen to	People
article			

Speaking: My news

4. YOUR TURN Work with a partner. When was the last time you did each of these things? Explain what each one was about.

- ☐ watched the news on TV
- ☐ watched the news online
- ☐ read an article in the paper
- ☐ read a review of a product, movie, or music album
- ☐ read or watched an interview

I watched the news on TV last night. I saw a report about . . .

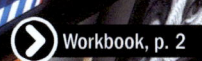
Workbook, p. 2

Reading Finding the Facts; Crazy About Comics; Cinderella's Closet
Conversation Expressing interest and disinterest
Writing A blog post about an event

It isn't always NEWS.

FINDING THE FACTS
Redo

You worked hard on your report for school. You read articles online. You even watched online videos. You thought you did well, but you got the report back from your teacher, and she said that you had to do it again. What did you do wrong? Well, when you were doing your research, you believed everything that was written on the Internet!

A lot of information on the Internet isn't true. Anyone can post information online. A lot of news *looks* real, but contains false information. Sometimes, an article is entirely false. Fake photographs have even been posted with some news stories. Because of this common problem, many websites have been developed to give people true information.

Snopes.com gives people information about urban legends, myths, and other false stories. Many people have used the website to find out whether a story is true or false. For example, there have been a lot of stories online that said that Bill Gates was giving people free laptops. However, Snopes.com reported this wasn't true.

Factcheck.org gives true information about what leaders in the United States say and do. It tells readers when stories aren't true. People who work at Factcheck.org believe that reporters should be honest all of the time and that the news should always be true.

Do you want true information about a person or event in history? WhoWhatWhen gives information about famous people and events from 1000 AD to today. You can even create a timeline of events based on a famous person's life. Do you want to know if the television was invented during Gandhi's lifetime? WhoWhatWhen can tell you!

Be careful when you write reports and use the Internet for research. Check your facts on websites like these and other sites that you know have true information!

> **DID YOU KNOW...?**
> Some websites create false news stories as a joke. These are called *satire websites*.

Reading: An article about checking facts

1. Look at the title and the pictures. Why do you think the boy might have to write his report again?

2. Read and listen to the article. What should students do before they write a report?

3. Read the article again. Answer the questions.

   1. Why is there a lot of false information on the Internet?
      _____

   2. Which fact-checking website would you use to find out if something the current US president said were true?
      _____

   3. Which website could you use to find out if it were possible for Elvis Presley to use a computer?
      _____

   4. Which website tells whether an urban legend is true or false?
      _____

4. **YOUR TURN** Work with a partner. What false stories have you read or heard about?

   > *I read that you can charge your smartphone with an onion, but it isn't true.*

4 | Unit 1

Grammar: Past tense review

5. Complete the chart.

Simple past
Use simple past statements to talk about past events and activities.

Regular	Irregular
What **did** you **believe**? I _____ everything on the Internet. We **didn't believe** the story.	What _____ she **write**? She **wrote** a report for school. She **didn't write** a blog post.

Past continuous
Use the past continuous to talk about activities that were in progress in the past. To form the past continuous use was/were + present participle (-ing form).

What _____ you _____ wrong?
I **was using** incorrect information. I **wasn't checking** my facts.

Present perfect
Use the present perfect to talk about experiences that happened at an indefinite time in the past. To form the present perfect, use has/have + the past participle.

Who **has used** Snopes.com?
Many people _____ the website! I **haven't used** it before.

> Check your answers: Grammar reference, p. 106

6. Complete the conversations with the correct form of the verbs in the questions. ✓ = yes, ✗ = no.

1. **A:** What were you watching last night?
   B: I _was watching_ (✓) the news. I _____ (✗) a movie.

2. **A:** Who has seen my keys?
   B: Peter _____ (✓) them. He _____ (✗) them today, though.

3. **A:** Where did Jackie go?
   B: She _____ (✓) to the store. She _____ (✗) to the market.

4. **A:** What were Tom and Jill posting online last night?
   B: They _____ (✓) a video. They _____ (✗) photos.

7. Write sentences. Use the form in parentheses.

1. the TV show / recorded / in April (past passive)
   The TV show was recorded in April.

2. the papers / not deliver (present perfect passive)
   _____

3. the report / file / in the main office (past passive)
   _____

4. the letters / open (present perfect passive)
   _____

5. the name of the reporter / not give (past passive)
   _____

Past passive and present perfect passive
Use the passive when it is not important who does the action, or when you don't know who does it.

Past passive
To form the past passive, use was/were + past participle.
The television **was invented** during Gandhi's lifetime. It **wasn't invented** during Abraham Lincoln's lifetime.

Present perfect passive
To form the present perfect passive, use has/have + been + past participle.
Fake photographs **have been posted** online. They **haven't been printed** in our newspaper.

Speaking: A newsworthy event

8. YOUR TURN Work with a partner. Talk about a time you did or saw something special on vacation.

> I went to a music festival last summer. It was in . . .

Find out about fake news and photos. How has technology changed the way we share information? (Workbook, p. 73)

1.1 REAL OR FAKE?

What Life WAS LIKE

Listening: Cell phones were huge!

1. Have you ever talked to your parents about what technology was like when they were young? How was it different from today?

2. Listen to Brandon talk to his mom about technology in the past. Check (✓) the things his mom DIDN'T have in high school.

   ☐ a smartphone   ☐ a phone in her room   ☐ a computer   ☐ a color TV

3. Listen again. Are the sentences true or false? Write *T* (true), *F* (false), or *NI* (no information).

   1. Brandon and his mom often watch old movies. ____
   2. Brandon's mom's best friend had a cell phone. ____
   3. Brandon's mom has a smartphone now. ____
   4. Brandon's mom had a computer in college. ____
   5. Brandon's mom did research at the library. ____
   6. Brandon's mom watched the news by herself. ____

Vocabulary: Time expressions

4. Underline the event that happened first. If the events happened at the same time, underline them both.

   1. I bought a new phone **after** I lost my old one.
   2. **As** I was watching a movie, my brother was playing a video game.
   3. I called Rick **as soon as** I found out the game was canceled.
   4. **Before** my dad left for work, he read the paper.
   5. **By the time** I got to the party, my friends were gone.
   6. **Every time** I had difficult homework, I asked my sister for help.
   7. I've watched video clips **since** my friend started posting them.
   8. I studied at the library **until** it was dark.
   9. **When** I got to the café, I sent Julia a text.
   10. **Whenever** I get together with my best friend, I feel happy.
   11. I read some reviews **while** I was online.

5. **YOUR TURN** Complete the sentences with a time expression from Exercise 4 and your own information.

   1. I've had a smartphone __since I was 12__.
   2. _____ something exciting happens, I call _____.
   3. _____ I turn 20, I _____.
   4. _____ I see my best friend, we _____.
   5. I do research online _____.

Grammar: Review of *used to* + infinitive and *would*

6. Complete the chart.

Use used to *or* would *for things that happened repeatedly in the past but don't happen now.*	
Where **did** she **use to do** research? She _____ **to do** it at the library. She **didn't use to have** a computer.	**Did** you _____ **to go** to the library? Yes, **I did**. No, **I didn't**.
When **would** you **watch** the news? I _____ it at 6:00. I **wouldn't watch** it online.	_____ they **watch** the news every night? Yes, they **would**. No, they **wouldn't**.
Use used to, *not* would, *for situations that happened in the past.*	
I **used to live** in Los Angeles. (NOT: ~~I would live~~ in Los Angeles.)	

> Check your answers: Grammar reference, p. 106

7. Complete the sentences with *would* when possible. When not possible, use *used to*.

My cousin ¹ _used to live_ (live) on a farm when he was a boy. As soon as he got up, he ² _____ (feed) the animals. He ³ _____ (not have) a computer or a smartphone when he was young. Every time he wanted to use a computer, he ⁴ _____ (go) to the library. I ⁵ _____ (not talk) to my cousin very much, but I ⁶ _____ (visit) him in the country sometimes. We ⁷ _____ (not play) inside – we were always outside. My sister and I ⁸ _____ (help) him with the animals. He ⁹ _____ (come) to our house in the city, too. He ¹⁰ _____ (love) playing my video games. When we got older, we ¹¹ _____ (not see) each other very much. I moved to the country, and my cousin moved to the city! Now, we both live in the city and see each other whenever we can. Where ¹² _____ (you / live) when you were young?

8. Rewrite the sentences. Change *used to* to *would*. If it's not possible, write X.

1. I used to swim every summer. ___*I would swim every summer.*___
2. Ellen used to be on a soccer team. _____
3. Jack and Terry used to play video games for hours. _____
4. I didn't use to have a phone in my room. _____
5. We didn't use to sleep late on the weekends. _____
6. Did you use to walk to school every day? _____
7. Where did Sara use to live? _____
8. When did they use to go on vacation? _____

> **Get it RIGHT!**
> Do not use **would** or **used to** for an event that happened once.
> I **watched** the news at 6:00 last night. (NOT: ~~I would watch the news at 6:00 last night.~~ ~~I used to watch the news at 6:00 last night.~~)

Speaking: My life in the past

9. **Work with a partner. Talk about your life 10 years ago. How does it compare to now? Use the ideas in the box and your own ideas.**

- how you got to school
- activities you did at school
- what technology you used/had
- what you did on the weekends

> I used to walk to school every day because I lived close to the school. But then we moved, so now I take the bus.

> I used public transportation when I was a kid. I would take the subway, and I take it now, too.

> **Say it RIGHT!**
> In sentences with **used to**, the **d** in *used* is often not pronounced and the **s** makes the /s/ sound.
> With **used** in the simple past, the **d** is pronounced and the **s** makes the /z/ sound. Listen to the differences in the sentences.
> She **used to** walk to school every day.
> He **used** public transportation.
> Pay attention to the way you say **used to** in Exercise 9.

 **REAL TALK** 1.2 WHAT MUSIC AND FASHION WERE YOUR PARENTS INTO?

Interests NOW and THEN

Conversation: Interests change.

1. **REAL TALK** Watch or listen to the teenagers talk about their parents' music and fashion in the past. Number the topics in the order you hear them.

_____ liked Michael Jackson	_____ liked the Beatles
_____ liked punk music	_____ liked pop music
_____ used to wear dresses with bows	_____ probably liked disco
_____ didn't like anything popular	_____ used to have pink hair

2. **YOUR TURN** What music and fashion were *your* parents into when they were growing up? Tell your partner.

3. Listen to Liz and Ivan talk about music. Complete the conversation.

USEFUL LANGUAGE: Expressing interest and disinterest

| crazy about | ✓really into | all about |
| not crazy about | not that into | can't stand |

Liz: I like your hair, Ivan.
Ivan: Thanks. I'm ¹ *really into* the punk look right now. The music, too.
Liz: What bands do you listen to?
Ivan: Well, I'm ² _____ the punk bands today. My mom used to listen to punk music, so I listen to all the bands she liked in the 1970s.
Liz: That's cool.
Ivan: What kind of music do you like?
Liz: Well, last year I was ³ _____ pop music, but this year I'm ⁴ _____ it. I listen to a lot of rap these days.
Ivan: I see. It's funny how interests change. Last year, I didn't know what punk music was, and now I'm ⁵ _____ it!
Liz: So what did you listen to last year?
Ivan: Rap music! Sorry, Liz, but now I ⁶ _____ it!
Liz: That's OK.

4. Practice the conversation with a partner.

5. **YOUR TURN** Work with a partner. Talk about your interests in the past and today. Use the situations in the chart or your own ideas.

What	When
music	last year and this year
fashion	five years ago and this year
sports/games	eight years ago and now

I'm really into rock music.

What bands do you listen to?

Last year, I really liked this local band, Volcanic Fire. But this year, I'm all about rock bands from the '80s like Joan Jett and the Blackhearts.

8 | Unit 1

CRAZY ABOUT COMICS

by Brian Campbell

I went to Comic-Con International in San Diego by myself last Saturday. It's an event for people who are crazy about comic books.

As soon as I got there, I went to a discussion group. Five comic book writers were talking about their comics. As I was leaving the room, I met one of the writers. It was an amazing experience because I myself hope to be a comic book writer someday! After that, I met a friend, and we bought comic books for ourselves. Some people who go to Comic-Con dress up as their favorite characters. I used to dress up as Rocket Raccoon, but this year, I went as Spider-Man. Comic-Con International is an amazing event. The best thing about it is meeting new people with similar interests.

Next year, Comic-Con International is in July. There are also Comic-Con events all over the world.

Reading to write: A blog post about an event

6. Look at the photo. What event do you think Brian went to? Read his blog post to check.

> **Focus on CONTENT**
> When you write about an event, present the information in this order:
> 1. Give general information about the event.
> 2. Give details about what you did or saw.
> 3. Give your opinion about the event.
> 4. Give information about the event in the future or similar events.

7. Read Brian's blog post again. What is the event? What did Brian do there? What does he think about the event?

> **Focus on LANGUAGE**
> You can use *reflexive* and *emphatic pronouns* in blogs. Use *emphatic pronouns* to emphasize a noun.
>
> | Reflexive | Emphatic |
> |---|---|
> | myself | I myself |
> | yourself / yourselves | you yourself / you yourselves |
> | herself / himself | she herself / he himself |
> | ourselves | we ourselves |
> | themselves | they themselves |
>
> I made dinner **myself**. My **mother herself** said it was delicious!

8. Find the reflexive and emphatic pronouns in Brian's blog.

9. Complete the sentences with pronouns from the Focus on Language box.
   1. The comic book writer _____ said that he was going to introduce a new character.
   2. I bought _____ three new video games.
   3. Lauren and Rafa learned about the problem _____ by reading articles online.
   4. We watched _____ in a video last night.
   5. You _____ said that the concert was boring.

Writing: Your blog post about an event

PLAN
You are going to write a blog post about an event. Think of an event you went to and write notes about it.

Name of the event	
Brief description of the event	
What you did or saw	
Your opinion of it	
Information about future or similar events	

WRITE
Write your blog post. Use your notes to help you. Write at least 125 words.

CHECK
Check your writing. Can you answer "yes" to these questions?

- Is information from the Focus on Content box in your blog post?
- Do you use reflexive and emphatic pronouns correctly?

Cinderella's Closet

Prom is a big dance that students in the United States go to in their last two years of high school. Girls usually wear beautiful dresses and boys often wear tuxedos. Prom can be very expensive, and some students can't afford the dresses and tuxedos. Two high school students, Stephanie Tomasetta and Katie Adams, wanted to change that.

Stephanie and Katie's organization, Cinderella's Closet, provides dresses and tuxedos for high school students in New Jersey who don't have enough money for prom clothes. They now have over 1,200 prom dresses. Each year, boys and girls come to "shop" for dresses and tuxedos. They wear them to prom and then return them. They also get shoes and jewelry. In 2014, over 500 students borrowed clothes for prom. Stephanie and Katie knew how to make the event special. Over 150 volunteers helped with the event. Most of the volunteers were high school students. Some of them were "personal shoppers." They helped other teens pick out clothing. Other volunteers gave girls advice on makeup.

Cinderella's Closet needs a lot of money for the dresses and tuxedos. For the past several years, Stephanie and Katie have become experts at raising money. One way they raise money is with a fashion show every year. People who attend the fashion show donate money. In 2014, they raised $40,000. It was a special event because teenagers designed and made the outfits for the show. About 40 high school boys and girls modeled the fashions for a big crowd. The audience voted on the best design. People who work in fashion also voted and gave several awards to the student designers.

Stephanie and Katie say that Cinderella's Closet isn't just about beautiful clothing. It's about making teenagers feel good about themselves, too.

Culture: An organization for prom fashions

1. Look at the photos and the title of the article. What do you think Cinderella's Closet is?

2. Read and listen to the article. Why did Stephanie and Katie start Cinderella's Closet?

3. Read the article again. Check (✓) the things that teenagers do for Cinderella's Closet.

   ☐ They sell dresses and tuxedos to students.
   ☐ They lend dresses and tuxedos to students.
   ☐ They volunteer and help other teens look for dresses.
   ☐ They donate money to the organization.
   ☐ They design clothes for the fashion show.
   ☐ They model at the fashion show.
   ☐ They work in fashion and voted at the fashion show.

4. **YOUR TURN** Work with a partner. What special dances or other events do you have at your school? What do teens wear or do for the events?

DID YOU KNOW...?

For some proms, students decorate their high school gyms for the dance. Other proms are at fancy hotels.

BE CURIOUS Find out about the Milan Fashion Show. Does the blogger want to be a model? Why or why not? (Workbook, p. 74)

1.3 MILAN'S FASHION WEEK

UNIT 1 REVIEW

Vocabulary

1. **Circle the correct answers.**
   1. As soon as I got home, I watched **the news** / **the article** on TV.
   2. After I wrote **a report** / **a reporter** for class, I emailed it to my teacher.
   3. I want to be **a headline** / **a reporter** for the school **paper** / **review** next year.
   4. My brother only reads the **headlines** / **paper**, but I like to read the entire **article** / **blogger**.
   5. Before I buy something online, I always read the **interview** / **reviews**.
   6. My aunt is **a report** / **a blogger**, and she does **interviews** / **news** with community members and then writes posts about them on her website.

Grammar

2. **Rewrite the sentences. Use the tense in parentheses.**
   1. I worked a lot yesterday. (past continuous)
      I was working a lot yesterday.
   2. Tara didn't pass her test. (present perfect)
      _____
   3. They wrote the story in two days. (past passive)
      _____
   4. Ricky works for a TV station. (simple past)
      _____
   5. Are you reading an interesting article? (past continuous)
      _____
   6. They have written the report in three languages. (present perfect passive)
      _____

3. **Complete the sentences with *would* when possible. When not possible, use *used to*.**
   1. When I was younger, I __would watch__ (watch) videos online. I _____ (look) at them all day long. I _____ (be) crazy about animal videos.
   2. My cousin _____ (live) in San Diego, but now he's in Denver. In San Diego, he _____ (go) to Comic-Con every year. He _____ (have) a comic book collection, but he sold it a few years ago.
   3. _____ (you / be) a reporter for your school paper? _____ (you / write) articles about important issues?

Useful language

4. **Circle the correct responses to complete the conversations.**
   1. **A:** Do you like punk music?
      B: ____. It's too loud, and I don't understand the words.
      a. I'm crazy about it.
      b. I'm not crazy about it.
   2. **A:** What do you think of big sunglasses?
      B: ____. I have three pairs!
      a. I'm really into them.
      b. I'm not really into them.
   3. **A:** What sports do you like to watch?
      B: ____. I like all the games, and I especially like the World Cup.
      a. I'm all about soccer.
      b. I can't stand soccer.

PROGRESS CHECK: Now I can . . .

- ☐ talk about my news-watching habits.
- ☐ talk about experiences in the past.
- ☐ talk about habits in the past.
- ☐ express interest and disinterest.
- ☐ write about an event.
- ☐ talk about a special event.

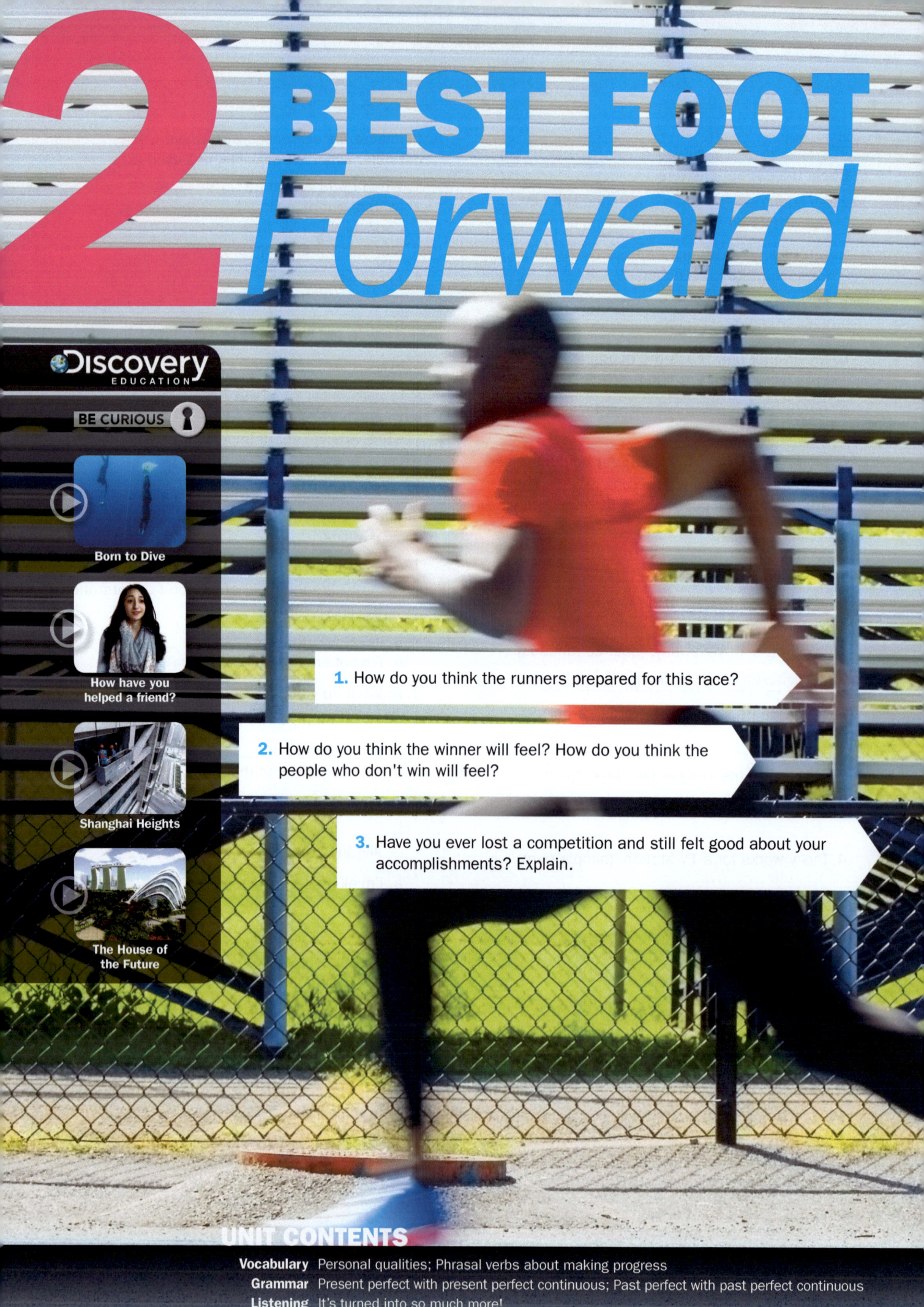

2 BEST FOOT Forward

Discovery EDUCATION
BE CURIOUS
- Born to Dive
- How have you helped a friend?
- Shanghai Heights
- The House of the Future

1. How do you think the runners prepared for this race?

2. How do you think the winner will feel? How do you think the people who don't win will feel?

3. Have you ever lost a competition and still felt good about your accomplishments? Explain.

UNIT CONTENTS

Vocabulary Personal qualities; Phrasal verbs about making progress
Grammar Present perfect with present perfect continuous; Past perfect with past perfect continuous
Listening It's turned into so much more!

Vocabulary: Personal qualities

1. Match the sentences with the correct pictures.

 a
 b
 c
 d
 e

1. __c__ She's very **talented**. Her pictures are really beautiful. And she's **determined**, too. She tries again and again until she gets it just right.
2. ____ He's really fun, and he's very **sociable**. He talks with everyone. He's really good with the **shy** kids, too – the ones who don't want to talk.
3. ____ He's **strict** and he makes his students work hard, but they love him and are very **motivated**.
4. ____ She's **passionate** about dancing. She loves it! And she's very **hardworking**, too. She spends all her free time at the dance studio.
5. ____ She's very **easy-going**. She never gets angry or **impatient** that I haven't practiced. And I'm not very good, so she has to be really patient!

 2. Listen, check, and repeat.

 3. Listen to people describing themselves. Match them to the personal qualities in Exercise 1.

1. _motivated_   5. _____   9. _____
2. _____   6. _____   10. _____
3. _____   7. _____
4. _____   8. _____

 Say it **RIGHT!**

In words with more than one syllable, one of the syllables is stressed more than the others. Listen to the stress in these words.

    •   •
mo-ti-va-ted   de- **ter**-mined

Listen to the rest of the words from Exercise 1 with more than one syllable. Which syllables are stressed?

Speaking: My helper

4. **YOUR TURN** Work with a partner. Think of a person who helps you in some way. Choose three adjectives from Exercise 1 that describe him or her. Tell your partner about the person.

> *My older brother helps me with my homework. He's very patient and . . .*

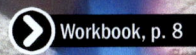 Workbook, p. 8

Reading A Natural Born Climber; Thanks for your help!; Leaving Home to Help
Conversation Showing concern
Writing A thank-you email for support

Unit 2 | 13

It's **HARD** work!

A NATURAL BORN CLIMBER

Brooke Raboutou has just turned 12, and she is one of the best rock climbers in the world, with seven world records. One of her coaches explains why she's so good. "She has incredibly strong fingers," he says. He adds that she also has the flexibility of a child. This really helps in climbing. It means she can do things older climbers have never dreamed of doing. Practice also helps. Brooke has been climbing regularly since she was four years old.

Brooke comes from a climbing family. Both of her parents are climbing champions. Her father has stopped climbing, but her mother, Robyn, who won the World Cup title four years in a row, is still climbing. She has been running a club for young climbers in Colorado since 2005. She coaches Brooke and her teammates. Brooke says her mom is a great coach. "She encourages me a lot. She gives me really good advice," Brooke says. "She's just a big part of my climbing life." Robyn can be strict, but she is also passionate. She has been passing this passion on to her daughter and students for years.

Brooke is very determined and has always been very motivated. This helps her when she's facing the challenges of this difficult sport. She's also hardworking. She hasn't gotten to the top of her sport by sitting around. "To be a really good climber, you can't just have it. You have to train really hard, so I take it pretty seriously," Brooke says. And that's what Brooke has been doing every day, at the club and at home. She even has a climbing wall in her basement.

But climbing isn't only hard work. It's fun, too. "When I'm on a high rock, I feel in control and just happy," Brooke says. "And when I look down, I'm not scared because I'm not scared of heights. But it's just so cool to think how small I am compared to the rock and how high up I am."

DID YOU KNOW...?
Rock climbing has been a sport for more than 150 years.

Reading: An article about a young rock climber

1. Look at the title and the picture. What do you think are three adjectives that describe Brooke?

2. Read and listen to the article. How does Brooke feel about rock climbing?

3. Read the article again. Answer the questions.

   1. What makes Brooke a good climber?

      _____

   2. What is Brooke's parents' connection to rock climbing?

      _____

   3. What does Brooke's mom do now?

      _____

   4. Why does Brooke think her mom is good at her job?

      _____

   5. How does Brooke feel when she's up high on a rock?

      _____

4. **YOUR TURN** Work with a partner. Have you tried rock climbing? What was it like? If not, would you like to try it? Explain.

Grammar: Present perfect with present perfect continuous

5. Complete the chart.

Present perfect continuous	
Use the present perfect continuous for experiences that happened at an indefinite time in the past and continue to the present.	
Where **have** you **been climbing**? I _____ at the club. I **haven't been climbing** in the mountains.	**Have** you **been training** a lot? Yes, I **have**. No, I _____.
What **has** she **been doing**? She **has been running** a club. She _____ **working** in an office.	_____ she _____ **climbing** for a long time? Yes, she **has**. No, she **hasn't**.
Present perfect vs. present perfect continuous	
Remember to use the present perfect for experiences that happened at an indefinite time in the past and are now complete. Use the present perfect to emphasize the result.	
He used to be a professional rock climber, but he _____ **stopped** climbing.	
Use the present perfect continuous to emphasize the action.	
She _____ **climbing** since she was four.	

> Check your answers: Grammar reference, p. 107

6. Write sentences with the present perfect continuous.

1. Cara / take / swimming lessons for six years *Cara has been taking swimming lessons for six years.*
2. they / work / here since 2013 _____
3. you / not live / in Vancouver for very long _____
4. Ricardo / text / Maria all day _____

7. Use the present perfect continuous when possible. When not possible, use the present perfect.

1. Olivia *hasn't finished* (not finish) high school yet.
2. She _____ (study) dance for three years.
3. She _____ (be) motivated all of her life.
4. Her parents _____ (help) her follow her dream of becoming a famous dancer.
5. They _____ just _____ (save) enough money for her to go to a dance school in New York City.
6. _____ you ever _____ (know) someone who followed their dreams?

> *Use the present perfect, not the present perfect continuous, with ever, never, just, already, and yet.*
>
> She **has already won** four competitions.
> (NOT: She's already been winning . . .)
>
> *Use the present perfect, not the present continuous, with know, have, and be.*
>
> I **have known** Brooke for many years.
> (NOT: I have been knowing Brooke . . .)

Speaking: What have you been doing?

8. YOUR TURN Work with a partner. Ask and answer questions about something you've been learning to do recently.

- ☐ How long have you been learning it?
- ☐ Why did you start?
- ☐ Who has been teaching you?
- ☐ What has been the most difficult thing to learn?

I've been taking piano lessons every weekend.

Have you been taking them for very long?

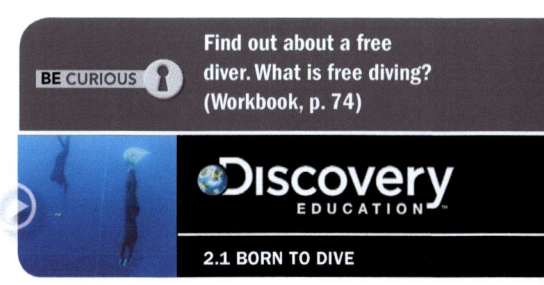

BE CURIOUS — Find out about a free diver. What is free diving? (Workbook, p. 74)

Discovery EDUCATION

2.1 BORN TO DIVE

> Workbook, p. 9

Helping HANDS

Listening: It's turned into so much more!

1. Have you ever taught someone how to do something? Was it difficult or easy?

2. Listen to an interview about a program a teenager started. What's the name of the program? What's its purpose?

3. Listen again. Answer the questions.
   1. Who are the teachers? Who are the students?
   2. How many people were in the program last year? How many are in it this year?
   3. What do the students learn to do? What do the teachers learn from the students?
   4. What was Helen's job in the past? What did she do at her job?
   5. Why is Jake surprised?

Vocabulary: Phrasal verbs about making progress

4. Read the sentences. Match the words with the definitions. Then listen and check.
   1. __g__ This project can **bring together** students and older people.
   2. ____ I hope my music hobby will **turn into** a career!
   3. ____ My grandmother wants to **sign up** for computer lessons.
   4. ____ They want to **keep up** with their grandkids.
   5. ____ We help them **set up** social networking pages.
   6. ____ We don't want them to **give up**.
   7. ____ We **get along** with each other.
   8. ____ They **pass on** their knowledge to young people.
   9. ____ They **count on** us to help them.

   a. to stop doing something
   b. to give something to someone
   c. to arrange to do an organized activity
   d. to have a good relationship (with someone)
   e. to get things ready for something
   f. to depend on someone or something
   g. to cause people to join each other
   h. to become something different
   i. to stay equal (with someone)

   > **Get it RIGHT!**
   > Some phrasal verbs are separable. An object can go after the preposition or between the verb and the preposition.
   > We helped **set up** _the site_.
   > We helped **set** _the site_ **up**.
   > Some phrasal verbs are not separable.
   > They **count on** _volunteers_ to help.
   > (NOT: ~~They count volunteers on to help.~~)

5. **YOUR TURN** Work with a partner. Ask and answer questions using phrasal verbs from Exercise 4.

   > Have you ever given up? Have you ever had a bad experience turn into something good?

   > What kinds of activities bring people together? Have you ever signed up for any of them?

   > Who do you get along with well? Do you count on those people? Do you ever feel like you have to keep up with them?

Grammar: Past perfect and past perfect continuous

6. Complete the chart.

Past perfect continuous

Use the past perfect continuous for experiences that started in the past and continued up until another time in the past.

What **had** they **been doing**? They _____ cell phones before the program started. They **hadn't been using** email.	_____ they **been using** cell phones? Yes, they **had**. No, they _____.

Past perfect vs. past perfect continuous

Remember to use the past perfect to refer to something that happened before a specific time in the past. Use the past perfect to emphasize the result.

Fifty people **had signed** up this year.   I **hadn't heard** of that job.

Use the past perfect continuous to emphasize the action.

I _____ **working** with Helen for 6 months.

> Check your answers: Grammar reference, p. 107

7. Complete the sentences using the past perfect continuous form of the verbs.

My parents ¹ *had been playing* (play) in different bands when they met at a music festival. My father ² _____ (sing) in a rock band, and my mother ³ _____ (play) the guitar in a country band. At the festival, they started talking to each other. After they ⁴ _____ (talk) for an hour, they realized they had a lot in common. They exchanged emails. They ⁵ _____ (not write) to each other for very long when they decided to form a band. They ⁶ _____ (tour) for about a year when they decided to get married. They toured together for three more years. They ⁷ _____ (not enjoy) life on the road when they decided to stop touring. That's when they started a music school. They ⁸ _____ (teach) students for about a year when I was born. Of course, they passed on their love of music to me!

8. Complete the sentences with the past perfect continuous when possible. When not possible, use the past perfect.

1. I *had liked* (like) music ever since I was a little kid.
2. I _____ (play) the piano for two years when my mother gave me her guitar.
3. I _____ (sign up) for classes as soon as I got my guitar.
4. I _____ (take) classes for a year when I started a band.
5. My band _____ (be) determined to make it big in music.

> Use the past perfect, not the past perfect continuous, with ever, never, just, already, and yet.
> I hadn't **ever heard** of that job.
> (NOT: I ~~hadn't ever been hearing~~ of that job.)
>
> Use the past perfect, not the past perfect continuous, with be, know, and like.
> She **had been** a typist in the '60s.
> (NOT: She ~~had been being~~ a typist in the '60s.)

Speaking: Self-improvement

9. YOUR TURN Work with a partner. Talk about something you did to improve a skill or talent.

> I had been studying French before I took a Spanish class.
> I hadn't been looking for a Spanish class for very long when . . .

> Workbook, pp. 10–11

Lending an EAR

Conversation: Finding solutions

1. **REAL TALK** Watch or listen to the teenagers talk about how they've helped people. Check (✓) the things they have helped with.

☐ not making a sports team	☐ the death of a pet	☐ difficult situations	☐ the loss of a parent's job
☐ not getting a coaching job	☐ getting people out of trouble	☐ speaking in public	☐ studying for an exam
☐ buying a new pet	☐ getting people into trouble	☐ watching too much TV	☐ finishing homework

2. **YOUR TURN** How have *you* helped a friend through a difficult situation? Tell your partner.

3. Listen to Mari tell Erica about a problem. Complete the conversation.

> **USEFUL LANGUAGE: Showing concern**
> ✓ Are you all right? | I'm sorry to hear that. | Is there anything I can do?
> I hope things get better. | What's the matter? | What's wrong with

Erica: Hey, Mari. ¹_____*Are you all right?*_____
Mari: Well, not really.
Erica: ²_____
Mari: It's my sister.
Erica: ³_____ your sister? Is she sick?
Mari: Oh, no, it's nothing like that. She's just really mad at me!
Erica: Why's that?
Mari: I borrowed her favorite sweater, and I ruined it.
Erica: ⁴_____
Mari: Thanks. I feel awful about it. And now she won't even talk to me.
Erica: ⁵_____
Mari: Yeah. Me, too.
Erica: ⁶_____
Mari: Maybe you could go shopping with me. I'd like to buy her a new sweater.
Erica: That's a great idea. That should make her happy, right?
Mari: I think so. But maybe I'll buy her two sweaters. Then she *has to* forgive me!

4. Practice the conversation with a partner.

5. **YOUR TURN** Work with a partner. Take turns talking about a problem and showing concern. Use the problems below or your own ideas.

Problem A	Problem B
You want to go to a concert with your friends, but your parents won't let you go.	Your brother or sister wants you to come to his/her soccer game, but you can't make it.

18 | Unit 2

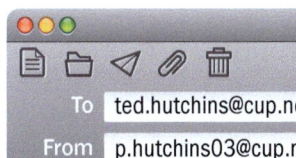

To: ted.hutchins@cup.net
From: p.hutchins03@cup.net
Subject: Thanks for your help!

Hi Grandpa,

I'm writing to thank you for listening to me and helping me with my new school. The work was harder than at my old school. I wasn't keeping up with the other students, and I'd felt like giving up. Thank you for telling me to explain the problem to my teachers. Soon, they realized I was determined to get better. Since then, they've been helping me a lot.

Making friends wasn't easy either. You know how shy I am, and it was hard to make friends. Thanks so much for your advice to smile and ask questions. Gradually, I started to feel more sociable. I've made a few good friends, and we get along really well. I had been spending a lot of time alone, but thanks to you, I'm busy with my friends all the time! I've attached a picture of me with a few of them. I really appreciate your help, Grandpa.

Thanks again,

Peter

Reading to write: A thank-you email for support

6. **Look at the photo. What do you think Peter is thanking his grandfather for? Read his email to check.**

   ### ◉ Focus on CONTENT
   Include these things in a thank-you email:
   - a greeting
   - a reason for writing
   - details: Include what he/she did to help you and how it helped.
   - a closing:
   If you send a photo, use:
   - by mail: *I've included a picture/photo of . . .*
   - by email: *I've attached a picture/photo of . . .*

7. **Read Peter's email again. What expressions from the Focus on Content box did he use? What two things did his grandfather tell him to do? How did it help?**

   ### ◉ Focus on LANGUAGE
   Use these transitional phrases to link your ideas. Use a comma after the phrases.
   - happening before something: *Before that, Prior to that,*
   - happening after something: *Since then, After that,*
   - happening quickly after something: *Soon, Immediately,*
   - happening slowly over time: *Slowly, Gradually,*

8. **What transitional phrases does Peter use in his thank-you email?**

9. **Circle the correct answers.**

   1. Janice had been practicing the piano every day for a year. **Before that / Slowly**, she got better.

   2. It started to rain during soccer practice. **Immediately / Gradually**, we went inside.

   3. Ted's parents bought a new boat. **Slowly / After that**, he started waterskiing.

Writing: Your thank-you email for support

◯ PLAN
You are going to write a thank-you email to someone for his/her support. Think of a time someone helped you. Complete the chart.

What he/she did to help you	How it helped

◯ WRITE
Write your thank-you email. Use your notes to help you. Include transitional phrases in your description of how the person helped you. Write at least 125 words.

◯ CHECK
Check your writing. Can you answer "yes" to these questions?

- Is information from the Focus on Content box in your email?
- Do you use transitional phrases correctly?

Leaving Home to HELP

Kwame lives in Ghana in an Ashanti village in the rainforest. He had been working in his village when he decided to leave home to go to school. He was determined to make a better life for himself. However, after he left, he realized the many good things about his home. After he finished school, he returned to his village. He wanted to make things better not only for himself, but also for his family and community. He started a school in his village. But that wasn't enough . . . he wanted to help others learn about the Ashanti people. As a child, he had learned to play the talking drum. The drum has been important to Ashanti people for many generations as a way to learn the language, communicate news, and for special ceremonies. Now, Kwame travels to schools in the cities to teach students about the talking drum and the Ashanti way of life. We spoke with Kwame to learn more.

Q 1 _____

A I'm passionate about my culture, and the talking drum is a big part of it. My uncle passed on the tradition to me, and I wanted to pass it on to others.

Q 2 _____

A I'm pretty shy, and as a result, no one was paying attention. Then I started playing the drum before I even spoke. That captured everyone's attention. The drum really does communicate. Students listen to the drum and then they want to listen to me. The drum helped me improve my presentation skills.

Q 3 _____

A Definitely how important my culture is. Also, how something as simple as a drum can bring people together. The more people understand about my culture, the more likely it is to survive. My family and community are counting on me!

Culture: An interview with an Ashanti person

1. Look at the photos. What do you think the article is about?

2. Read the interview. Complete the interview with the questions. Then listen and check your answers.

   What's the most important thing you've learned from your experience?

   Why did you decide to teach others about the talking drum?

   What has been the hardest part about teaching others about your culture?

3. Read the interview again. Are the sentences true or false? Write *T* (true), *F* (false), or *NI* (no information).

   1. Kwame didn't like working in his village. ____
   2. He wanted to help himself more than he wanted to help his family. ____
   3. He goes to schools to teach people about his culture. ____
   4. Kwame's father taught him to play the talking drum. ____
   5. Kwame isn't shy anymore. ____

4. **YOUR TURN** Work with a partner. Do you know someone who has left home to help his or her family? Do you know someone who has helped his or her family in another way? What did they do?

DID YOU KNOW...?

There are many types of Ashanti drums. The talking drums are called *atumpan*.

BE CURIOUS Find out about Sun Feng's job. What's difficult about it? (Workbook, p. 75)

Discovery EDUCATION

2.3 SHANGHAI HEIGHTS

UNIT 2 REVIEW

Vocabulary

1. Complete the sentences with the correct words.

determined	passionate	strict
easy-going	shy	talented
impatient	sociable	

1. Lola is extremely _____. She plays the piano well.
2. My sister is very _____. She never gives up!
3. Don is pretty _____. He gets along with everyone, but he doesn't talk very much. However, his sister is very _____. She talks to anyone!
4. My boss is very _____. We can't be late to work, and he gets so angry about the littlest things. I wish he were _____.
5. Tonya is so _____. She runs with her friends, and she gets frustrated when they can't keep up with her.
6. Barry is _____ about so many things, but he loves rock climbing the most.

Grammar

2. Correct the sentences.

1. Tonya was studying dance for four years, and she's in an advanced dance class now.
2. I've been knowing Tom for 16 years.
3. Jared has took six rock-climbing trips this past year.
4. How have you been do in your art classes?
5. We used to go to summer camp, but we not having gone in years.
6. You haven't been ride your bike by my house lately.

3. Write sentences with past perfect continuous when possible. When not possible, use the past perfect.

1. we / have / work / for 6 hours
   _____
2. Rick / be / passionate / about photography since 2005
   _____
3. Eve and Jun / never / go / to that school
   _____
4. Anna / not study / all day
   _____
5. I / just / see / a fantastic movie
   _____

Useful language

4. Choose the correct answers.

1. **A:** Are you **all right / anything**?
   B: No, not really. I'm having trouble in one of my classes.
   A: I'm sorry. I hope things get **better / matter**.
2. **A:** What's the **wrong / matter**?
   B: My parents won't let me go the movies.
   A: Is there **anything / hope** I can do?
3. **A:** What's **wrong / sorry** with Julie?
   B: I think her grandmother is sick.
   A: I'm sorry to hear **better / that**.

PROGRESS CHECK: Now I can . . .	
☐ talk about a person's qualities.	☐ show concern.
☐ talk about recent events.	☐ write a thank-you email.
☐ talk about personal experiences.	☐ talk about someone who has helped his/her family.

CLIL PROJECT

2.4 THE HOUSE OF THE FUTURE, p. 116

3 Planning for the Future

Discovery EDUCATION

BE CURIOUS

What a Waste!

Are you saving up for something special?

Mission: Possible?

1. What is the person doing? Where is she?

2. What do you think she is thinking about?

3. What do you think about when you think about the future?

UNIT CONTENTS
Vocabulary Verbs of the future; Achievements
Grammar Future review; Future continuous and future perfect
Listening The waters around you

Vocabulary: Verbs of the future

1. Match the sentences with the correct pictures.

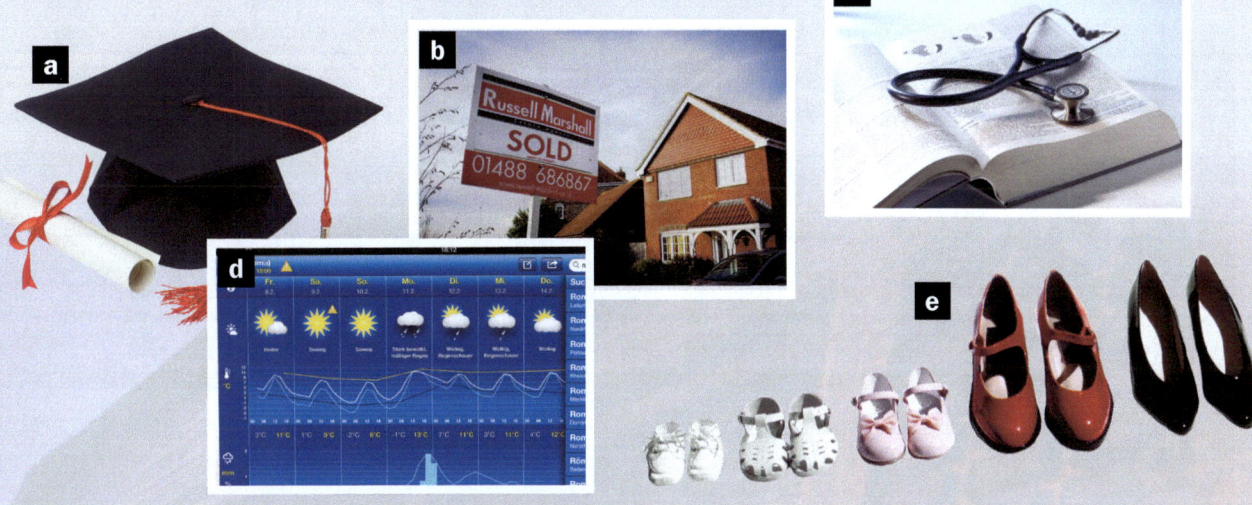

1. __e__ Children **grow up** so fast.
2. ____ If you **plan** to **become** a doctor, you have to **keep on** studying after college.
3. ____ Meteorologists try to **predict** the weather.
4. ____ Many high school students **graduate** in May.
5. ____ People often **move** to new homes because of work and **end up** in new cities.

 2. Listen, check, and repeat.

3. Complete the sentences with the correct verbs from Exercise 1.

Hi, I'm Todd. I live in Jackson, Wyoming. I've lived here since I was a baby, and it was a great place to ¹ __grow up__ . I'll ² _____ from high school in May. I'm really excited! I ³ _____ to go to college in the fall. I want to ⁴ _____ a computer engineer. Of course, I'll have to ⁵ _____ studying after college if I want a really good job. After that, I'll probably ⁶ _____ to California. All of the successful software designers ⁷ _____ there. I ⁸ _____ that I'll eventually come back to Jackson, but not until I'm much older, like when I retire!

Speaking: Plans change

4. YOUR TURN Work with a partner. Talk about someone you know who . . .

- ☐ wants to move to another country in the future.
- ☐ wants to become a doctor when he/she grows up.
- ☐ plans to keep on studying after high school.
- ☐ plans to graduate early.

My cousin wants to move to Argentina in a few years.

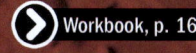 Workbook, p. 16

Reading A Career in Space; Leaving School Early; School in the Cloud
Conversation Expressing cause and effect
Writing An opinion essay

A FAR AWAY FUTURE

A CAREER IN SPACE

Are you planning to become an astronaut? Do you think you'll move to the space station one day? If so, plan to study A LOT before you graduate from space school.

David Gomez is thinking about a career in space. He is determined to become an astronaut for the National Aeronautics and Space Administration (NASA) in Houston, Texas, someday. Last year, he went to space camp and learned what it takes to be an astronaut. First, he needs to get a college degree in engineering, science, or math. Then he needs to have three years of professional experience or 1,000 hours as a pilot. Finally, he needs to pass a medical exam. If he gets into NASA's Astronaut Corps, his training will look something like this:

He will have two years of training. He'll have science and technology classes. He'll also learn medical skills. As an astronaut, he's going to need to know what to do in an emergency. He'll also learn how the International Space Station (ISS) works. He will take scuba diving courses, too. Astronauts train underwater to understand what it is like in space with no gravity. In addition, he'll take Russian classes. When he finishes training, he can be sent on a space mission. He'll learn even more on the job.

David is confident he'll get into NASA's program. He's already preparing for his future career. Next year, he's taking advanced science and math classes. He's also going to take Russian after school. After he graduates, he's going to move to Houston and go to college there.

He's extremely motivated and excited about his future career. He plans to move to the ISS someday. We predict he'll end up working for NASA and that his dream will come true!

DID YOU KNOW...?
Astronauts who live on the ISS live there for 3 to 6 months at a time.

Reading: An article about becoming an astronaut

1. Look at the pictures. What do you think David wants to become?

2. Read and listen to the article. What does it give information about?
   a. different careers at NASA
   b. what it takes to become an astronaut
   c. how to survive on the International Space Station

3. Read the article again. Then read the sentences and write *B* (before training), *D* (during training), or *A* (after training).
   1. Find out how the ISS works. _____
   2. Get 1,000 hours of flying experience. _____
   3. Get a college degree. _____
   4. Go on a mission. _____
   5. Learn medical skills. _____
   6. Learn to scuba dive. _____
   7. Pass a medical exam. _____
   8. Possibly live in the ISS. _____

4. **YOUR TURN** Work with a partner. Would you like to become an astronaut? Why or why not?

Say it RIGHT!

When a word that starts with **h** links to the words before it, the **h** can be silent. Listen to the differences in these sentences.
H pronounced: First, **he** needs to get a college degree.
Silent **h**: Then **he** needs to have three years of professional experience.
Listen to and repeat these sentences from the article. Circle the words with pronounced **h**'s. Cross out the words with silent **h**'s.
1. If he gets into NASA's Astronaut Corps, his training will look something like this.
2. When he finishes training, he can be sent on a space mission.
3. After he graduates, he's going to move to Houston.
4. He's extremely motivated and excited about his future career.

Grammar: Future review

5. Complete the chart.

will	be going to
Use will for predictions.	Use going to for planned actions and events.
What classes **will** David **take**? He _____ Russian classes. He **won't take** French.	Where **is** he **going to live**? He **is going to live** in Houston. He _____ in his hometown.
Present continuous	**Simple present**
Use the present continuous for planned actions and events.	Use the simple present for scheduled future events.
What classes **is** he **taking** next year? He _____ advanced science. He **isn't taking** art classes.	Where _____ he _____ to go? He **plans** to go to the ISS. He **doesn't plan** to go to Russia.

> Check your answers: Grammar reference, p. 108

6. Circle the correct answers.

Today is Aaron Lucas's first day at his dream job as a train driver, and Penn Station is his destination. The train ¹**leaves / is leaving** Boston at 1:40 p.m. and ²**isn't arriving / arrives** about 4 hours later. Next week, he ³**is going to drive / drives** further – from Boston to Chicago. It's a long trip! It ⁴**will take / is taking** about 23 hours. The good news is that he ⁵**doesn't travel / isn't traveling** alone. His family ⁶**makes / is making** the trip to Chicago, too.

7. Write sentences with the future forms given.

1. Taylor and Joe / travel / to Colombia next year (*be going to*)
   Taylor and Joe are going to travel to Colombia next year.

2. cars / be / driverless in the future (*will*)
   _____

3. Martin / have / a soccer game next Friday (*simple present*)
   _____

4. I / not take / Russian next year (*present continuous*)
   _____

5. You / not like / that movie (*will*)
   _____

6. Sarah / study / science in college (*be going to*)
   _____

Speaking: Your future – near and far

8. YOUR TURN Work with a partner. Talk about your future plans for the times below. How sure are you? Use *will* for predictions. Use *be going to*, the present continuous, or the simple present for planned events.

| tomorrow | next week | next year |
| in 5 years | in 10 years | |

I'll become a chef in five years. I'm planning to take cooking classes next year.

BE CURIOUS Find out about e-waste. What is it? (Workbook, p. 76)

Discovery EDUCATION
3.1 WHAT A WASTE!

A Better FUTURE

Listening: The waters around you

1. Do you ever swim or do sports in the ocean? What do you do? Have you ever noticed trash in the ocean?

2. Listen to a show about Dive for Debris. What does the organization do?

3. Listen again. Circle the correct answers.
   1. The divers in Dive for Debris are _____.
      a. professional divers
      b. volunteers
   2. Divers collect trash in an area _____.
      a. once
      b. many times
   3. In the future, Dive for Debris will work with _____.
      a. waste management companies
      b. local schools and teachers
   4. About _____ volunteers have collected litter in the ocean.
      a. 100
      b. 1,600

Vocabulary: Achievements

4. Match the pictures with the correct words. Then listen, check, and repeat.
   1. _g_ become famous
   2. ___ break a record
   3. ___ develop a project
   4. ___ do volunteer work
   5. ___ make a million dollars
   6. ___ start a business
   7. ___ support the community
   8. ___ win an award

5. **YOUR TURN** Work with a partner. Rank the achievements from Exercise 4 in order of importance for you. Share your ideas with a partner and explain why.

> *Doing volunteer work is number 1 for me. I think it's important because . . .*

Grammar: Future continuous and future perfect

6. Complete the chart.

Future continuous

Use the future continuous to describe something that will be in progress in the future. To form the future continuous, use **will + be + the -ing form of a verb**.

Who **will** be **volunteering**? Many more divers _____. **I won't be volunteering**.	_____ you **be volunteering**? Yes, I **will**. No, I _____.

Future perfect

Use the future perfect to describe something that is going to be finished at a certain time in the future. To form the future perfect, use **will + have + past participle**.

How much trash **will** she **have collected** in 20 years? She _____ a lot of trash. She **won't have earned** much money.	**Will** she **have collected** a lot of trash? Yes, she _____. No, she **won't have**.

▶ Check your answers: Grammar reference, p. 108

7. Put the words in the correct order to complete the sentences.

1. making / will / dollars / a / Janet's company / be / million

   Janet's company will be making a million dollars by 2020.

2. have / the organization / supported / will

   In 2020, _____ the community for 50 years.

3. be / Danilo / the / will / beach / cleaning up

   By this time tomorrow, _____.

4. picked up / they / have / will

   By the end of the day, _____ all of the trash?

5. will / started / company / you / have / your

   In September, _____ a year ago.

6. living / I / will / be

   _____ in Chicago in August.

Get it RIGHT!

Use the correct word order for questions with the future perfect.

Will she **have** collected a lot of trash? (NOT: **Will have** ~~she collected a lot of trash~~?)

8. Complete the sentences with the future continuous or future perfect.

1. Lucy _will have seen_ 20 landmarks by the time she returns from her trip.
2. In January, I _____ (know) my best friend for 15 years.
3. _____ you _____ (volunteer) at the community clean up tomorrow? We really need your help!
4. My father _____ (not work) at the community center on Saturday. He has a doctor's appointment.
5. By this afternoon, Jeremy _____ (hear) the results of his interview.
6. What _____ you _____ (do) tomorrow morning? Can you help me with something?

NOTICE IT

Remember, *be*, *know*, *understand*, *like*, *want*, and *need* aren't usually used in continuous forms. In addition, many sense verbs, like *feel*, *see*, and *hear* aren't usually used with the continuous.

Speaking: Predictions for my future

9. YOUR TURN Work with a partner. Talk about your life in 30 years. What will you be doing? What will you have achieved?

> In 30 years, I'll be living in Tokyo. I'll have learned Japanese, and I'll be working for a computer company. I'll . . .

Ohayou gozaimasu.

▶ Workbook, pp. 18–19

 **REAL TALK** 3.2 ARE YOU SAVING UP FOR SOMETHING SPECIAL?

Saving for the FUTURE

Conversation: Planning and budgeting

1. **REAL TALK** Watch or listen to the teenagers talk about what they are saving money for. Complete the items.

   1. concert _____
   2. an electric _____
   3. a secondhand _____
   4. _____ in two years
   5. a summer _____

2. **YOUR TURN** Are *you* saving up for something special? What? Tell your partner.

3. Listen to Nora talking with Mr. Lee about the budget for a school trip. Complete the conversation.

USEFUL LANGUAGE: Expressing cause and effect

as a result | consequently | because of | since | ✓so that | thanks to

Mr. Lee: Thanks for helping me with the budget for our school trip, Nora. Just think, this time next month, you'll be riding horses at a ranch!

Nora: I know! Everyone's really excited.

Mr. Lee: Your class has saved a lot of money for the trip ¹___so that___ students don't have to pay. But I don't think we have enough for everything we've planned. ²_____, we're going to have to make some cuts.

Nora: Well, I just talked to Lauren Rigby. And ³_____ her, the cost of horseback riding at the ranch is going to be cheaper.

Mr. Lee: Really? Why?

Nora: ⁴_____ the owners are Lauren's aunt and uncle, they're going to give us a discount.

Mr. Lee: That's nice. So, we should have enough money for food. I'm not sure if we have enough for transportation, though. ⁵_____ the number of people going, we have to rent one of the bigger buses, and they're pretty expensive.

Nora: What if we get parent volunteers to drive us? ⁶_____, we'd save a lot of money.

Mr. Lee: That's a good idea, Nora.

4. Practice the conversation with a partner.

5. **YOUR TURN** Work with a partner. Have a conversation about a budget for one of the items below or your own idea.

   a school dance | a new sports center for the school | an after-school club

28 | Unit 3

LEAVING SCHOOL EARLY
Should students be allowed to leave school before they are 18?

by Rita Newman

In the United States, the school-leaving age is different from state to state, but it is usually 16 years old, meaning some students can legally leave school before their senior year. Personally, I don't think it's a good idea to make everyone stay until they are 18.

Obviously, students who want to go to college will stay in school until they are 18 anyway, but not everyone enjoys studying. Many young people would rather work or take a training course. They want to learn skills so that they will be able to get jobs.

Certainly, students who don't want to stay in school will behave badly. What's more, they will create problems for other students and teachers. It is better to allow students to leave and pursue other things.

Consequently, I'm against forcing students to stay in school, at least until schools can provide a wider range of training courses and work experience.

Reading to write: An opinion essay

6. Look at the title and the photo. What do you think Rita's opinion will be? Read her essay to check.

> ◉ *Focus on* **CONTENT**
> When you write an opinion essay, organize it like this:
> - introduction (1 paragraph): Introduce the topic and state your opinion.
> - body (1 to 3 paragraphs): Give reasons for your opinion.
> - conclusion: State your opinion again.

7. Read Rita's essay again. What reasons does Rita give for her opinion?

> ◉ *Focus on* **LANGUAGE**
> Use adverbs to show how you feel about your opinions:
> - to show something is in your opinion: *personally*
> - to show that everyone knows it: *obviously, clearly*
> - to show it's certain to happen: *certainly, surely, definitely, inevitably*
> - to show the result of something you said: *therefore, consequently, accordingly*
>
> Use connecting words and phrases to add additional ideas: *in addition, what's more, also*

8. Which adverbs does Rita use in her essay? Which connecting phrase does she use?

9. Circle the correct answers.

1. **Obviously** / **Personally**, science is important.
2. Everyone should know how food is grown. **Therefore** / **What's more**, I think high school students should take a food science class.
3. Crime is a problem in this area. **In addition** / **Surely**, we need more police officers.
4. Teenagers should start saving money for their futures. They should **inevitably** / **also** start to explore career options.

 Writing: Your opinion essay

☐ **PLAN**
You are going to write an opinion essay. Choose one of the questions below and complete the chart.

- Should teenagers work before they are 16?
- Should parents give teenagers spending money?

Question	
Your opinion	
Reasons for your opinion	

☐ **WRITE**
Write your opinion essay. Use your notes to help you. Include an introduction, body, and conclusion. Use adverbs and connecting phrases. Write at least 125 words.

☐ **CHECK**
Check your writing. Can you answer "yes" to these questions?

- Is information from the Focus on Content box in your essay?
- Do you use adverbs and connecting phrases correctly?

Workbook, pp. 20–21

School in the CLOUD

What do you think school will be like in the future? In 1999, Sugata Mitra had an idea for a school of the future. He got his idea when he put a computer in a classroom full of students who had never used one before. Amazingly, the students taught themselves how to use it. To Mitra, this was not so amazing. He believed that children could teach themselves just about anything! He imagined students in a classroom with an adult who gave them questions to answer, like "Why do animals cry?" or "Why is the sky blue?" Students would be in charge of their own learning and would work together using the Internet to answer those questions.

In 2013, Mitra started such a school, called a *School in the Cloud lab*, in a high school in England. Soon after, three School in the Cloud labs opened in India.

School in the Cloud also has SOLEs – Self-Organized Learning Environments. A SOLE is similar to a lab, but it's done after school and on the weekends, and students are not in a classroom. They work together over the Internet. Any adult can start a SOLE. SOLE leaders are volunteers, and they're called *Grannies*. Their job is to help children learn. They post a question to students online, and students work however they want to find the answers. Grannies are there to encourage students and help them as they discover answers.

Mitra calls his schools a "global experiment," and he hopes to create more of them around the world. His dream is likely to come true. In 2013, he won an award to develop his project – one million dollars. He feels this money will help fund more schools that allow children to learn by discovery.

Culture: An article about a new way of learning

1. Look at the title. What do you think School in the Cloud is?

2. Read and listen to the article. What's the article's purpose?

   a. To teach people how to start a SOLE

   b. To explain what School in the Cloud is

   c. To compare School in the Cloud to a traditional classroom

3. Read the article again. Are the sentences true or false? Write *T* (true), *F* (false), or *NI* (no information).

   1. Sugata Mitra gives teachers ideas for questions to ask students. ____

   2. The first School in the Cloud started in India. ____

   3. "Grannies" get paid to work with students. ____

   4. At School in the Cloud students can work together. ____

   5. Mitra hopes to have one million schools in the future. ____

   6. Mitra thinks students are able to learn by themselves. ____

4. **YOUR TURN** Work with a group. Imagine what school will be like in 100 years. Share your ideas.

   I think that classrooms will be in space in 100 years. Students will learn while . . .

DID YOU KNOW...?
Some experts predict that about 5 billion people will be using the Internet by 2020.

BE CURIOUS Find out about space travel. What problem do astronauts have? (Workbook, p. 77)

3.3 MISSION: POSSIBLE?

UNIT 3 REVIEW

Vocabulary

1. **Complete the sentences with the correct forms of words.**

become	grow up	plan
✓ end up	keep on	predict
graduate	move	

   1. Becky won an award on a talent show, and she _ended up_ becoming famous.
   2. I need to _____ studying after high school if I want to start a business.
   3. After _____ to New York City, I immediately started doing volunteer work.
   4. I _____ to study math in college.
   5. My sister will have _____ from high school by the time I start middle school.
   6. Why do you want to _____ an astronaut?
   7. I _____ that I will break a record at the race tomorrow.
   8. Do you want to become famous when you _____?

Grammar

2. **Rewrite the sentences. Use the future forms given.**

   1. I'm doing volunteer work on Saturday. (be going to)

      I'm going to do volunteer work on Saturday.

   2. I'm planning on making a million dollars someday. (will)
      _____

   3. Josh isn't going to work after school next week. (present continuous)
      _____

   4. What time does the train leave on Monday? (be going to)
      _____

   5. The party will start at 10:00 a.m. on Friday. (simple present)
      _____

   6. He isn't going to be an astronaut when he grows up. (will)
      _____

3. **Correct the future continuous and future perfect mistakes in the sentences.**

   1. Lyle will have ~~saving~~ _saved_ $1,000 by September.
   2. Have you be diving with the group on Sunday?
   3. Gina and Tom will be save money after they get jobs.
   4. How many years won't she have flown before she goes on the space shuttle?
   5. Mary won't be lived in Denver long by the time I move there.
   6. I won't attending Carl's graduation party next weekend.

Useful language

4. **Complete the sentences with the correct words.**

   1. Vicky is sick. C_____, she can't go to space camp.
   2. We don't have to pay for our class trip b_____ _____ a donation from a business.
   3. I'm saving up my money s_____ t_____ I can buy a bicycle.
   4. The bus broke down this morning. A_____ a r_____, Caleb was late to work.
   5. We applied to the program early s_____ it usually fills up fast.
   6. T_____ _____ my aunt, I have a summer job.

PROGRESS CHECK: Now I can . . .

☐ talk about people's plans for the future.
☐ talk about my plans for the near and distant future.
☐ make predictions about the future.
☐ express cause and effect.
☐ write an opinion essay.
☐ discuss what schools will be like in the future.

4 What's Cooking?

Discovery EDUCATION
BE CURIOUS

- The Origin of Argan Oil
- What would you make if you had to cook for your family?
- Fruits of the Sea
- You Are What You Eat

1. What do you think the people are making?
2. What problems are they having?
3. Do you cook? Are you a messy or a neat cook?

UNIT CONTENTS
Vocabulary Cooking verbs; Adjectives describing foods
Grammar First conditional review; zero conditional; Second conditional review
Listening A taste test

Vocabulary: Cooking verbs

1. Label the pictures with the correct words.

bake   boil   chop   fry   grate   grill   mix   ✓roast   slice

1. _roast_    2.  _____   3.  _____   4.  _____   5. _____

6.  _____   7.  _____   8.  _____   9. _____

2. Listen, check, and repeat.

3. Work with a partner. What can you do with these foods? Check (✓) the correct columns and then discuss.

	bake, fry, roast, and grill	boil	chop	mix	slice
1. chicken					
2. cheese					
3. onions					
4. spices					
5. strawberries					

You can bake, fry, roast, and grill chicken.

You can also boil it and then use it to make chicken salad.

NOTICE IT
bake = to cook something in an oven
roast = to cook something in an oven on high heat so it turns brown on top
chop = to cut something into small pieces
slice = to cut something into thin, flat pieces

Speaking: A good recipe

4. **YOUR TURN** Choose a simple recipe you know. Write the steps. Add as many steps as you need.

First, . . . → Then . . . → Next, . . . → Finally, . . .

First, fry the beef.
Then grate cheese and . . .

5. Work with a partner. Tell your partner how to make your recipe.

Nachos are easy to make. First, fry some beef. Then grate cheese and chop onions and peppers while the beef is frying. Next, . . .

▶ Workbook, p. 22

Reading Food for Thought; A Traditional Dish; Pots and Pans of the Past
Conversation Cooking instructions
Writing An article about a family dish

DANGEROUS *Foods?*

FOOD FOR THOUGHT

What do you want to know about food? Ask our experts.

Why does chopping onions make you cry? Are they dangerous?

A poisonous gas comes out of an onion when you cut or fry it. If the gas gets into your eyes, your body makes tears to wash it out. So, the next time you chop an onion, do it under running water. When you cut an onion under running water, the gas won't get into your eyes.

I heard fugu is poisonous. Can people eat it?

Fugu is the world's most poisonous fish, but you can eat it! It's a very expensive fish, and it's popular in Japan. The fish has some very poisonous parts, but you can eat the rest of it. Specially trained fugu chefs learn how to slice the fish very carefully to get rid of the poisonous parts. If you are ever in Japan and want to try fugu fish, you'll have to be very careful. You'll have to go to a restaurant with a fugu-trained chef, unless you want it to be your last meal!

Can garlic get rid of evil?

According to legend, garlic can protect people from vampires. Of course, vampires are only in the movies, but garlic can protect us from other things. For example, mosquitos find their victims by smell. And they don't like the smell of garlic! When you eat garlic, the smell comes through your skin. If your skin smells like garlic, a mosquito probably won't bite you!

Why are so many people allergic to peanuts?

Peanut oil contains a chemical called *glycerol*, which can be used to make dynamite. Many people are allergic to glycerol. They get sick, have trouble breathing, or get a rash after eating food with glycerol in it. Many dogs are allergic to peanuts, too! Even the smallest piece of peanut can cause serious problems for people or animals with peanut allergies. You'll need to get to a hospital immediately if you have an allergic reaction to a peanut.

Reading: An article about dangerous foods

1. Look at the pictures. What foods do you see?

2. Read and listen to the article. What bad things are mentioned about the foods? What good thing is mentioned about one of the foods?

3. Read the article again. What advice does the website give for . . .

   1. chopping onions? _____
   2. eating peanuts if you're allergic? _____
   3. eating fugu fish? _____
   4. avoiding mosquito bites? _____

4. **YOUR TURN** Work with a partner. Answer the questions.
   1. Are you allergic to any foods? Which ones?
   2. Would you try fugu fish? Why or why not?
   3. What other dangerous foods do you know about?

DID YOU KNOW...?

Eating a lot of onions can make you sleepy. If you have problems sleeping, have some onion soup for dinner!

Grammar: First conditional review; zero conditional

5. Complete the chart.

> *Use the first conditional to show results or possible results of future actions. Use if, when, or unless and the simple present in the main clause. Use will (not) and the base form of a verb in the result clause.*
>
> **If** your skin **smells** like garlic, a mosquito probably **won't bite** you!
> You**'ll have to go** to a restaurant with a fugu-trained chef, **unless** you _____ it to be your last meal!
>
> *Use the zero conditional to show a result of an action that is always true. Use if, when, or unless and the simple present in the main clause and the simple present in the result clause.*
>
> A poisonous gas **comes** out of an onion **when** you _____ or **fry** it.
> **If** the gas **gets** into your eyes, your body _____ tears to wash it out.

▶ Check your answers: Grammar reference, p. 109

6. Circle the correct answers.

1. I never eat fish because when I (**eat**) / **will eat** it, I **get** / **will get** really sick.
2. I hope we don't get grasshoppers this year. If grasshoppers **attack** / **will attack** our crops, they **destroyed** / **will destroy** the food.
3. You **get** / **will get** a lot of mosquito bites unless you **put** / **will put** on some bug spray.
4. I **don't try** / **won't try** sushi when I **go** / **will go** to Japan next week.
5. My mom **uses** / **will use** a lot of garlic when she **cooks** / **will cook** pasta on Sundays.
6. Your breath **smells** / **will smell** if you **eat** / **will eat** that garlic bread.

Get it RIGHT!

When talking about the future, use the simple present in the main clause with **if**, **when**, and **unless**. Do not use **will**.
If your skin **smells** like garlic, a mosquito won't bite you. (NOT: ~~If your skin **will smell** like garlic, a mosquito won't bite you.~~)

7. Write zero or first conditional sentences.

1. if / Jackie / drink / coffee tonight → not sleep well
    If Jackie drinks coffee tonight, she won't sleep well.

2. when / we / grill / steaks → we usually / put / a lot of salt on the meat
    _____

3. Johnny / not eat / those vegetables → unless / you / put / butter on them
    _____

4. I always / get / a rash → if / I / eat / strawberries
    _____

5. when / water / reach / 32° → it / boil
    _____

6. I / eat / chicken → unless / it / be / fried
    _____

Speaking: Party time!

8. YOUR TURN Work with a partner. Talk about what makes a party good and bad.

> *I like parties with music!*
>
> > *Not me. It's hard to talk when there's music.*
> > *I like parties with interesting food.*
>
> > *Me, too. But only if the food isn't spicy.*
> > *If the food is too spicy, I don't eat it.*

BE CURIOUS — Find out about argan oil. What is it used for? (Workbook, p. 78)

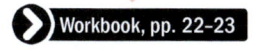

Discovery EDUCATION
4.1 THE ORIGIN OF ARGAN OIL

Unusual FOODS

Listening: A taste test

1. Do you like to try new foods? Why or why not?

2. Listen to three teens taking a taste test. Check (✓) the foods they try.

   a. ☐ jellyfish
   b. ☐ swordfish 
   c. ☐ fried chicken 
   d. ☐ fried alligator tail 
   e. ☐ chapulines/grasshoppers 
   f. ☐ beef tacos 

3. Listen again. Did the teens like the food? Complete the chart with *Yes* or *No*.

	Dale	Josie	Kristen
Food 1	Yes		
Food 2			
Food 3			

Vocabulary: Adjectives describing foods

4. Match the definitions (a–j) with the adjectives in sentences 1–10. Then listen and check.

   1. __j__ I don't eat cookies. I prefer **savory** snacks, like nuts and chips.
   2. ____ These strawberries are **delicious**! I love them!
   3. ____ Quick, give me some water! This sauce is really **spicy**!
   4. ____ This meal is totally **disgusting**! I hate it.
   5. ____ Did you forget to put spices on the meat? It tastes very **bland**.
   6. ____ Wow! This cake is very **sweet**!
   7. ____ This lemonade is very **sour**. It needs more sugar.
   8. ____ Yuck! This coffee doesn't have any sugar in it. It's really **bitter**.
   9. ____ Have you tried these apples? They're so **crunchy**!
   10. ____ I can't eat this soup because it's too **salty**!

   a. having a lot of sugar
   b. hard and makes a sound when you eat it
   c. tasting or looking terrible
   d. tasting very good
   e. having a lot of salt
   f. having an acid-like taste
   g. strong flavor; the opposite of sweet
   h. having strong spices that cause a burning feeling in your mouth
   i. not having a strong flavor
   j. spicy or salty and not sweet

5. **YOUR TURN** Work with a partner. Name foods that the adjectives in Exercise 4 describe. Do you like them?

   Lemons are sour. I don't like lemons, but I like lemonade.

   I like lemons on grilled fish. It's a savory dish.

Grammar: Second conditional review

6. Complete the chart.

> Use the second conditional to describe imaginary situations and possible consequences. Use **if** or **unless** + simple past for the imaginary situation. Use **would (not)** + base form of the verb for the possible consequence.
>
> ### Yes/No questions
>
> **Would** you **eat** it again **if** you **had** the chance?
> Yes, I _____. / No, I **wouldn't**.
> **If I saw** it on a menu, I **would eat** it again.
> I **wouldn't eat** it again _____ you **paid** me.
>
> ### Wh- questions
>
> **If** I **wanted** to eat *chapulines* again, where _____ I **get** them?
> You probably **wouldn't find** them **unless** you **went** to Mexico.
>
> *For be, use was or were after I.*
>
> I'd try *chapulines* if I _____ in Mexico. If I **were** in Mexico, I'd try *chapulines*.

> Check your answers: Grammar reference, p. 109

7. Circle the correct answers.

1. Rafa **didn't eat** / **wouldn't eat** snake unless he **was** / **would be** very hungry!
2. **Did** / **Would** you try jellyfish if you **got** / **would get** the chance?
3. If Laura **had** / **would have** to choose between giving up chocolate or pizza, she **gave up** / **would give up** chocolate!
4. If I **were** / **would be** a fugu chef, I **were** / **would be** very worried about poisoning my customers!
5. Unless I **picked** / **would pick** them myself, I **ate** / **wouldn't eat** wild mushrooms. They could be poisonous!
6. If someone **offered** / **would offer** you an unusual food, what you **would** / **did** you do?

> **NOTICE IT**
> *Was* and *Were* are both possible after *I* in the second conditional. *Was* is informal and *were* is more formal in style.
> *If I was alone on an island, I'd . . .*
> *If I were alone on an island, I'd . . .*

8. Match the beginnings of the sentences in the zero, first, and second conditional to their endings.

1. When I make eggs, _e_
2. If I go to Japan, ___
3. If I tried catfish, ___
4. I wouldn't eat raw fish ___
5. I'll order fish tacos ___
6. I always use beef ___

a. if I go to a Mexican restaurant.
b. I would probably like it.
c. when I make nachos.
d. unless it were sushi.
e. I boil them until they're hard.
f. I'll eat sushi.

Speaking: Food talk

9. YOUR TURN Work with a partner. Ask and answer the questions.

1. If you had dinner with a famous person, who would you eat with? Why? What would you eat?
2. What foods wouldn't you eat unless you had no other choice?
3. If you were to eat only one food for the rest of your life, what would it be?

> *If you had dinner with a famous person, who would you eat with?*
>
> > I'd eat with Demi Lovato because . . .

> **Say it RIGHT!**
> Listen to the questions. Notice the stress on the <u>word after the verb</u> in the *if* clause. Notice the stress <u>on the verb</u> in the clause asking about the possible consequence.
> *If you had **dinner** with a famous person, who would you **eat** with?*
> *What food would you **eat** if you were **alone** on an island?*
> Practice correct stress and intonation in the questions in Exercise 9.

> Workbook, pp. 24–25

REAL TALK 4.2 WHAT WOULD YOU MAKE IF YOU HAD TO COOK FOR YOUR FAMILY?

Family RECIPES

Conversation: It's a one-pot meal!

1. **REAL TALK** Watch or listen to the teenagers talk about what they would cook for their families. Complete the phrases they say.

   1. steak and _____ a big green _____
   2. pasta and _____
   3. a _____ steak
   4. do the grocery _____
   5. I'd _____ breakfast. _____ and pizza
   6. _____ on the side

2. **YOUR TURN** What would *you* make if you had to cook for your family for a day? Tell your partner.

3. Listen to Josh getting cooking instructions from his mom. Complete the conversation.

USEFUL LANGUAGE: Cooking instructions

| a pinch of | ✓ first of all | let it simmer |
| pour it into | stir it for | then add |

Mom: Hi, Josh. I'm going to be home late. I need you to make dinner.
Josh: Really?
Mom: Yes. We're having spaghetti. It's so easy – it's a one-pot meal!
Josh: Um, OK. What do I do?
Mom: ¹ *First of all*, put the beef in a pan and fry it. While you're frying the beef, chop an onion and some garlic.
Josh: OK.
Mom: ² _____ the onion and garlic to the beef, and fry it for a few more minutes.
Josh: OK. What's next?
Mom: Open a can of tomato sauce, and ³_____ the pan.
Josh: OK. Do I need to mix it together?
Mom: Of course! ⁴_____ a couple of seconds.
Josh: Do I need to add any spices?
Mom: Yes. Add ⁵_____ salt and a little pepper.
Josh: Great. And that's it?
Mom: Yes. Just ⁶_____ until I get home. You know, cook it just a little . . . not a full boil. Then we'll cook the pasta when I get home.
Josh: OK, mom, but that's another pot – spaghetti is a two-pot meal!
Mom: Oh, Josh! It's still easy!

4. Practice the conversation with a partner.

5. **YOUR TURN** Work with a partner. Take turns giving cooking instructions. Use the recipe for vegetable stir fry or your own ideas.

VEGETABLE STIR FRY

1. Cut vegetables.
2. Heat oil in a pan on very high.
3. Put vegetables into the pan.
3. Stir it for 5 to 10 minutes.
4. Pour soy sauce over the vegetables.
5. Add pepper and a pinch of salt.
6. Stir and fry for 2 more minutes.

A TRADITIONAL DISH
posted by Allison Bently

I live in Ironwood, Michigan, in the United States. We have a great deal of delicious food, but our most famous dish is the pasty. To make a pasty, put enough meat and vegetables on the dough to fill it, and fold it over so it looks like the letter D. Then bake it.

Pasties are usually served hot and are easy to eat with your hands. Traditional pasties are filled with beef, potatoes, onions, and carrots, but today, they're also made with chicken. There's even a taco pasty and a pizza pasty!

Pasties came from Cornwall, England. In the 1850s, British miners came to work in Ironwood. They introduced pasties. The miners left a long time ago, but the pasties stayed. Now, it's such a traditional food in my town. You can eat pasties all over England, but in the United States, you can only find them in a few places, like Ironwood!

Reading to write: An article about a local dish

6. Look at the photo. What dish do you think Allison is writing about? What's in it? Read her article to check.

   ### Focus on CONTENT
   When you write about a local dish, include these things:
   - the name of the dish
   - the main ingredients
   - how it's made
   - variations
   - how it's eaten
   - the history of the dish

7. Read Allison's article again. What information did she give for each item in the Focus on Content box?

   ### Focus on LANGUAGE
   Use these words to describe amounts or degrees of something without using numbers:
   a lot of / a great deal of: There are **a lot of** vegetables in stir fries.
   not much, too much: There's **not much** salt in this chicken dish, but there's **too much** pepper.
   (not) enough: Be sure to put **enough** pepper in the soup.
   such, so: This is **such** a good dish! It's **so** delicious.

8. Which words from the Focus on Language box does Allison use in her article?

9. Circle the correct answers.
   1. There aren't **enough / too much** spices in this dish.
   2. This soup is **such / so** salty!
   3. There's **a great deal of / much** cheese in the lasagna.
   4. There's **so / too much** salt on this chicken.
   5. This is **such / much** a good cookie recipe.

Writing: An article about a family dish

○ **PLAN**
Choose a dish that is a specialty in your family. Complete the chart.

The name of the dish	
The main ingredients	
How it's made	
Variations	
How it's eaten	
The history of the dish	

○ **WRITE**
Write an article about your dish. Use your notes to help you. Write at least 125 words.

○ **CHECK**
Check your writing. Can you answer "yes" to these questions?

- Is information from the Focus on Content box in your article?
- Do you use words to describe amounts or degrees of things correctly?

Pots and Pans of the PAST

THE MOROCCAN TAGINE

A traditional tagine is made of clay or ceramic. The bottom of the pot is wide and circular. The top is triangular. People in Morocco and other North African countries have used the tagine for hundreds of years to make meat or vegetable stews. The ingredients are chopped and put into the tagine. In the past, the tagine was put on very hot coals. Today, it is often used on top of the stove. After the stew simmers for hours, it is served in the tagine. Traditionally, everyone at the table shares this one-pot meal, eating from the tagine with bread instead of forks.

A MĀORI HĀNGI

A long time ago, the Māori people in New Zealand didn't have any pots for cooking. They roasted, baked, and grilled food on an open fire. They also created a way to cook with steam called *hāngi*. First, they put stones in a fire. Then they dug a big hole in the ground and prepared the food – fish or chicken, potatoes, and vegetables. When the stones were hot, they put them in the hole. Cabbage leaves were put on top of the hot stones and a great deal of water was poured over it. Then the food was put on top of the cabbage, and a wet cloth was put over the food. The steam from the water cooked the food. Today, people still use this method of cooking for special feasts. However, they often put the food in metal baskets.

THE MAYA MORTAR AND PESTLE

You may think that traditional foods of long ago were bland, but that's not true. Many cultures used spices thousands of years ago. Many native people of Mexico ate spicy foods. Groups like the Maya used a mortar and pestle to grind spices. The mortar is a small bowl and the pestle is a thick stick. In the past, they were made from basalt – a type of black rock. Today, some mortar and pestles are made from basalt, but they're also made from metal, ceramic, and wood. The spices go in the mortar, and they are ground with the pestle. This technology is thousands of years old, but people continue to use it in their kitchens today.

Culture: An article about traditional cooking

1. Look at the photos. What foods do you see?

2. Read and listen to the article. Match each item with its description and its use.

   1. tagine ____ ____
   2. hāngi ____ ____
   3. mortar and pestle ____ ____

   a. used to steam food
   b. used to grind spices
   c. pot to put on a fire
   d. a bowl and a stick
   e. method of cooking in the ground
   f. used to make stews

3. Read the article again. Write *T* (tagine), *H* (hāngi), or *M* (mortar and pestle).

   1. The food is cooked and served in the same pot. ____
   2. It can be made from ceramic. ____ ____
   3. It has two parts. ____ ____
   4. No pots or bowls are used for cooking. ____ ____
   5. It's used to heat up food. ____ ____

4. **YOUR TURN** Work with a partner. What other traditional ways of cooking do you know?

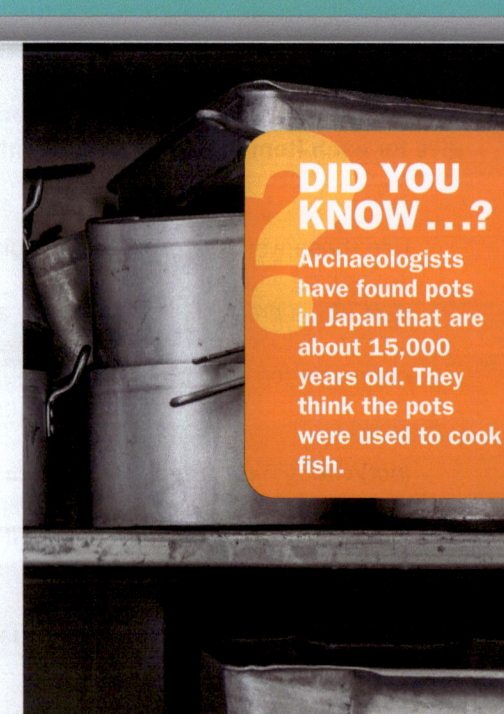

DID YOU KNOW...?

Archaeologists have found pots in Japan that are about 15,000 years old. They think the pots were used to cook fish.

BE CURIOUS Find out about fish in Japan. What are some of the kinds of seafood that people in Japan eat? (Workbook, p. 79)

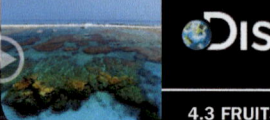

Discovery EDUCATION

4.3 FRUITS OF THE SEA

UNIT 4 REVIEW

Vocabulary

1. Circle the correct answers.

   Spicy Chili

   First of all, ¹**fry / slice** beef in a pan. ²**Boil / Chop** an onion and add it to the pan with the beef. Add a can of tomatoes and a cup of water. Add some pepper and a pinch of salt. Don't make it too ³**sour / salty**. Add other spices so that it's not ⁴**bland / spicy**. ⁵**Slice / Mix** it together. Let it ⁶**boil / grill** for 10 minutes and then simmer for 30 minutes. Put the chili in a bowl when it's done. ⁷**Grate / Mix** cheese and put it on top of the chili. Mmm . . . it's ⁸**disgusting / delicious**!

Grammar

2. Complete the sentences with the correct form of the words.

   1. If you fry garlic, it _____ (release) the flavor.
   2. I _____ (go) to a Hāngi if I go to New Zealand.
   3. Larry _____ (not buy) a tagine unless it's on sale.
   4. If it _____ (rain), we won't eat outside.
   5. Meat cooks when it _____ (be) on top of hot stones.
   6. If I make pasta, I _____ (invite) you over for dinner.

3. Write second conditional sentences and questions.

   1. if / I / have / time ➔ I / make / dinner tonight / .
      _____
   2. Carlos / take / cooking classes ➔ if / he / have / enough money / .
      _____
   3. I / not eat / dessert ➔ unless / it / be / chocolate / .
      _____
   4. if / Janet / be / really hungry ➔ she / get / fast food / .
      _____
   5. you / make / the food ➔ if / you / have / a party / ?
      _____
   6. if / you / buy / a mortar and pestle ➔ where / you / buy / it / ?
      _____

Useful language

4. Put the phrases in the correct order in the correct sentences.

of / a / pinch	all / of / first	simmer / it / let
add / then	it / for / stir	into / pour / it

   1. This recipe only calls for _____ salt.
   2. After the stew comes to a boil, _____ for an hour.
   3. _____ , chop the vegetables. Next, grate the cheese.
   4. Measure a cup of water and _____ the pot.
   5. Fry the chicken in a pan. _____ spices.
   6. Put the fruit in a bowl with juice and _____ a minute.

PROGRESS CHECK: Now I can . . .

- ☐ talk about how to prepare a simple dish.
- ☐ talk about party preferences.
- ☐ discuss imaginary situations in the future.
- ☐ give instructions for cooking.
- ☐ write about a family dish.
- ☐ talk about traditional ways of cooking.

CLIL PROJECT

4.4 YOU ARE WHAT YOU EAT, p. 117

5 Fame and Fortune

Discovery EDUCATION
BE CURIOUS

- A Cool Experiment
- How do you prepare for a sports event?
- Trendsetters

1. Who do you think the photographers are taking pictures of?

2. Do famous people walk on red carpets in your country? For what events?

3. If you were famous, what would you like to be famous for?

UNIT CONTENTS

Vocabulary Verbs expressing opinions; Adverbs of degree
Grammar Defining and non-defining relative clauses; Tag questions
Listening I see your point, but . . .

Vocabulary: Verbs expressing opinion

1. Circle the correct answers.

Meet Cathy, a very opinionated person!

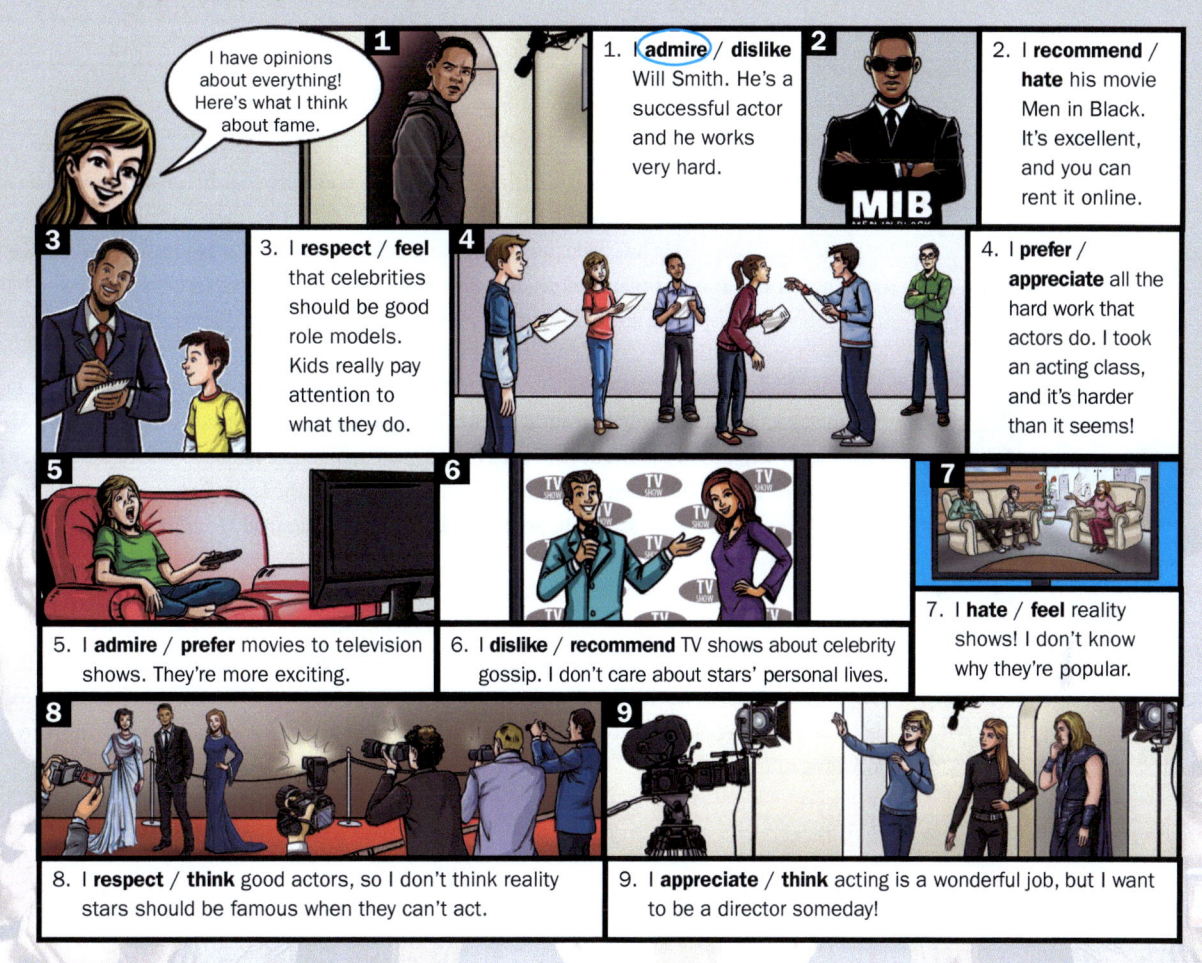

I have opinions about everything! Here's what I think about fame.

1. I **admire** / dislike Will Smith. He's a successful actor and he works very hard.
2. I **recommend** / **hate** his movie Men in Black. It's excellent, and you can rent it online.
3. I **respect** / **feel** that celebrities should be good role models. Kids really pay attention to what they do.
4. I **prefer** / **appreciate** all the hard work that actors do. I took an acting class, and it's harder than it seems!
5. I **admire** / **prefer** movies to television shows. They're more exciting.
6. I **dislike** / **recommend** TV shows about celebrity gossip. I don't care about stars' personal lives.
7. I **hate** / **feel** reality shows! I don't know why they're popular.
8. I **respect** / **think** good actors, so I don't think reality stars should be famous when they can't act.
9. I **appreciate** / **think** acting is a wonderful job, but I want to be a director someday!

2. Listen, check, and repeat.

Speaking: Movies and Music

3. YOUR TURN Work with a partner. Give your opinion about one of these topics.

Movies and actors	Music and musicians
What movies do you recommend?	Are there any songs you hate? Why?
What do you like and dislike about going to the movies?	What singer do you admire? Why?
What actor do you respect? Why?	Do you feel that singers should be good role models? Why or why not?

I recommend Avatar. It's such a great movie. I prefer watching it on a big screen, but you can watch it on your computer. In fact, I feel like watching it right now!

NOTICE IT
Feel and *think* are often followed by *that* to express an opinion, but *that* is optional.
I feel/think that movie actors are better than TV actors.
I feel/think movie actors are better than TV actors.
Feel can often be followed by other expressions, such as *like* and *as if*.
I feel like watching a movie. = This is what I want to do.
I feel as if you're not listening to me. = It seems to me that you're not listening to me.

Workbook, p. 30

Reading Celebrity Causes; The Book Is Better!; Getting Paid for Your Opinions
Conversation Making a point
Writing A comparison/contrast essay

Star POWER

Many celebrities do more than sing, dance, act, or play sports. A lot of people with star power give time and money to causes they care about.

Bono, who is the lead singer of the Irish rock band U2, is admired for his charity work. His interest in giving started in 1985 when his band performed at Live Aid, which was a concert to raise money for people in Ethiopia. He has been giving time and money to various organizations ever since. He has even started his own organizations, like the ONE Campaign. The ONE Campaign, which began in 2004, helps poor people around the world. Bono strongly feels that it's possible to end poverty.

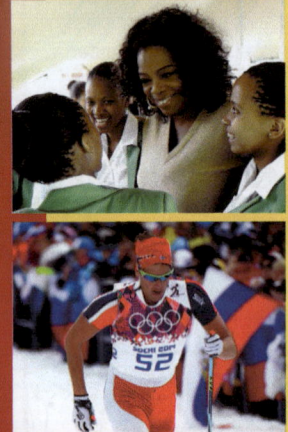

Oprah Winfrey, who became famous in the 1980s for a popular talk show, is another big giver when it comes to causes. People around the world appreciate Oprah for her generosity. The Angel Network, which Oprah started in 1998, has raised more than $50,000,000. Some of the money helped people whose homes had been ruined in Hurricane Katrina in the United States in 2005. A lot of the money was used for a girls' school in South Africa. Oprah passionately feels that everyone deserves a good education.

Sometimes, celebrities work together for a cause. During the 2014 Winter Olympics, over 100 **Olympic athletes** worked together to fight global warming. They saw the effects of global warming firsthand in Sochi, Russia, where the Olympics took place. The warmer weather affected the snow for skiing and snowboarding events. The athletes asked world leaders to do more to stop global warming.

Celebrities that give money to organizations often help bring attention to important causes. As a result, other people, who might not have known about the causes, care about them, too.

Reading: An article about celebrity causes

1. Look at the pictures. What causes do you think the people care about?

2. Read and listen to the article. Match the people with the correct causes.

   1. Bono ___
   2. Oprah ___ ___
   3. Olympic athletes ___

   a. helping hurricane survivors
   b. global warming
   c. ending poverty
   d. education

3. Read the article again. Are the sentences true or false? Write *T* (true), *F* (false), or *NI* (no information).

   1. Bono prefers singing to doing charity work. ___
   2. The ONE Campaign helps people in Ethiopia. ___
   3. Oprah's Angel Network only helps people in natural disasters. ___
   4. All of the girls at Oprah's school in South Africa do well in class. ___
   5. Olympic athletes have not noticed global warming over the years. ___
   6. People often become interested in causes that celebrities are involved with. ___

4. **YOUR TURN** Work with a partner. Do you think celebrities should use their fame to support causes and start organizations? Why or why not?

Grammar: Defining and non-defining relative clauses

5. Complete the chart.

Use defining relative clauses with who, which, that, where, and whose to give necessary information about a noun. The sentence has a different meaning without the clause.

People _____ **make clothing** should be treated fairly.
Celebrities **that give money to organizations** often help bring attention to important causes.
Some of the money went to help people _____ **homes had been ruined**.

Use non-defining relative clauses with who, which, where, and whose to give additional information about a noun. The clause can be left out of the sentence and it still makes sense.

Bono, _____ **is the lead singer of U2**, is admired for his charity work.
The Angel Network, **which Oprah started in 1998**, has raised more than $50,000,000.
They saw the effects of global warming in Sochi, _____ **the Olympics took place**.

> Check your answers: Grammar reference, p. 110

6. Circle the correct answers.

I hate reality TV stars ¹(who) / whose don't have any talent. I never watch the shows ²which / where have people living together. I do like reality shows ³that / whose are talent competitions. There were auditions for a singing competition show ⁴that / where I live. I have a cousin ⁵which / who tried out for the show, and he made it! Watch him on TV next week. He's the singer ⁶whose / that voice sounds like Elvis Presley!

7. Combine the sentences. Make the second sentence a non-defining relative clause with who, which, where, or whose.

1. Lilly gave money to the ONE Campaign. She likes Bono's music.

   Lilly, who likes Bono's music, gave money to the ONE Campaign.

2. The city of Sochi is warmer than it used to be. The 2014 Winter Olympics took place in Sochi.

   _____

3. Brad Pitt is a famous actor. His Make It Right organization helped hurricane survivors.

   _____

4. *Reality Gossip* is my favorite TV show. I watch it five nights a week.

   _____

5. We've lived in Hollywood for two years. Many celebrities live there.

   _____

Get it RIGHT!

Don't repeat the subject in a relative clause.
Lilly, **who likes Bono's music**, gave money to the ONE campaign. (NOT: Lilly, **who she likes Bono's music**, gave . . . .)
Don't repeat a direct object in a relative clause.
My cousins gave money, **which they raised in two weeks,** to a charity. (NOT: My cousins gave money, **which they raised it in two weeks**, to a charity.)

Speaking: Who would you help?

8. YOUR TURN Work with a partner. If you were a celebrity, which organization would you most want to help? Why? Discuss your ideas using relative clauses.

an organization that helps . . .		
wild animals	people in poverty	people get jobs
sick people	stop global warming	educate children

I'd want to help an organization that helps wild animals. My cousin, who has traveled to Asia, told me that tigers are in danger.

> Workbook, pp. 30–31

BE CURIOUS Find out about global warming. Why is Eric Gustafson doing an experiment? (Workbook, p. 80)

Discovery EDUCATION
5.1 A COOL EXPERIMENT

Making MILLIONS

Listening: I see your point, but . . .

1. Do you ever disagree with a friend's opinion? What do you do when you disagree?

2. Listen to Jack and Mae disagree about a topic. Who thinks actors and athletes make too much money?

3. Listen again. Are the sentences true (*T*) or false (*F*)?
   1. Mae and Jack liked the movie. ____
   2. The main actor in the movie isn't very popular. ____
   3. Mae thinks that movie tickets are too expensive. ____
   4. Jack thinks that Lionel Messi only makes money for playing soccer. ____
   5. Jack feels that players should get a lot of money because they could get hurt. ____
   6. Mae and Jack don't agree on anything. ____

Vocabulary: Adverbs of degree

4. Read the sentences and circle the sentence that is true for each situation. Then listen and check.
   1. Josh went to bed at 3:00 a.m. and got up at 6:00 a.m. He **hardly** slept at all.
      a. He didn't sleep much.　　　b. He slept a lot.
   2. Sandra makes $10 an hour. Vicky makes $11 an hour. Vicky makes **slightly** more money than Sandra.
      a. Vicky makes a little bit more.　　　b. Vicky makes a lot more.
   3. When I got home, **nearly** all of the lights were on.
      a. None of the lights were on.　　　b. Most of the lights were on.
   4. Laura was **pretty** excited to see her favorite singer at the concert.
      a. She was excited.　　　b. She wasn't excited at all.
   5. Martin, who is on two different soccer teams, is a **fairly** good player.
      a. He is good at soccer.　　　b. He isn't good at soccer.
   6. I saw an **absolutely** amazing movie, which my favorite actor was in.
      a. It was very good.　　　b. It was almost good.
   7. Usain Bolt, who has won many Olympic races, is an **extremely** fast runner.
      a. He's kind of fast.　　　b. He's very fast.
   8. Those bananas are **perfectly** fine. Don't throw them away.
      a. You shouldn't eat the bananas.　　　b. You can eat the bananas.

5. **YOUR TURN** Work with a partner. Do you think famous actors and athletes make too much money? Why or why not?

> *I think that professional athletes should be paid a lot because they work extremely hard. Nearly all of the athletes I like deserve the money they make.*

Grammar: Tag questions

6. Complete the chart.

Use tag questions to find out new information, to find out if someone agrees or disagrees with you, or to confirm something you believe is true. Tag questions are common in spoken English. If the statement is affirmative, the tag question is negative. If the statement is negative, the tag question is affirmative.

Simple present of *be*	Simple past of *be*
That's crazy, _____ it?	The acting **was** fabulous, **wasn't** it?
He**'s not** an actor, **is** he?	The acting **wasn't** good, _____ it?

Simple present	Simple past
That **seems** like too much, **doesn't** it?	She **admired** that actor, _____ she?
That **doesn't seem** fair, _____ it?	We **didn't see** that movie, **did** we?

Modals
Actors **shouldn't make** so much money, **should** they?
The actors _____ **get** a large portion of the money, **shouldn't** they?

> Check your answers: Grammar reference, p. 110

7. Circle the correct answers.

1. He'll make a lot of money for that movie, **will** / **(won't)** he?
2. Carl didn't agree with you, **did** / **didn't** he?
3. Robert Downey Jr. is the highest paid actor in Hollywood, **is** / **isn't** he?
4. You haven't seen that movie yet, **have** / **haven't** you?
5. Actors shouldn't care what people think about them, **should** / **shouldn't** they?
6. You can go to the soccer game, **can** / **can't** you?
7. That wasn't a famous actor in the café, **was** / **wasn't** it?
8. Mary and Ron dislike reality TV shows, **do** / **don't** they?

8. Complete the sentences with the correct tag questions.

1. Sandra Bullock gives a lot of money to charity, ___*doesn't she*___?
2. Basketball players make a lot of money doing TV commercials, _____?
3. You're buying the new Beyoncé album, _____?
4. Tom didn't make much money playing soccer last year, _____?
5. Larry shouldn't give up his dream of becoming famous, _____?
6. Jennifer Lawrence hasn't acted in a comedy, _____?
7. Angelina Jolie and Brad Pitt are married, _____?
8. You weren't at the last World Cup, _____?

Speaking: It was great, right?

9. YOUR TURN Work with a partner. What does your partner think about these topics? Guess using tag questions.

a popular movie	a famous soccer player
a hip-hop musician	a reality TV star

You liked the Avengers movies, didn't you?

Yes, I did. The special effects were absolutely amazing, weren't they?

Yeah. And the acting was great, right?

Say it RIGHT!

Listen to the sentences. When you are sure about an answer, your voice goes down with the tag question. When you are unsure, your voice goes up.

*You liked the movie, **didn't you**?*
= You're pretty sure the person liked the movie, and you want confirmation.

*You liked the movie, **didn't you**?*
= You don't know if the person liked the movie, and you want to find out.

Use the correct intonation when you ask questions in Exercise 9, depending on how sure you are of your partner's answers.

NOTICE IT

The tags **right** and **OK** can be used after statements with any verb tense.
*Let's stop talking and go to lunch, **OK**?*
*You haven't seen the Avengers movies, **right**?*

REAL TALK 5.2 HOW DO YOU PREPARE FOR A SPORTS EVENT?

Lights, Camera, ACTION!

Conversation: Getting ready for the game

NOTICE IT

British English	American English
crisps	potato chips
match	game
take-away meal	take-out meal

1. **REAL TALK** Watch or listen to the teenagers talk about how they prepare for a sports event. Check (✓) the things they mention.

   ☐ buying good shoes ☐ getting more sleep ☐ practicing
   ☐ drinking water ☐ listening to music ☐ stretching
   ☐ getting food ☐ listening to the coach ☐ swimming

2. **YOUR TURN** How do *you* prepare for a sports event? Tell your partner.

3. Listen to Elsa and Marcos talking about two soccer teams. Complete the conversation.

   USEFUL LANGUAGE: Making a point
   - as far as I'm concerned
   - it seems to me that
   - Not necessarily!
   - ✓ of course
   - That's a good point.
   - You're absolutely right.

   Elsa: I can't wait for the soccer championship on Saturday.
   Marcos: Me, neither. It's going to be a great game. ¹ _Of course_, Bayside is going to win.
   Elsa: ² _____ Clifton has an excellent head coach this year. I think they'll win.
   Marcos: No way! Bayside has won three years in a row, and they have the better team.
   Elsa: Well, they started pretty strong this year but ³ _____ they haven't been playing as well the last few weeks.
   Marcos: True, but that's because their star player was injured. He's better now, and he'll be playing on Saturday.
   Elsa: Oh, I didn't know that. But ⁴ _____, Clifton still has a chance. I mean, they won their last 10 games. And since they've never won the championship, they're going to really fight for it.
   Marcos: ⁵ _____ But they're going to have to fight extremely hard!
   Elsa: ⁶ _____ It's going to be exciting either way.

4. Practice the conversation with a partner.

5. **YOUR TURN** Work with a partner. Discuss one of the questions below or your own idea. Each person takes a different side, even if you don't really agree with it. Support your opinions with reasons.

	Student A	Student B
Which singer is better?	Katy Perry	Demi Lovato
Which team is better?	Real Madrid	Santos

THE BOOK IS BETTER!
by Ethan Beck

Both the first Harry Potter book, *Harry Potter and the Sorcerer's Stone* and the first Harry Potter movie with the same name are extremely good. In my opinion, the book is slightly better.

There are many similarities between the book and the movie. The characters in the movie are as interesting as the book's characters. In addition, many parts of the plot are the same in the book and the movie, especially the first scene.

There are also some differences. First of all, Harry Potter has green eyes, but Daniel Radcliff, who played Harry Potter, has blue eyes. Secondly, many of the characters' parts in the movie are not nearly as big as they are in the book. For example, Nicholas Flamel, who created the stone, is barely seen in the movie. Mrs. Figg isn't in the movie at all!

Although both the book and the movie are good, I feel that the book is better because we learn more about the characters.

Reading to write: A comparison/contrast essay

6. Look at the title of Ethan's essay and the photos. What do you think it's about? Read his essay to check.

> ### Focus on CONTENT
> When you write a comparison/contrast essay, include this information:
> - introduction: State your opinion.
> - body: Give similarities and differences in two separate paragraphs.
> - conclusion: Restate your opinion.

7. Read Ethan's essay again. What's his opinion? What similarities and differences does he give?

> ### Focus on LANGUAGE
> Use *(not) as . . . as* to compare or contrast two things.
> The book is **as good as** the movie.
> The movie is **not as long as** the book.
> You can also use adverbs with *(not) as . . . as*.
> The characters are **just** as **interesting** as the plot.
> That movie star is **nowhere near** as **rich** as his wife.
> The first scene is **not nearly** as **exciting** as the last.
> The second book is **not quite** as **good** as the first.

8. Find the phrases in Ethan's essay with *(not) as . . . as*.

9. Complete the sentences with the correct form of *(not) as . . . as*.

1. The movie *Alice in Wonderland* is <u>just as strange as</u> the book. (just / strange)
2. In the book, the Cat in the Hat is _____ he is in the movie. (not nearly / tall)
3. The movie *Charlotte's Web* is _____ the book. (magical)
4. The movie is _____ the book. (not quite / good)
5. In the movie *The Jungle Book*, the Croc is _____ he is in the book. (nowhere near / scary)
6. The book *Polar Express* is _____ the movie. (not colorful)

Writing: Your comparison/contrast essay

PLAN
Choose a book that has been made into a movie to write about. Complete the diagram.

(Venn diagram: The book. | Both | The movie.)

WRITE
Write a comparison/contrast essay. Use your notes to help you. Use *(not) as . . . as* and adverb + *(not) as . . . as*. Write at least 150 words.

CHECK
Check your writing. Can you answer "yes" to these questions?

- Is information from the Focus on Content box in your essay?
- Do you use *(not) as . . . as* and adverb + *(not) as . . . as* correctly?

Getting Paid for Your OPINIONS

It seems that everyone is a critic these days. People are saying what they think about movies, TV shows, books, fashion, and celebrities on social networking pages and blog posts. But what does it take to become a critic that people listen to and respect?

First of all, to be a good critic, you need to be a good writer. Your ideas need to be clear and organized. You also have to develop your own style. Is your writing smart and serious? Or is it humorous and quirky? People have to want to read your opinions and care about what you say! Secondly, you need to have a lot of experience in your field. Critics often make comparisons in their reviews. So, if you're a movie critic, you need to know about a lot of different movies – past and present. You should also know about actors, directors, and even cinematography (how the movie is filmed). If you're a book critic, you need to have read a lot of books and be familiar with many authors. Thirdly, decide what media you want to use. Do you want to write for a magazine or a website? Do you want to make video reviews or work on a TV show?

It can be extremely difficult to make a career as a critic, but these people did it.

TARAN ADARSH is a movie critic in India. He started working for a weekly movie magazine at 15. Today, he reviews Bollywood movies online and hosts a TV show, which includes movie reviews and interviews with Bollywood stars.

JACKSON MURPHY, who goes by the name Lights Camera Jackson, is a teenage movie critic in the United States. He writes online movie reviews that are extremely popular.

KELLY OSBOURNE, who is British, is a famous fashion critic. She was on a TV show called *Fashion Police*. She says what she likes and dislikes about clothes that celebrities wear.

If they do it, you can, too, right?

Culture: An article about becoming a critic

1. Look at the title. What ways do you know that people can get paid for their opinions?

2. Read and listen to the article. What three things does the article say you need to do to be a critic?

3. Read the article again. Match the beginnings of the sentences with the correct endings.

   1. You need to have an interesting writing style ____
   2. Movie critics need to know ____
   3. Critics not only write, ____
   4. Taran Adarsh is ____
   5. Jackson Murphy is ____
   6. Kelly Osbourne is ____

   a. a movie critic and TV host.
   b. a fashion critic.
   c. about actors and directors.
   d. so that people want to read your opinions.
   e. a young movie critic.
   f. but they also give their opinions on Web videos and TV.

4. **YOUR TURN** Work with a partner. Imagine you are a movie, book, or fashion critic on a TV show. Give your opinion about a recent movie, book, or fashion trend.

DID YOU KNOW...?
Most critics try not to include "spoilers" in their reviews. A spoiler is when you tell someone information about a movie that gives away a surprise.

BE CURIOUS Find out about trends and trendsetters. What do Saeko and Yuko do? (Workbook, p. 81)

Discovery EDUCATION

5.3 TRENDSETTERS

UNIT 5 REVIEW

Vocabulary

1. Circle the correct answers.
   1. We **appreciate** / **think** movie stars who help other people.
   2. I **feel** / **respect** that you care too much about following trends.
   3. Mike **dislikes** / **prefers** reading to watching movies.
   4. I really **admire** / **recommend** my sister for becoming her soccer team's captain.
   5. Lori **hates** / **appreciates** reality TV, and she gets mad at me when I watch it.
   6. Kayla **feels** / **recommends** Ursula K. Le Guin's books.
   7. My mother **hates** / **thinks** that I should watch less TV.
   8. I **respect** / **prefer** my science teacher for all of his hard work.

Grammar

2. Put the words in order to make sentences.
   1. who / I / slightly strange / comedians / prefer / are

      _____
   2. to schools / she / that / gives / nearly all her money / need help

      _____
   3. started a trend / the athlete, / who / won a gold medal, / in sports clothing

      _____
   4. were fairly expensive, / we / which / last week / bought concert tickets,

      _____
   5. whose / moved / to Hollywood / house we bought / the actor

      _____
   6. in the city, / our favorite singer / where / we met / we went / to a concert

      _____

3. Match the beginnings of the sentences with the correct tag questions.
   1. Nancy was perfectly calm before the concert, ____
   2. Julie works extremely hard, ____
   3. Vanessa isn't in that movie, ____
   4. Jin-Hee hasn't donated to our cause, ____
   5. Paulina will make a new album, ____
   6. Kate didn't win the race, ____

   a. is she?
   b. did she?
   c. won't she?
   d. wasn't she?
   e. has she?
   f. doesn't she?

Useful language

4. Circle the correct answers.

   Lynn: I really dislike reality TV shows. [1]**It seems to me that / That's a good point** the people who are on them are famous for doing nothing!

   Jeff: [2]**Of course / Not necessarily!** For example, on *Project Runway*, the reality stars are pretty good fashion designers.

   Lynn: Well, [3]**as far as I'm concerned / that's a good point**. But I don't mean shows like that. I mean ones where it's just about people's everyday lives. [4]**As far as I'm concerned / You're absolutely right**, they're just a waste of time.

   Jeff: [5]**It seems to me that / You're absolutely right!** I hate those kinds of reality shows, too. [6]**Not necessarily / Of course**, a lot of people disagree. They're extremely popular.

   Lynn: I know! Nearly all of my friends like them.

PROGRESS CHECK: Now I can . . .

☐ express opinions about different topics. ☐ make a point.

☐ give reasons why I'd support a cause. ☐ write a comparison/contrast essay.

☐ ask questions to confirm and find out information. ☐ give my opinion about a movie, book, or fashion trend.

Uncover Your Knowledge
UNITS 1–5 Review Game

TEAM 1 START

1. In 30 seconds, tell a teammate about how your interests in movies or music have changed from five years ago. Use expressions like *(not) crazy about* or *really into/can't stand*.

2. Use each of these phrasal verbs in a sentence: *sign up, give up, get along, turn into*.

3. Tell a teammate about something that happened last weekend. Use the verbs *watch* and *hear*. Then say what you were doing while those things happened.

4. In 60 seconds, explain the difference between a reporter and a blogger, and in what media you'll find an article, a news report, and an interview.

5. Role-play a difficult situation with a teammate. Show concern that your teammate's best friend is moving away. Your teammate responds.

6. Name the top three priorities you have in life, and explain why they are important to you.

7. Say 3–5 rules to have a good party. Talk about things that are possible and things that are always true.

8. In 30 seconds, describe someone in class using three adjectives of personal qualities. Your teammates must guess who it is.

9. Play "cause and effect." Tell a teammate a cause, such as *One day, I'll have earned a million dollars…* Your teammate responds with a phrase such as *since* or *because of* to introduce the effect: *since I learned to speak English well*. See how many you can say in 2 minutes.

10. Describe two things that you didn't use to do 10 years ago that you do now. Then describe two things that you often did 10 years ago that you don't do now.

11. Talk about your plans for the future. Use the verbs *predict, graduate, plan,* and *become*.

INSTRUCTIONS:

- Make teams and choose game pieces.
- Put your game pieces on your team's START.
- Flip a coin to see who goes first.
- Read the first challenge. Can you do it correctly?

    Yes → Continue to the next challenge.

    No → Lose your turn.

The first team to do all of the challenges wins!

- GRAMMAR
- VOCABULARY
- USEFUL LANGUAGE

TEAM 2
START

Use *be going to* and *will* to make predictions and talk about another classmate's plans for the next five years.

In 15 seconds, name seven different ways to cook food.

Role-play with a teammate. Your teammate is a famous athlete or celebrity. You are a reporter. Ask questions about where and how long they've been playing or performing. The teammate answers.

Tell a partner how to cook your favorite dish. Use cooking instructions, the steps in the process, and amounts.

Describe how your English was before you took this class. How long had you been studying before and how had your English been?

Predict achievements for two of your classmates. Use at least two of these nouns: *an award, a record, volunteer work, a business, a project.*

With a teammate, ask and answer three questions to find out information or if someone agrees/disagrees, or if something is/isn't true. Use tag questions.

Describe two foods you like and two that you don't like. Use adjectives such as *crunchy* or *sour* to describe them.

Make predictions about what a famous celebrity and/or athlete will have achieved in the next five years.

Say five sentences about what you did last night. Use these adverbs of degree: *pretty, nearly, hardly, extremely, perfectly.*

Share an opinion with your teammate. Your teammate should disagree politely and explain why. Continue the conversation for 30 seconds, remembering to use phrases to make a point.

Ask a teammate four questions about what he/she would/wouldn't eat in imaginary situations. Use *would (not)* in your questions. Your teammate answers.

Use different verbs to express opinions about movies, music, and sports. Say one positive and one negative sentence about each topic.

Use relative clauses (*who, where,* or *whose*) to talk about your favorite and least favorite athletes and celebrities.

Units 1–5 Review | 53

6 It's the Little Things

Discovery EDUCATION

BE CURIOUS

- Survival Objects
- What's your favorite gadget? 
- The Start of the Web 
- Inside the Guitar 

1. What are the objects in the photo? What objects are they made out of?

2. Do you think it's a good idea? Why or why not?

3. Do you ever use objects for other purposes? Explain.

UNIT CONTENTS

Vocabulary Everyday objects; Modifiers
Grammar Passive infinitive; Review of causative *have/get*
Listening All kinds of unusual things

Vocabulary: Everyday objects

1. Label the pictures with the correct words.

a candle   a fan   a light bulb   a remote control   an air conditioner
a charger   ✓ a heater   a plug   a switch   matches

1. _a heater_ 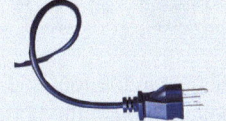   2.  _____   3.  _____   4. _____

5.  _____   6.  _____   7.  _____   8. _____

9. _____   10. _____

> **NOTICE IT**
> A system that cools a house or car is sometimes called **air conditioning** instead of **an air conditioner**.
> *It's hot in the car. Can you turn on the air conditioning?*

2. Listen, check, and repeat. (6.01)

3. What are the objects in Exercise 1 used for? Complete the chart.

to provide light or to light something	_a candle_	_____	_____
to heat or cool something	_____	_____	_____
to turn something on	_____	_____	
to give electricity to something	_____	_____	

Speaking: We need it!

4. YOUR TURN Work with a partner. Discuss why the objects from Exercise 1 are important. Which three do you think are the most important?

> *A heater is important because it helps us stay warm when it's cold.*

▶ Workbook, p. 36

Reading Light in a Bottle; Let's Hear It for Headphones!; Before There Was Texting
Conversation Buying a gadget
Writing A product review for a gadget

Useful INVENTIONS

Light in a Bottle

Imagine a light bulb that doesn't need electricity or plugs and doesn't cost anything to run. Alfredo Moser invented the bottle lamp in Brazil more than 10 years ago. He was trying to help people in his hometown, which often had problems with electricity. Sometimes there was only enough electricity for the factories, and people's homes and small businesses were left in the dark. One day, Moser and his friend were talking about how a light should be created for emergencies. One of them suggested using water in a bottle to reflect the light from the sun. Moser likes to be challenged. He thought, *Why not use water to make a lamp?* It was a great way to create a lamp that didn't have to be plugged in.

His invention is very simple. Start with a clear, plastic bottle. First, fill it with water. Then add some bleach to keep the water clean and clear. Finally, the bottle needs to be closed with a black top. The black top attracts the sun. When the lamp is finished, cut a small hole in the roof and push the bottle through it. The sunlight comes in through the bottle and lights the room below. The light is much stronger than light from a candle!

Moser's lamp bottles were installed in the local supermarket. Moser was happy to help his community. He didn't expect to be known around the world for his invention, but that's just what happened. Ten years later, the MyShelter Foundation in the Philippines heard about Moser's invention. The organization helps people in poor areas and specializes in building houses with recycled materials. They use plastic bottles to make walls and windows, but they had never thought of using them to make light. Now there are Moser lamps in more than 140,000 homes throughout the Philippines. The idea has spread to several other countries, too. Moser's bottle lamps have definitely made life easier for a lot of people!

Reading: An article about an invention

1. Look at the pictures. What is the invention? What everyday object is it made from?

2. Read and listen to the article. Complete the chart.

1. Inventor	
2. Country	
3. Reason for the invention	
4. Where it was first used	
5. Where it was used 10 years later	

3. Read the article again. Number the steps to making a bottle light.

   ____ Make a hole in the roof.   ____ Put the bottle in the hole.
   ____ Put bleach in the water.   ____ Put the top on the bottle.
   ____ Get a plastic bottle.   ____ Put water in the bottle.

4. **YOUR TURN** Work with a partner. In what other ways can people use plastic bottles or other everyday objects?

   You can keep rice in plastic bottles.

   Yeah. You can use old candles to fix furniture.

DID YOU KNOW...?

In India, people use bottle lamps in schools, and they also use them to grow food in some areas. In Bangladesh, the lights are used in small businesses.

Grammar: Passive infinitive

5. Complete the chart.

The passive is the main verb + to be + a past participle. The main verb usually expresses thinking or speaking, for example: be, have, know, want, need, expect, like, believe, and ask.

Present	Past
The bottle **needs** _____ **closed** with a black top. Moser **likes to be challenged**.	The lamp **didn't have to be plugged** in. He **didn't expect** _____ **known** around the world for his invention.

> Check your answers: Grammar reference, p. 111

6. Write sentences in the passive infinitive. Use the simple present for the main verb.

1. Brett / want / know / for his Web designs
   Brett wants to be known for his Web designs.

2. we / ask / inform / about all new projects
   _____

3. Carmela / not like / tell / what to do
   _____

4. the store lights / need / turn off / at night
   _____

5. the air conditioner / be / fix / next week
   _____

6. Lynn / expect / greet / at the inventor's workshop
   _____

7. Rewrite the sentences. Use the modals in parentheses.

1. The switch needs to be turned off. (must)
   The switch must be turned off.

2. The matches need to be dry before you can use them. (should)
   _____

3. The tablet needs to be repaired. (must)
   _____

4. Susana is to be picked up after school. (had better)
   _____

5. The new smartphone is expected to be sold in the fall. (might)
   _____

> *The passive with a modal can sometimes be used to convey a similar meaning to a passive infinitive sentence.*
>
> The bottle **needs to be closed** with a black top. → The bottle **must be closed** with a black top.
>
> *To form the passive with modals, use modal + be + past participle.*
>
> A light **should be created** for emergencies.

Speaking: More inventions

8. YOUR TURN Work with a partner. Think of three inventions for each category. Which invention is the most useful in each category?

1. Things that need to be plugged in
2. Things that don't need to be plugged in
3. Things that could be used at school and at home
4. Things that should be repaired regularly

> *Computers need to be plugged in.*
>
> *Yeah. And smartphones need to be plugged in.*

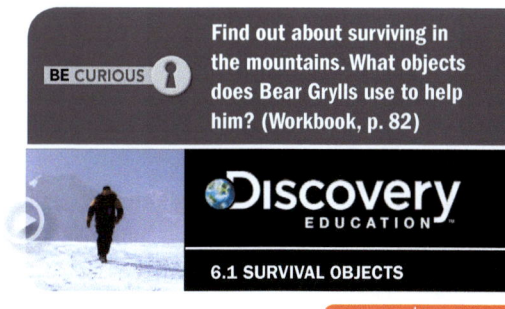

BE CURIOUS Find out about surviving in the mountains. What objects does Bear Grylls use to help him? (Workbook, p. 82)

Discovery EDUCATION

6.1 SURVIVAL OBJECTS

Buying and FIXING

Listening: All kinds of unusual things

1. Have you ever shopped at a market? What did they sell? Did you buy anything?

2. Listen to a man looking for a cheap, useful object at a market. Number the objects in the order he talks about them. Which object does he buy?

   _____ a. solar charger
   _____ b. handheld fan
   _____ c. floor lamp/heater

3. Listen again. Match the objects (a–c) to the sentences (1–6).

   1. These objects are expensive. _____ _____
   2. This object does two different things. _____
   3. This object is available in different colors. _____
   4. This object is available in different styles. _____
   5. This object can be sent to your house. _____
   6. This object uses sunlight. _____

> **NOTICE IT**
> *Kind of* has two meanings:
> A modifier that means *fairly*: *My smartphone is **kind of** small.*
> A phrase that means *a type/sort of*: *The AL20 is a **kind of** smartphone.*

Vocabulary: Modifiers

4. Read the sentences and check (✓) the correct column. Then listen and check your answers.

	−	+	++
1. This charger is **kind of** big. I'd rather have a smaller one.		✓	
2. The light bulb is **extremely** bright. It will be great for reading.			
3. That lamp is **ridiculously** expensive. It's $1,000!			
4. That invention is **not really** useful. I don't think anyone will buy it.			
5. That fan is **totally** safe. There's no way you could cut your finger on it.			
6. That air conditioner is **so** old. I don't even think it works anymore.			
7. That case is **a little bit** small for my phone. It doesn't quite fit.			
8. That heater is **far too** pricey. We can find a much cheaper one online.			

5. **YOUR TURN** Work with a partner. Talk about the items that you have. Use the adjectives below and modifiers from Exercise 4.

Item	Adjectives
phone	small, expensive
tablet or computer	big, new
bicycle	pricey, light
desk	old, heavy

> *My phone is extremely small. It was kind of expensive.*
>
> *Really? My phone wasn't really expensive. It . . .*

> **Say it RIGHT!**
> The phrase **kind of** often sounds like *kind-a*. However, when the following word starts with a vowel, the *f* is usually pronounced. Listen to the sentences.
> *My phone was **kind of** small.*
> *My phone was **kind of** expensive.*
> Pay attention to the way you pronounce **kind of** in Exercise 5.

Grammar: Review of causative *have/get*

6. Complete the chart.

Use causative *have/get* in situations where someone else does something for you or when it's not important who is doing the action. You can use *have* or *get*. They have similar meanings.
Use *have/get* + an object + past participle with the present, past, and future.

	Active	Passive/Causative
Simple present	Someone **cleans** her house on Thursdays.	She **has** her house **cleaned** on Thursdays.
Simple past	Someone **delivered** the lamp today.	We **got** the lamp **delivered** today.
Present continuous	No one **is sending** the lamp to the man's house.	The man **isn't having** a lamp _____ to his house.
Future with *will*	I **will ask** someone **to make** a designer battery charger for my sister.	I **will get** a designer battery charger _____ for my sister.
Modals	**Should** I **ask** someone **to wrap** them for you?	Should I **have** them _____ for you?

▶ Check your answers: Grammar reference, p. 111

7. Look at Sandra's calendar. Write sentences about her activities.

Monday	Tuesday	Wednesday	Thursday	Friday
get / clothes / clean	have / car heater / check	*Today – Now* get / hair / do	get / computer / upgrade	get / camera / fix

1. On Monday, *Sandra got her clothes cleaned* _____.
2. On Tuesday, *she* _____.
3. Today, _____.
4. Tomorrow, _____.
5. On Friday, _____.

8. Rewrite the sentences. Change the active to passive.

1. Someone painted our nails at the new salon. (get) *We got our nails painted at the new salon.*
2. Someone will fix Laurie's bike next week. (have) _____
3. Someone won't fix my phone until next week. (have) _____
4. Someone is repairing Sam's skateboard. (get) _____
5. Someone was painting your house last week. (have) _____
6. Someone had stolen Marta's purse at the mall. (get) _____

Speaking: It's broken!

9. YOUR TURN Write notes about problems you had with objects that you couldn't fix yourself.

My tablet crashed, my bicycle broke, . . .

10. Work with a partner. Talk about the problems from Exercise 9 and what you got/had done about them.

> My tablet crashed last week. I had it fixed right away. The computer technician got it done in one day!

> My bicycle broke. I didn't get it fixed yet, but my sister will try to fix it tomorrow.

Get it RIGHT!

Use **get**, not **have**, when the subject is doing the action for someone else. The computer technician fixed the tablet. She **got** it **done** for me in one day. (NOT: She **had** it **done** for me in one day.)

REAL TALK 6.2 WHAT'S YOUR FAVORITE GADGET?

Gadgets are GOOD!

Conversation: Getting gadgets

1. **REAL TALK** Watch or listen to the teenagers talk about their favorite gadgets. Check (✓) their favorite items.

   ☐ an alarm clock ☐ a desk lamp ☐ a phone ☐ a stress ball
   ☐ a camera   ☐ a flashlight ☐ a reading light ☐ a tablet

2. **YOUR TURN** What's *your* favorite gadget? Tell your partner.

3. Eddie is shopping for a new phone. Listen and complete the conversation with the words in the box.

   USEFUL LANGUAGE: Buying a gadget
   ✓ Could you show me | How good is | Is it . . . to use? | Does it have | How long does | Which model is

   Eddie: Excuse me. ¹ *Could you show me* some of your smartphones?
   Clerk: Sure. Did you have one in mind?
   Eddie: Not really. ² _____ the best?
   Clerk: I like this one – the TS500.
   Eddie: OK. ³ _____ easy _____
   Clerk: Oh, yes. It's extremely user-friendly.
   Eddie: Great. And ⁴ _____ the battery last?
   Clerk: About 8 hours.
   Eddie: That's not bad. ⁵ _____ the sound?
   Clerk: It's pretty good.
   Eddie: I see. And can I put a lot of songs on it? How much memory does it have?
   Clerk: You can download thousands of songs. You can get it with 16G, 32G, or 64G of memory.
   Eddie: OK. I need 32G. ⁶ _____ a camera?
   Clerk: Of course! Anything else?
   Eddie: Oh, yeah. How much does it cost?
   Clerk: For the 32G? $150.
   Eddie: Hmm . . . that's a little bit pricey, but I'll take it.

4. Practice the conversation with a partner.

5. **YOUR TURN** Work with a partner. Take turns asking a clerk about a gadget. Use one of the items below or your own ideas.

Gadget	A tablet	An e-reader
Model	Storm5000	Etric6
Battery life	10 hours	20 hours
Sound quality	extremely good	not really good
Memory	64G or 128G	8G or 16G
Camera	yes	no
Price	64G = $350 128G = $450	8G = $75 16G = $125

NOTICE IT
The *G* in *16G* means gigabytes. It is often pronounced as "gig" or "gigs."

★★★★☆ HEADPHONES!
posted by Ji Ah Rhee on January 6, 2015

I bought the Magicmusic G42 Headphones at magicmusic.com for $39.99.

The design is modern, and they are available in black and red. The headphones have a noise-canceling switch. It doesn't need to be turned on, but when it's on, you hear only your music, not the noise in the room. While most headphones have short cords, these have an extremely long one. They also come with a travel case that's kind of cool.

The sound quality is ridiculously good! It sounds like your favorite bands are right in front of you. The headphone volume goes from quiet to extremely loud. One problem: The headphones arrived broken! I had the package sent back, and the company did replace the headphones right away.

These headphones are a great value for the money. Whereas other headphones have stopped working after a few months, these headphones are lasting a long time. I've been totally happy with them and recommend them to other music lovers.

Reading to write: A product review for a gadget

6. Look at the photo, title, and number of stars. What did Ji Ah buy? Did she like it? Read her product review to check.

● *Focus on* CONTENT
When you write a product review for a gadget, include these things:
- the name of the product, price, and where you bought it
- the design and features
- the quality (what works and what doesn't)
- your opinion of the product and recommendation

7. Read Ji Ah's product review again. What information did she give for each item in the Focus on Content box?

● *Focus on* LANGUAGE
Use *while* and *whereas* to compare one product to another. They have the same meaning.
While the older model only has 32G of memory, the new model has 128G.
The new model has 128G of memory, **while** the older model only has 32G.

Whereas a tablet has a short battery life, an e-reader has a long one.
An e-reader has a long battery life, **whereas** a tablet has a short one.

8. Find the sentences in Ji Ah's product review with *while* and *whereas*.

9. Are *while* and *whereas* used correctly? Write **Y** (yes) or **N** (no).
1. The lamp has a light bulb, whereas it's also a heater. __N__
2. While most battery chargers are far too big, this one is extremely small. ____
3. The new air conditioner has 10 cooling settings, whereas the old model only had five. ____
4. While energy-efficient light bulbs use less electricity, so I bought some. ____
5. Whereas a typical fan has to be plugged in, this one is cordless. ____
6. Candles are useful in a storm, while your flashlight has to have batteries. ____

Writing: Your product review for a gadget

○ **PLAN**
Choose a gadget to review. Complete the word web.

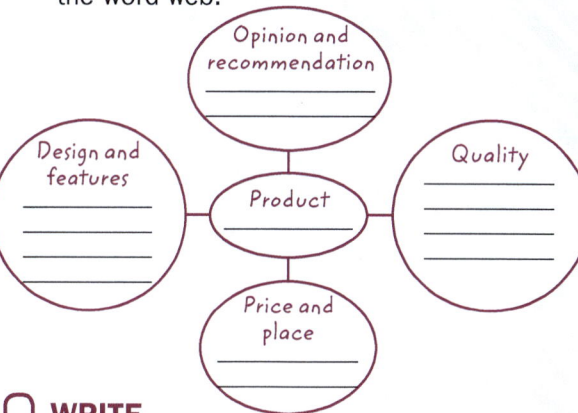

Word web with center "Product" and branches: Opinion and recommendation, Quality, Price and place, Design and features

○ **WRITE**
Write your product review. Use your notes to help you. Include the parts of a product review and *while* and *whereas* to make comparisons. Write at least 150 words.

○ **CHECK**
Check your writing. Can you answer "yes" to these questions?
- Is information from the Focus on Content box in your review?
- Do you use *while* and *whereas* correctly to make comparisons?

Before There Was TEXTING

Our world today is filled with gadgets that make our lives easier – and paperless! The invention of the Internet has also decreased our use of paper. We send emails and text messages electronically, and we sometimes do our homework online. We don't even think about the importance of paper. Whereas the Internet has helped us communicate in today's world, paper has been helping people communicate for centuries.

Writing existed before paper, but it was difficult. People wrote on clay tablets, shells, bones, and pieces of wood. Then paper came along and changed the world – slowly. The exact date of the invention of paper isn't known, but people in Egypt made paper about 5,000 years ago. Very thin pieces of papyrus plants were cut to be used as paper. Even though the word *paper* comes from *papyrus*, this invention didn't travel far. It wasn't until about 2,000 years ago that paper started to travel the globe.

Historians say that Cai Lun, a Chinese court official, was tired of carrying his books. During his time, books were written on pieces of bamboo, and they were extremely heavy. Cai Lun found a way to make paper from small pieces of bark from trees. He mixed them with water and pounded them with a wooden tool. Finally, he put them on cloth to let the water dry. The end result – a thin sheet of paper! After Cai Lun's invention, papermaking quickly spread throughout Asia, to places like Korea and Japan. About 1,000 years later, papermaking made its way to India, and in the 11th century, to Europe. In the late 1600s, people in what is now the United States were making paper. It wasn't until the 1800s, when paper factories started in Australia, that paper had made it all the way around the world.

Paper was one of the first tools used to help people spread information – through books, letters, and newspapers. You could say that paper was the world's first communication gadget!

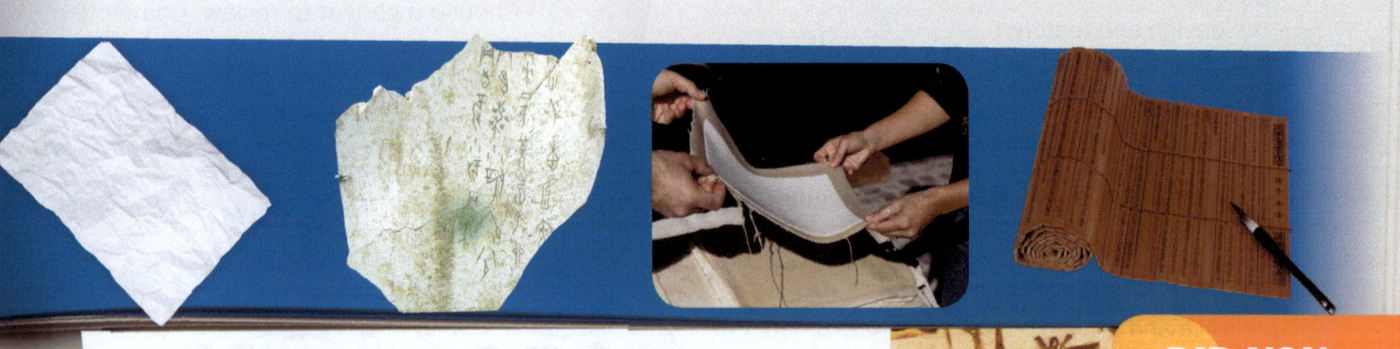

Culture: An article about the invention of paper

1. Look at the title. Why do you think paper is an important invention?

2. Read and listen to the article. Number the photos in the article in the correct order.

3. Read the article again. Correct the sentences.
   1. The Internet ~~increased~~ *decreased* the amount of paper we use.
   2. Before paper, people wrote on clay tablets, shells, bones, and pieces of plants.
   3. People made paper in Egypt about 2,000 years ago.
   4. Cai Lun invented paper because he didn't like writing in books.
   5. Cai Lun mixed pieces of tree bark and cloth to make paper.
   6. Paper could be found all over the world in the 1600s.

4. **YOUR TURN** Work with a partner. What other inventions changed the world? How did they change things?

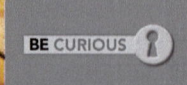

DID YOU KNOW...?
People wrote on silk cloth in China before paper was invented, but it was far too expensive for most people.

BE CURIOUS Find out about the history of the Internet. In what ways did the Internet change over time? (Workbook, p. 83)

Discovery EDUCATION

6.3 THE START OF THE WEB

UNIT 6 REVIEW

Vocabulary

1. Read the sentences. Write the missing words in the puzzle. Find out what Lorenzo needs to get by filling in the gray boxes.

   1. Can you find the ___ to turn off this lamp?
   2. Those energy-efficient ___ bulbs are kind of expensive.
   3. The blades in that old ___ look dangerous.
   4. Can you turn on the ___? It's so cold in here.
   5. The ___ to my computer doesn't fit in the wall socket.
   6. Do you have any ___ so that I can light this candle?
   7. I'm so excited about my new ___ conditioner because it has a remote control.

Grammar

2. Put the words in the correct order to make sentences.

   1. to / Chao / expected / for his work / paid / be

      _____

   2. by our friends / liked / be / to / we / want

      _____

   3. be / the invention / needs / by January / finished / to

      _____

   4. locked / the doors / be / at 9:00 p.m. / are / to

      _____

3. Write sentences with *get/have* something done. Use the tense in the parentheses for the main verb.

   1. I / have / my teeth / clean / next week (present continuous)

      _____

   2. Elsa / not have / her house / paint / this year (future with *will*)

      _____

   3. they / get / their skateboards / fix / before the competition (past perfect)

      _____

Useful language

4. Complete the conversation.

   | Could you show me | Does it have | Is it … to use? |
   | How long does | How good is | Which model is |

   Anne: ¹_____ some air conditioners, please?

   Clerk: Sure. What would you like to see?

   Anne: ²_____ the cheapest?

   Clerk: The Saver500 is the cheapest.

   Anne: ³_____ difficult _____

   Clerk: Oh, no. Not at all.

   Anne: ⁴_____ a remote control?

   Clerk: No, I'm sorry. It doesn't.

   Anne: Oh, OK. ⁵_____ the cooling system?

   Clerk: It's very good. And the Saver500 is on sale!

   Anne: Really? ⁶_____ the sale last?

   Clerk: Until Saturday.

PROGRESS CHECK: Now I can . . .

☐ talk about everyday objects and why they're important.
☐ talk about new uses for everyday objects.
☐ talk about inventions.
☐ ask and answer questions about buying a gadget.
☐ write a product review for a gadget.
☐ talk about how inventions have changed the world.

CLIL PROJECT

6.4 INSIDE THE GUITAR, p. 11

7 Have a Ball!

Discovery EDUCATION

BE CURIOUS

- Let's Celebrate
- What's the worst party you've ever been to?
- Like Father, Like Daughter

1. What is this woman doing?
2. Why do you think she's doing this?
3. Do you have a similar celebration in your country? What is it for?

UNIT CONTENTS

Vocabulary Celebration phrases; Descriptive adjectives
Grammar Verb + -ing form (gerund) or infinitive; -ing form (gerund) as subject; by/for + -ing form
Listening Surprising celebrations

Vocabulary: Celebration phrases

1. Match the phrases with the correct pictures.

a. dress up
b. give a present
✓ c. have a good time
d. hold a contest
e. play music
f. prepare special food
g. put up decorations
h. set off fireworks
i. watch a parade

1. _c_
2. ___
3. ___
4. ___
5. ___
6. ___
7. ___
8. ___
9. ___

2. Listen, check, and repeat.

3. Complete the paragraph with the phrases from Exercise 1.

This year, I'm going to have a New Year's Eve party. I'm going to ¹ _put up decorations_ in my home. They'll be black, white, and silver. I'm also going to ² _____, like some great desserts that my parents will help me make. I'm going to ask all of my friends to ³ _____ for the party. You know, wear fancy dresses and suits. I'll also ⁴ _____ – the best-dressed person gets a prize! Of course, I'll ⁵ _____ at the party. I've already downloaded my favorite songs of this year. At night, my older brother will ⁶ _____ – just small ones, of course. They'll look great in the night sky. I'm sure everyone is going to ⁷ _____. It will be the best party ever! My best friend is going to stay the night. It's her birthday the next day, so I'll ⁸ _____ her _____. I bought her a new case for her phone. Then we're going to ⁹ _____ downtown. The city has one every year on New Year's Day.

Speaking: How do you have a good time?

4. YOUR TURN Work with a partner. When do you do the things in Exercise 1? Tell your partner. Ask each other follow-up questions.

> My school holds a talent contest every year.

> Have you ever entered it?

> Yes, I have. Last year, my friends and I dressed up as rock stars and sang a song.

> Did you have a good time?

Workbook, p. 44

Reading How to Plan a Party; A Great Family Party!; Korea: Coming of Age
Conversation Making exclamations
Writing A description of a celebration

PARTY Planning

HOW TO PLAN A PARTY

Everybody loves going to parties! But some people don't enjoy hosting them because it can be very stressful. Are you planning to have a party? Read these how-to tips to make party planning easy!

1. **Choose the time, date, and place.** Give your guests advanced notice. Teens have busy lives, and you want to make sure the most people possible can come. Decide how many people you are going to invite before you pick the place. Will they all fit at your house? Do you need to have the party at a bigger place, like a park or a restaurant?

2. **Pick a theme.** Is it a party for a birthday, holiday, or other special occasion? Are you having a "just because" party? Consider having a theme party. For example, ask guests to dress up as their favorite cartoon characters or super heroes. Maybe the theme is related to the time of year, like "Winter Wonderland," "Think Spring," or "Summer Blast."

3. **Plan your party.** Decide what food you want to make and if you are going to put up decorations. Are you going to hold a contest or have games? Will you play music at the party or have a band? If you have a theme party, you can plan your party around the theme. For example, for a "Winter Wonderland" party, you might put up decorations of snowflakes and snowmen. You might serve cold foods, like ice cream. Don't forget to plan a budget. Figure out how much everything is going to cost. Are you going to buy food, make food, or ask your friends to bring something to share?

4. **Invite your friends.** Send out invitations. You can send emails, texts, or make an invitation to post online. Be sure to let your friends know whether or not they can invite guests. You don't want to invite 20 people and have 40 show up!

With a little planning, your party is sure to be successful, and you'll enjoy the party as much as your friends do!

Reading: A how-to article about planning a party

1. Look at the pictures and the title. What do you think you will learn from this article?

2. Read and listen to the article. Number the steps in order.

    ____ Plan the menu and activities for your party.

    ____ Decide what kind of party you are going to have.

    ____ Tell your friends about the party.

    ____ Decide when and where you are going to have the party.

3. Read the article again. Then read the sentences. Which steps from Exercise 2 are the people following? Write 1, 2, 3, or 4.

    1. Carrie is going to have her guests play card games. ____

    2. Leo decided to have his party at a skate park. ____

    3. Tom is having his guests dress up in sports uniforms. ____

    4. Luke is having his party on April 16. ____

    5. Jing posted an invitation on her Web page. ____

    6. Sylvia is going to have her brother's band play music at the party. ____

    7. Patricia is having a "Back to School" party. ____

4. **YOUR TURN** Work with a partner. Have you ever planned a party? What was it like? What kinds of parties do you like to go to?

DID YOU KNOW...?

Some people pay party planners to plan parties for them. Party planners are popular for big events like weddings, special birthday parties, and graduations.

Grammar: Verb + -ing form (gerund) or infinitive

5. Complete the chart.

Many verbs are followed by the -ing form of a verb or an infinitive.
Some verbs can be followed by either an -ing form or an infinitive with no change in meaning. Others can be followed by either an -ing form or an infinitive, but the meaning changes.

Verb + -ing form:	
consider discuss enjoy finish keep miss	**Consider having** a theme party. Some people **don't enjoy** _____ them.
Verb + infinitive:	
decide learn expect need plan want	Decide what food you **want** _____. Do you **need to have** the party at a bigger place?
Verb + -ing form or infinitive:	
begin hate like love prefer start	Everybody **loves** _____ to parties! Everybody **loves to go** to parties!
Verb + -ing form or infinitive with change in meaning:	
forget remember try	Don't **forget** _____ a budget. (= not forget to do something) I'll never **forget going** to my first birthday party. (= not forgetting that something happened)

> Check your answers: Grammar reference, p. 112

6. Circle the correct answers. Sometimes both answers are possible.
1. I like (**going**) / (**to go**) to parties on the weekends.
2. Remember **inviting** / **to invite** Susan to your party.
3. I prefer **watching** / **to watch** parades on TV.
4. We plan **dressing up** / **to dress up** for the holiday party.
5. The city decided **setting off** / **to set off** fireworks on Friday night.
6. Sarah finished **putting up** / **to put up** decorations at 9:00 p.m.

7. Write sentences. Use the simple past and -ing forms (gerunds) or infinitives.
1. I / learn / play / the violin six years ago
   I learned to play the violin six years ago.
2. we / discuss / prepare / special food for the party
   _____
3. Terry / start / take / photos at the graduation ceremony
   _____
4. Emily / expect / hear / from her cousin last week
   _____
5. They / hate / go / home after a school party
   _____

Say it RIGHT!
When a verb is followed by an infinitive, **to** usually sounds like *ta* and isn't stressed. Listen to the sentences.
*I learned **to** play the violin six years ago. My parents love **to** hear me play.*
Work with a partner. Read the sentences in Exercise 7. Practice reducing **to**.

Speaking: An end-of-school party

8. YOUR TURN Work in groups. Design your ideal school-leaving party. What type of party will it be? Formal or informal? Make a list of the activities.

> *I can't imagine having a formal party. Let's make it informal.*
> *But dressing up would be fun!*

9. YOUR TURN Present your party to the class. Which party sounds the most fun?

BE CURIOUS Find out about celebrations around the world. What holidays celebrate the change in seasons? (Workbook, p. 84)

Discovery EDUCATION
7.1 LET'S CELEBRATE

Let's CELEBRATE!

Listening: Surprising celebrations

1. Have you ever been to an unusual celebration or festival? What was it for? What was it like?

2. Listen to a show about some unusual celebrations. Circle the correct answers.
   1. The festival in Harbin, China, has **artwork** / **fireworks**.
   2. For the festival in Ivrea, Italy, people throw about **4,000** / **1,000,000** oranges.
   3. The festival in Lopburi, Thailand, starts **in the morning** / **at night**.

3. Listen again. Match the places (1–3) with the correct sentences (a–f).
   1. Harbin ____ ____   2. Ivrea ____ ____   3. Lopburi ____ ____

   a. There's singing and dancing.   d. People dress up in costumes.
   b. It's amazing at night.   e. The weather is cold.
   c. People feed animals.   f. It celebrates a past event.

Vocabulary: Descriptive adjectives

4. Replace the underlined words with the correct words. Then listen and check.

colorful	lively	peaceful	traditional
crowded	messy	scary	
✓ impressive	noisy	stunning	

   1. The dancers at the festival were <u>amazing and extremely talented</u>. *impressive*
   2. Jana's dress is <u>blue, yellow, green, red, and pink</u>.
   3. The street was so <u>full of people</u> that I couldn't find a good place to watch the parade.
   4. We made the party <u>exciting and full of energy</u> by playing music.
   5. Our house was <u>dirty</u> after the party, and we spent the next day cleaning it up.
   6. The fireworks were very <u>loud</u>. My little sister hated them.
   7. Last year, there was a fight at our New Year's party, but this year it was <u>calm and quiet</u>.
   8. My friend had a costume party, and I wore something <u>that made people afraid</u> – I dressed up as a vampire.
   9. The sand sculptures for the contest were <u>very beautiful</u>. They were so beautiful that they made me speechless.
   10. We learned some <u>old and historic</u> dances for a school play about our country.

5. **YOUR TURN** Work with a partner. Which celebration would you like to go to the most? Why?

   > I'd like to go to the festival in Lopburi because it seems lively and . . .

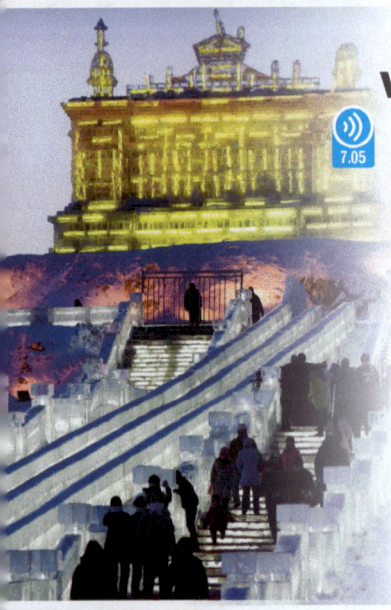

Grammar: -ing form (gerund) as subject; by/for + -ing form

6. Complete the chart.

> You can use the -ing form as the subject of a sentence. When it's the subject, the verb is singular.
>
> **Traveling** to Italy is always great.
> **Watch**_____ the monkeys is very entertaining.
> **Not going** to the festival would be a mistake.
>
> The -ing form can also be used after *by* to show how to do something and after *for* to show the purpose or use of something.
>
> Let's start _____ **returning** to Harbin.
> The weather is perfect **for making** ice statues.

> Check your answers: Grammar reference, p. 112

7. Write sentences using gerunds as subjects.

1. go / to the Sundance Film Festival / be / my favorite thing to do
   Going to the Sundance Film Festival is my favorite thing to do.

2. show / independent films at Sundance / support / talented directors, writers, and actors
   _____

3. have / a movie / at Sundance / be / a great honor
   _____

4. not arrive late / to a Sundance movie / help / you get a better seat
   _____

5. watch / Sundance movies / make / me happy
   _____

8. Complete the sentences with the -ing form of the verbs and by or for.

1. The city used an open field ___*for setting off*___ (set off) fireworks.
2. I mostly use my new smartphone _____ (take) photos.
3. We'll start the party _____ (play) music.
4. We'll celebrate the New Year _____ (watch) a parade.
5. Let's make the room look special _____ (put up) decorations.
6. The community park is a great place _____ (have) a family reunion.

Speaking: A lively celebration

9. **YOUR TURN** Work with a partner. Ask and answer questions about a festival, celebration, or other event you've been to.

1. What was the event? What was it like?
2. What was your reason for going?
3. How did going to the event make you feel?
4. What would others experience and learn by going to the event?

> *I went to the Garlic Festival in the park last summer. Going to the event made me want to eat garlic! It was crowded and . . .*

The Sundance Film Festival takes place in Sundance, Colorado, every year. The movies shown at the festival do not have big budgets like Hollywood movies.

REAL TALK 7.2 WHAT'S THE WORST PARTY YOU'VE EVER BEEN TO?

Party *Time!*

Conversation: Planning a party is difficult.

1. **REAL TALK** Watch or listen to the teenagers talk about the worst parties they've been to. Match the parties (1–6) with the reasons the parties were bad (a–f).

   1. _____ A party last month
   2. _____ A spring dance
   3. _____ Someone's own party
   4. _____ A wedding reception
   5. _____ A costume party
   6. _____ A best friend's birthday

   a. Parents staying for the movie
   b. A chocolate fountain not working correctly
   c. Getting the day wrong
   d. Dressing up for the wrong theme
   e. Not being able to play music
   f. Having to cancel the party

2. **YOUR TURN** What's the worst party *you've* ever been to? Tell your partner.

3. Listen to Drew helping Ellen plan her birthday party. Complete the conversation.

USEFUL LANGUAGE: Exclamations

Great idea! | How | ✓ is so | That'd be | That's such a | What a

Ellen: It's my birthday next week, and I haven't done anything for the party yet. I don't want it to be the worst party ever. Planning a party ¹___*is so*___ difficult!

Drew: Don't worry. I'll help you. What needs to be done?

Ellen: Well, I haven't decided what music to play.

Drew: I have tons of music. I can organize a playlist at home and bring it.

Ellen: ²_____ great! Thanks.

Drew: What about food? Do you know what you're going to have?

Ellen: Well, I decided to have a rainbow theme. Maybe the food could have something to do with that.

Drew: ³_____ cool theme! You could have food the color of the rainbow. Red cake, yellow and orange vegetables, things like that.

Ellen: ⁴_____ good idea! Let's make a list. And we can make a list of decorations, too.

Drew: ⁵_____ I'll help you put up the decorations the day before the party.

Ellen: ⁶_____ nice of you! Thanks.

Drew: No problem. I love planning parties.

Ellen: I'm feeling better about it, thanks to you. Let's start working on those lists.

4. Practice the conversation with a partner.

5. **YOUR TURN** Work with a partner. Take turns helping each other plan a party or event. Use one of the items below or your own ideas.

   | a class trip | a holiday party |
   | a pool party | a school dance |

Party Planner
THEME:
DATE:
BUDGET:
GUESTS:

💬 A Great Family Party!

posted by Amy Jackson | January 15

My grandparents were born on the same day. Last July, they were 70 years old, so we had a party with family, friends, and neighbors. The party was in my grandparents' yard because their house is too small for a big party. We did everything ourselves. My mom and dad prepared special food, and my cousins and I put up decorations.

First we had lunch at the party, and the food was so delicious! After eating, we watched a film my aunt had made with photos and videos of my grandparents. Then my little brother played "Happy Birthday" on his guitar. He was so nervous, but my grandparents loved listening to it. He played it again, and everyone sang. Finally, everyone gave my grandparents presents.

At night, we danced to my grandparents' favorite music. The party was so amazing! I wanted to dance all night, but I was too tired.

Reading to write: A description of a celebration

6. Look at the title and the photo. What do you think Amy and her family celebrated? Read her description to check.

⊙ Focus on CONTENT
When you write a description of a celebration, include this information:
- the reason for the celebration
- the place of the celebration
- how you prepared for it
- what happened at the celebration

7. Read Amy's description again. What information does she include for each category in the Focus on Content box?

⊙ Focus on LANGUAGE
Use *so* + adjective to emphasize an adjective.
*The party was **so lively**!*

Use *too* + adjective to say there was more than needed or wanted.
*We didn't set off fireworks at the party because it was **too dangerous**.*

8. Find the sentences in Amy's description with *so* and *too*.

9. Complete the sentences with *too* when possible. When it's not possible, use *so*.

| crowded | delicious | exciting | noisy | scary | slow |

1. The dance was _____! We had a great time dancing and talking with friends.
2. The festival was _____. You couldn't walk down the streets.
3. We couldn't dance because the music was _____.
4. My aunt and uncle prepared special food for the party. It tasted _____.
5. We couldn't talk to each other because the party was _____.
6. I screamed when I saw Connor. His costume was _____!

✏️ Writing: Your celebration

○ PLAN
Choose a celebration to describe and take notes.

Celebration	
The reason	
The place	
How you prepared for it	
What happened	

○ WRITE
Write a description of a celebration. Use your notes to help you. Use *so* and *too*. Write at least 150 words.

○ CHECK
Check your writing. Can you answer "yes" to these questions?

- Is information from the Focus on Content box in your description?
- Do you use *so* and *too* correctly?

➤ Get it RIGHT!
Be careful not to confuse *so* and *too*. Sometimes a sentence works with both words, but they have different meanings.
*She is **so** happy.* = She is very happy.
*She is **too** happy.* = She should be sadder.

Workbook, pp. 48–49

Korea: COMING OF AGE

Many cultures celebrate "coming of age." This expression means that you go from being a child to becoming an adult. In Latino cultures, this happens for girls at 15 with *quinceañera* parties. Many teens in the United States have "sweet sixteen" parties. In Jewish cultures, boys and girls have *bar mitzvahs* and *bat mitzvahs* when they turn 13. In Korea, on the third Monday of May, 19-year-olds celebrate their Coming of Age Day in the year they turn 20.

In some ways, it is a very serious and symbolic day. The soon-to-be ex-teenagers are acknowledged as adult members of society. They are reminded of the responsibility and pride involved in leading the future of Korea. Coming of age also means teens can do things that adults do, like voting, driving, and getting married.

Participants wear traditional Korean clothing, known as *hanbok*. The clothes are bright and colorful. Men often tie their hair into knots on top of their heads and wear traditional hats made of bamboo and horsehair, called *gat*. Women roll their braided hair into a bun, which is held in place with a *binyeo*, a long, decorative hairpin.

During the ceremony, the young people often sit in the center of a stadium, boys on one side and girls on the other. The children bow to their parents out of respect. In turn, the parents also bow to their children to recognize their children's promise to be responsible adult citizens. And then there's the fun part – people give the "new adults" presents. For girls, the most popular presents are jewelry, bags, flowers, and makeup. Boys often get watches or electric shavers.

The ceremony is hundreds of years old, and it was popular between the 1300s and 1900s. The ceremony became popular again in the 1970s. Parents fear that the traditional coming-of-age day festival is being lost in Korea. Many young Koreans think 20 is too old to become an adult. They feel like they are adults already and don't take part in the ceremony. Other young people decide to have more modern versions of the ceremony. For those who do participate, it is an extremely important and exciting day.

Culture: An article about coming of age in Korea

1. Look at the photos. How old do you think the people are? What are they wearing?

2. Read and listen to the article. What is the Korean celebration? Why is it important?

3. Read the article again. Circle the correct answers.
   1. People around the world celebrate becoming an adult at **the same** / **(different)** ages.
   2. In Korea, people are considered adults at age **19** / **20**.
   3. The boys and girls wear **traditional** / **modern** hairstyles.
   4. The children bow to their parents out of **responsibility** / **respect**.
   5. The ceremony was started again in the **1300s** / **1970s**.

4. **YOUR TURN** Work with a partner. Discuss the questions.
   1. At what age are people in your country considered adults? Are there any coming-of-age celebrations or traditions?
   2. At what age can you do these things in your country: vote, drive, get married?

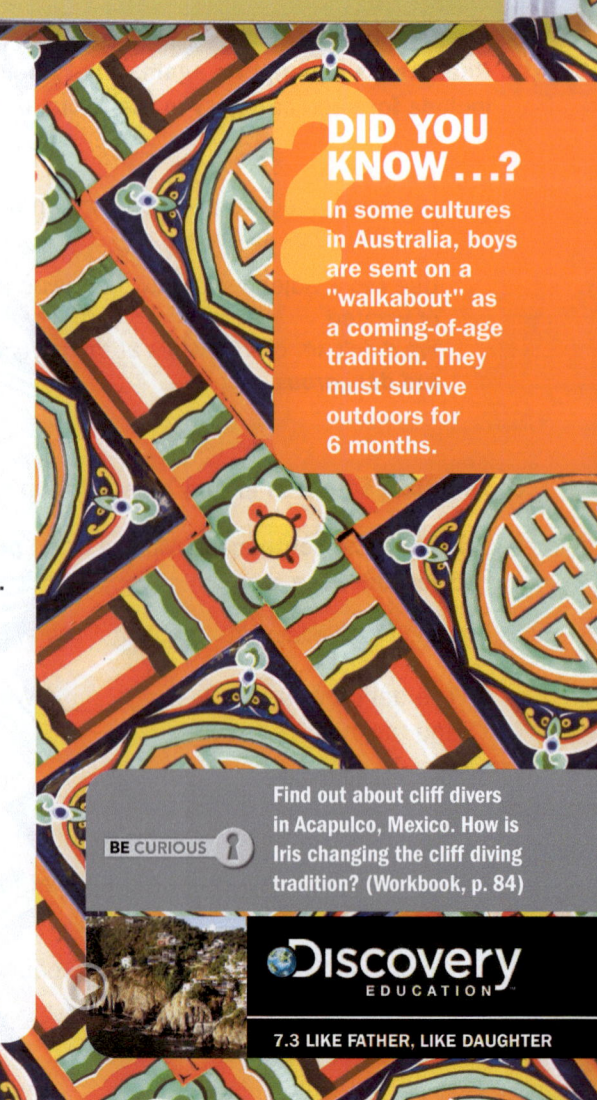

DID YOU KNOW…?
In some cultures in Australia, boys are sent on a "walkabout" as a coming-of-age tradition. They must survive outdoors for 6 months.

BE CURIOUS Find out about cliff divers in Acapulco, Mexico. How is Iris changing the cliff diving tradition? (Workbook, p. 84)

Discovery EDUCATION
7.3 LIKE FATHER, LIKE DAUGHTER

UNIT 7 REVIEW

Vocabulary

1. **What are the objects used for? Label the pictures with the correct phrases.**

dress up	give a present
play music	prepare special food
put up decorations	set off fireworks

   1. 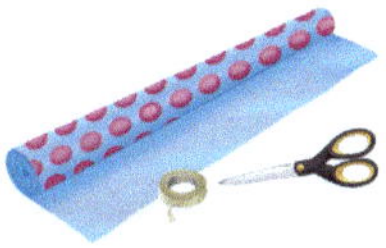 _____
   2. _____ 
   3.  _____
   4. _____ 
   5.  _____
   6. _____

Grammar

2. **Complete the sentences with -ing forms (gerunds) or infinitives.**

   1. Will you consider _____ (come) to my party?
   2. Gina forgot _____ (lock) the door.
   3. We thought the festival would be peaceful, but it began _____ (get) so noisy.
   4. I miss _____ (go) to school dances now that I've graduated.

3. **Correct the mistakes.**

   1. Seeing the Battle of the Oranges were impressive.
   2. We raised money for our school for holding a talent contest.
   3. No spending money on decorations was a great way to save money.
   4. We got around the crowded festival for walking on side streets.
   5. Give presents is my favorite part of celebrating the holiday season.
   6. My sister gets paid by singing at birthday parties.

Useful language

4. **Circle the correct exclamations.**

   1. **A:** Let's go watch the parade tomorrow.
      B: ____ idea!
      a. Great   b. How

   2. **A:** Are you done planning your party?
      B: No. Budgeting ____!
      a. that'd be difficult   b. is so difficult

   3. **A:** Look at my costume for the festival.
      B: ____ a colorful dress!
      a. What   b. It's so

   4. **A:** Let's have a party for Father's Day.
      B: ____ nice.
      a. What   b. That'd be

   5. **A:** I want to set off fireworks tonight.
      B: ____ bad idea! It's so dangerous.
      a. That's such a   b. Great

   6. **A:** I just won a dance contest.
      B: ____ impressive!
      a. How   b. What an

PROGRESS CHECK: Now I can . . .

- ☐ talk about party preparations and activities.
- ☐ plan an end-of-school party.
- ☐ describe events and festivals.
- ☐ comment using exclamations.
- ☐ write a description of a celebration.
- ☐ talk about coming-of-age celebrations.

8 Mysteries and Secrets

Discovery EDUCATION
BE CURIOUS

- A Lost Civilization
- What's the biggest lie you've ever been told? 
- Mysteries of the Brain 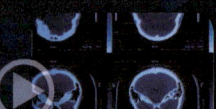
- Reliving History 

1. What is the scuba diver doing?
2. What do you think the diver will learn?
3. What mysteries do you know about?

UNIT CONTENTS

Vocabulary Adjectives with *un-*; Reporting verbs
Grammar Time clauses; Present participle clauses; Reported speech; Indirect questions
Listening A mysterious act of kindness

Vocabulary: Adjectives with *un-*

1. Complete the sentences. Add *un-* to the words.

✓ believable	known	necessary
expected	likely	solved
important	lucky	usual

1. The stories about the Bermuda Triangle are <u>unbelievable</u>! I can't imagine that so many ships were lost in that part of the ocean.

2. The hurricane was _____. We had no idea it was coming.

3. The news about the storm was so _____ that it wasn't even in the paper.

4. The location of the sailboat is _____. Rescue workers have been looking for it for 2 days.

5. It's _____ that we will ever know everything there is to know about the ocean, but researchers are constantly uncovering its secrets.

6. The scuba diver was sick the day her dive team saw a giant squid without her. She was _____.

7. Bringing our swimsuits to the beach was _____. We weren't able to swim because there were sharks in the water.

8. The Loch Ness monster is one of the world's _____ mysteries. No one has proven that it exists.

9. Dan saw an _____ animal in the water. It was very strange, and he had never seen anything like it before.

NOTICE IT
The prefix *un-* can also be used before verbs to give an opposite meaning.
*un*cover   *un*do   *un*lock   *un*pack

2. Listen, check, and repeat.

Speaking: Unusual events

3. YOUR TURN Work with a partner. Use the adjectives in Exercise 1 with and without *un-* to describe one of the following situations. Ask each other questions.

Situations	Questions
a dream you had recently	What happened (next)?
a mystery you heard or read about	What was it like?
recent extreme weather	How did you/he/she/it feel?
an interesting book or movie you've seen	When did you have/see/read/hear about it?

I had an unusual dream last night.

What happened?

I was in charge of an important event. I had to unlock the door to a room, but the key was too small.

What happened next?

This part is unbelievable! The . . .

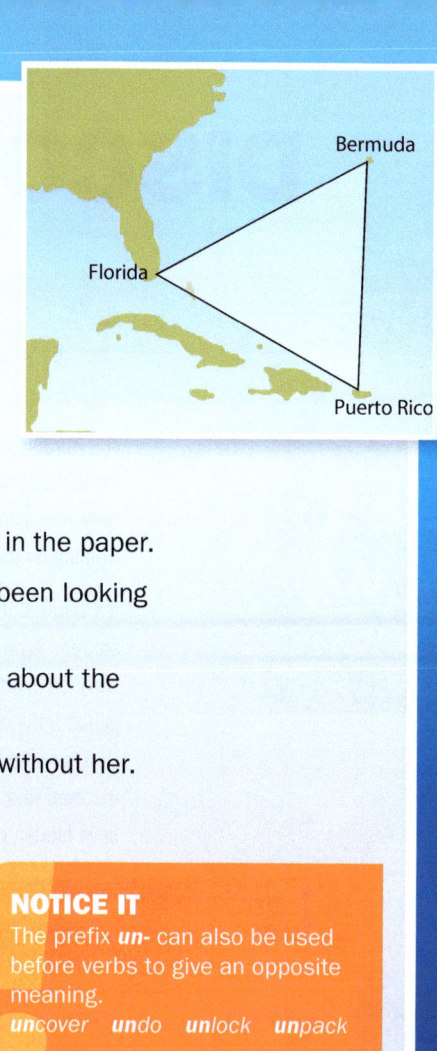

▶ Workbook, p. 50

Reading A Secret Under the Street; The Secret Room; An Unbelievable Book
Conversation Confirming and denying
Writing A story about a secret

DISCOVERIES

A SECRET UNDER THE STREET

The Atlantic Avenue Tunnel was made in 1844 before the subway system was created in New York City. Steam trains traveling between New York City and Boston went through the tunnel. The trains drove by Atlantic Avenue in Brooklyn, New York, coming in and out of the tunnel. As Brooklyn got busier, the train became more dangerous to people walking on the street. So, in 1861, steam trains were no longer allowed in the city, and the tunnel was closed.

It's 1980. Bob Diamond, a 19-year-old engineering student, is on a mission to uncover a secret. He hears a story on a radio program about the unused tunnel that is under the very busy street in Brooklyn, where he lives. Bob is excited when he hears that John Wilkes Booth, the man who killed President Lincoln in 1865, might have hidden pages from his journal in the abandoned tunnel. After hearing about the mysterious tunnel, he decides to start looking for it.

Bob finds an old map with the tunnel on it after searching city records for 8 months. It shows a circle above the tunnel, and Bob thinks it might be an entrance. When Bob goes to the place on the map, he finds a manhole cover and convinces men from a gas company to let him go down the hole. He crawls underground until he hits a brick wall. He knocks down part of the wall, and he's hit with unexpected cold air. It's the tunnel!

Bob's discovery is unbelievable! He never finds John Wilkes Booth's journal, but the tunnel is exciting enough. After the news spreads, he becomes a local hero. The city puts him in charge of the tunnel. He starts giving tours and also starts the Brooklyn Historic Railway Association. As soon as he found the tunnel, he knew he had to share it with others, and he wants to make this unknown city secret known to all!

Reading: An article about an old train tunnel

1. Look at the pictures. What do you think the man discovered? How old do you think it is?

2. Read and listen to the article. What is the purpose of the article?

    a. to inform the reader about secret train tunnels in cities

    b. to tell a story about a man's search for and discovery of a secret tunnel

    c. to give information about transportation in New York City in the past

3. Read the article again. Are the sentences true or false? Write *T* (true), *F* (false), or *NI* (no information).

    1. Bob Diamond wanted to become a train engineer. _____

    2. Bob does a lot of research to find the train tunnel. _____

    3. A subway replaced the Atlantic Avenue Tunnel. _____

    4. It took Bob more than a year to find the tunnel. _____

    5. Bob found a secret journal of a famous person in the tunnel. _____

    6. Bob gave tours of the tunnel to inform people about its history. _____

4. **YOUR TURN** Work with a partner. What things can you visit to learn about the past in your area? Were any of the things discovered in recent times?

DID YOU KNOW...?
Bob Diamond and others believe there is an old steam train buried in another part of the tunnel.

Grammar: Time clauses; present participle clauses

5. Complete the chart.

Use time clauses to show the order of events in the past, present, and future.
Use **before** to show that the event in the time clause happened second.
The Atlantic Avenue Tunnel was made in 1844, _____ the subway system was created. └── FIRST EVENT ──┘   └── SECOND EVENT ──┘
Use **after** to show the event in the time clause happened first.
_____ the news spreads, Bob becomes a local hero. └── FIRST EVENT ──┘ └── SECOND EVENT ──┘
Use **when** to show that both events happened at the same time.
They will search for a steam train in the tunnel _____ they have enough money.
You can use the **-ing** form (gerund) of a verb after **before** and **after**.
Before searching for the tunnel, Bob heard about it on a radio program. Bob finds an old map **after** _____ city records for 8 months.

Get it RIGHT!
When talking about the future, the time clause is usually in the present tense, not the future with **will**.
When they **have** enough money, they'll search for the steam train. (NOT: **When** they ~~will have~~ enough money, they'll search for the steam train.)

> Check your answers: Grammar reference, p. 113

6. Put the words in the correct order to make sentences.

1. an hour before / had waited / we / for / the tunnel / we saw *We had waited for an hour before we saw the tunnel.*
2. we / visit / seeing the tunnel, / the museum / after / will _____
3. the ancient pyramids / go to Mexico / we / will / when we / visit _____
4. online after / Maria usually / secret caves / posts photos / exploring _____

7. Circle the correct answers.

Scientists thought there were nine planets in our solar system ¹(**until**) / **every time** they discovered a tenth planet with a telescope. Scientists called the unnamed planet *2003 UB313* ²**while / before** they gave it its official name – Eris. ³**After / Before** they found Eris in 2003, they took photos of it. ⁴**When / Until** they studied the photos, they thought Eris was bigger than Pluto. However, they realized this wasn't true ⁵**every time / once** they did more research. Scientists have been discussing what the definition of a planet is ⁶**since / as** 2003, when Eris was discovered. Eris is now considered a dwarf planet. ⁷**As soon as / Until** news about Eris was shared with the world, people wanted to know about the tenth planet.

Other times clauses can be used to show:
- events happening at the same time: **while**, **as**
- one event quickly following another: **as soon as**, **once**
- when an action started in the past: **since**
- an action continuing up to another action: **until**
- repeated events are connected: **every time**

Speaking: My discovery

8. YOUR TURN Work with a partner. Pretend you made a discovery. Use one of the ideas below or your own idea. Tell your partner how you found it and what you'll do with it.

| an old book | a secret cave | a new star |

> I found an old book while I was cleaning our basement. Once I figure out how much it's worth, I will . . .

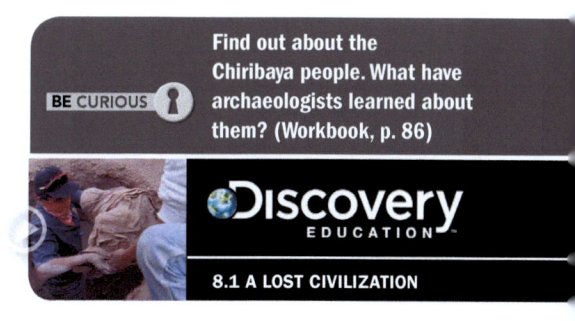

BE CURIOUS Find out about the Chiribaya people. What have archaeologists learned about them? (Workbook, p. 86)

Discovery EDUCATION
8.1 A LOST CIVILIZATION

Workbook, pp. 50–51

Solving MYSTERIES

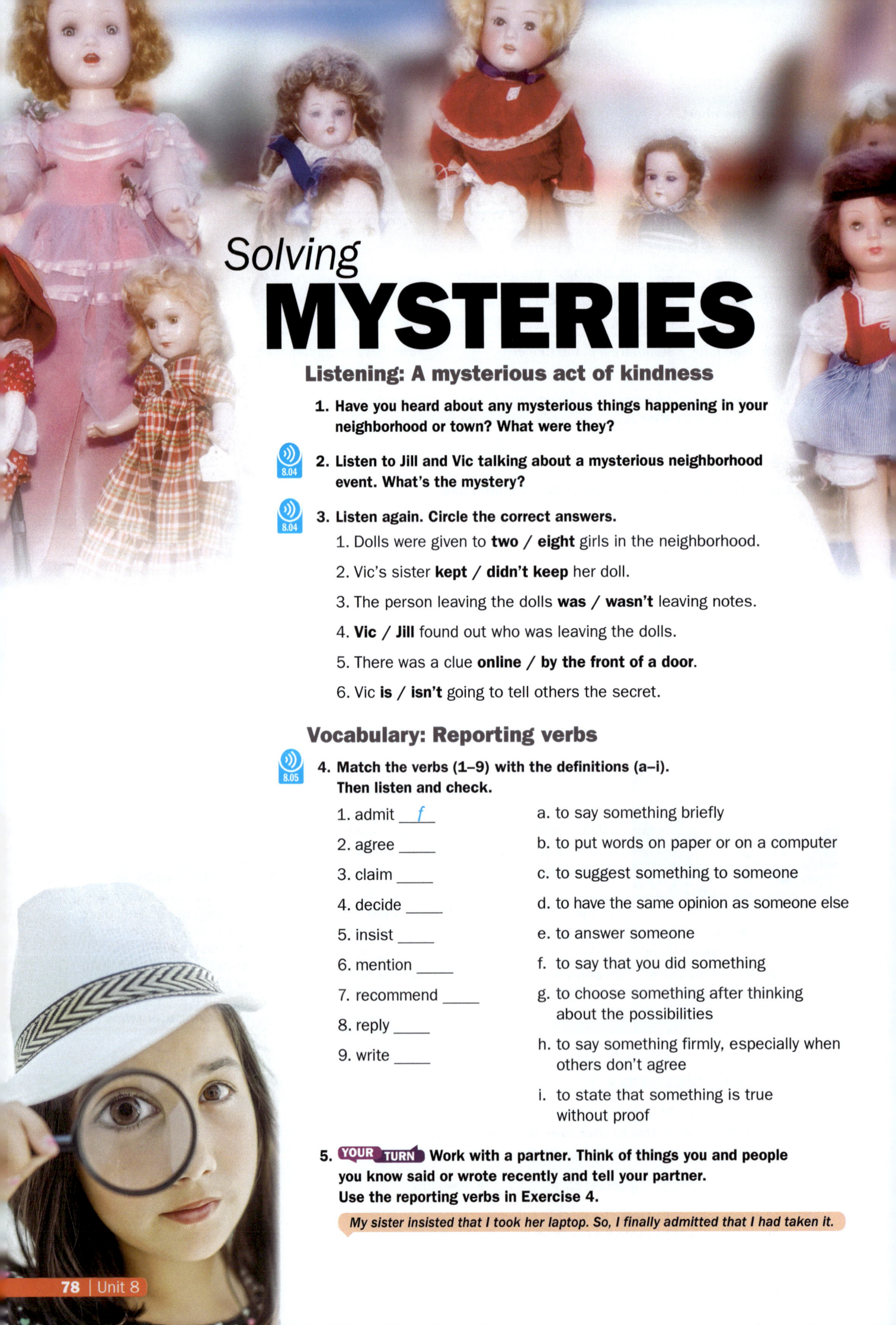

Listening: A mysterious act of kindness

1. Have you heard about any mysterious things happening in your neighborhood or town? What were they?

2. Listen to Jill and Vic talking about a mysterious neighborhood event. What's the mystery?

3. Listen again. Circle the correct answers.

   1. Dolls were given to **two / eight** girls in the neighborhood.
   2. Vic's sister **kept / didn't keep** her doll.
   3. The person leaving the dolls **was / wasn't** leaving notes.
   4. **Vic / Jill** found out who was leaving the dolls.
   5. There was a clue **online / by the front of a door**.
   6. Vic **is / isn't** going to tell others the secret.

Vocabulary: Reporting verbs

4. Match the verbs (1–9) with the definitions (a–i). Then listen and check.

   1. admit *f*
   2. agree ____
   3. claim ____
   4. decide ____
   5. insist ____
   6. mention ____
   7. recommend ____
   8. reply ____
   9. write ____

   a. to say something briefly
   b. to put words on paper or on a computer
   c. to suggest something to someone
   d. to have the same opinion as someone else
   e. to answer someone
   f. to say that you did something
   g. to choose something after thinking about the possibilities
   h. to say something firmly, especially when others don't agree
   i. to state that something is true without proof

5. **YOUR TURN** Work with a partner. Think of things you and people you know said or wrote recently and tell your partner. Use the reporting verbs in Exercise 4.

   My sister insisted that I took her laptop. So, I finally admitted that I had taken it.

Grammar: Reported speech; indirect questions

6. Complete the chart.

Use reported speech and reported questions to tell others what another person said. In both reported speech and reported questions, the verbs usually change tenses.

Quoted speech	Reported speech
She said, "I **am leaving** the dolls."	She admitted that she **was leaving** the dolls.
She said, "I **was watching** TV."	She wrote that she _____ **been watching** TV.
He asked, "**When will** you **be talking** to her?"	He asked me **when** I **would be** _____ to her.
He asked, "**Are** you **keeping** her secret?"	He asked me **if** I **was keeping** her secret.

Infinitives can be used with these reporting verbs: agree, claim, decide.

I **agreed to keep** it a secret.	She **claimed** _____ **know** who had done it.

The -ing form can be used with these reporting verbs: recommend, insist on, admit to.

She **insisted** _____ **keeping** the doll.	I **recommend posting** a question online.

Imperative clauses

Change an imperative to a reported imperative using infinitive verbs.

Quoted imperative	Reported imperative
He said, "**Tell** me about it!"	He told her **to tell** him about it.
She said, "**Don't tell** anyone."	She said **not** _____ anyone.

> Check your answers: Grammar reference, p. 113

7. Change the direct speech to reported speech.

1. "I'll be going to a detective school." (she / mention)
   She mentioned that she would be going to a detective school.

2. "I was reading a mystery book all day." (she / claim)
   _____

3. "We'll solve this mystery." (they / insist on + -ing form)
   _____

4. "Don't look in that closet." (he / say)
   _____

5. "Are you trying to solve the mystery?" (he / ask us)
   _____

6. "Tell me the ending of the story." (I / say)
   _____

8. Write indirect questions for the witness of a robbery.

1. What's your name?
   Can you tell me your name?

2. What happened?
   _____

3. When did the robbery take place?
   _____

4. Did you do anything to try to stop the robbers?
   _____

5. Were you frightened?
   _____

Indirect Questions

Can you tell me . . . ?, Could you tell me . . . ?, I wonder . . . , and *I don't know* are used to form indirect questions.

Direct	Indirect
What's going on?	**Can you tell me** what's going on?
Why was she doing it?	**I wonder** why she was doing it.
Did she admit to the crime?	**I don't know** if she admitted to the crime.

Say it RIGHT!

Listen to the indirect questions. Notice the rising and falling intonation.
Can you tell me what happened?
I wonder what happened.
Pay attention to the way you pronounce indirect questions in Exercise 9.

Speaking: Where were you last night?

9. YOUR TURN Make notes about an imaginary crime you saw. Work with a partner. Student A is a police officer and Student B is a witness. Use the questions in Exercise 8 and your own ideas to ask and answer questions about what you saw. Then swap roles.

> Workbook, pp. 52–53

REAL TALK 8.2 WHAT'S THE BIGGEST LIE YOU'VE EVER BEEN TOLD?

Truths and Lies

Conversation: It's a lie!

1. **REAL TALK** Watch or listen to the teenagers talk about lies they've been told. Match the people to the lies they told.

   1. A classmate _____
   2. An ex-best friend _____
   3. A brother _____
   4. Everyone _____
   5. A grandma _____
   6. A boy in class _____

   a. insisted that a fruit tasted great.
   b. explained that vegetables did amazing things.
   c. claimed that there wasn't school tomorrow.
   d. said it was an ocean-themed party.
   e. announced that his cousin was famous.
   f. mentioned that her grandma wasn't well.

2. **YOUR TURN** What's the biggest lie *you've* ever been told? Tell your partner.

3. Listen to a famous soccer player being interviewed. Complete the conversation.

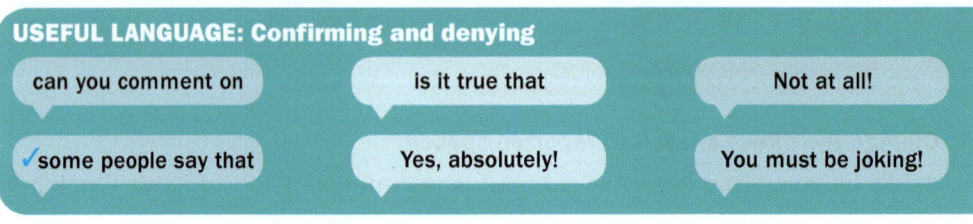

   USEFUL LANGUAGE: Confirming and denying

   | can you comment on | is it true that | Not at all! |
   | ✓ some people say that | Yes, absolutely! | You must be joking! |

   Host: Today I'm interviewing a world-famous soccer player. Lucas, there are a lot of things I need to ask you.

   Lucas: No problem. Ask away!

   Host: OK. So, you're only 19 years old, you have a five-year contract, and ¹ *some people say that* you earn over $100,000 a week.

   Lucas: Ha! ² _____ I make a lot less than that, and many players on the team make more than me.

   Host: OK. But ³ _____ you just bought a new sports car?

   Lucas: ⁴ _____ That is true. It's always been my dream to own one.

   Host: Nice! Now, let's talk about the team. A teammate claimed that you don't get along with your coach. ⁵ _____ the situation?

   Lucas: It's a lie! I don't know if my teammate even said that.

   Host: I see. Hey, I've heard that you've been having an unlucky streak. True?

   Lucas: ⁶ _____ I mean, no way. I've been playing better than ever!

   Host: Well, thank you, Lucas. That clears some things up for us.

4. Practice the conversation with a partner.

5. **YOUR TURN** Work with a partner. Take turns asking about situations and confirming and denying them. Use one of the situations in the box or your own ideas.

Situation 1	Situation 2
Student A: You are a TV host asking a famous actor about these situations. You heard: • he/she had an argument with another famous actor • he/she is going to quit acting **Student B:** You are the actor. Confirm or deny the situations with your own ideas.	**Student A:** You are a radio host asking a researcher about a mystery. You heard: • he/she saw an unusual sea creature • he/she was attacked by the sea creature **Student B:** You are the researcher. Confirm or deny the situations with your own ideas.

The Secret Room

by Loretta Price

Mom's high heels

Grandpa's shoes

Our favorite trunk

When my brother and I were young, we had a secret playroom in the attic. We used to sneak up there when my parents were downstairs. The first time we were in the attic, we found a locked box. We searched all over until we found the key. We unlocked the box and it was full of old clothes – not only our parents' clothes, but also our grandparents' clothes! After that, we would go up there whenever we could. We used to dress up in the clothes and pretend that we lived in the past.

Last week, when talking with our parents, we admitted playing in the attic as kids. My dad replied that they had known all along! They had decided not to tell us in order to let us think we were being sneaky. My brother and I agreed that we were glad. It had been fun thinking we had a secret.

Reading to write: A story about a secret

6. Look at the photo. What do you think is in the box? Read Loretta's story to check.

⊙ Focus on CONTENT
When you write a story, include these things:
- an introduction: what the story is about
- background information: who, where, when
- what happened: the events in order
- a conclusion: why the story was special or what you learned

7. Read Loretta's story again. What information does she give for each item in the Focus on Content box?

⊙ Focus on LANGUAGE
Use *in order to, so that,* and *not only . . . but also* to connect ideas.
I got online **in order to** read more about the mystery.
The soccer player did an interview **so that** he could tell the truth about his life.
The detective **not only** solved the crime, **but** she **also** caught the thief.

8. Find the sentences in Loretta's story with the connectors from the Focus on Language box.

9. Circle the correct answers.

1. I used to tell stories **so that / in order to** make my friends laugh.
2. The thief **not only / so that** lied about his actions, but he also asked his friend to lie.
3. Did you follow that man **so that / but also** you could help solve the mystery?
4. The book was not only old, **in order to / but also** valuable.
5. We told the truth **in order to / so that** not get in trouble.

▶ Workbook, pp. 54–55

Writing: Your story about a secret

○ PLAN
Choose a secret or mystery to write a story about. It can be something that happened to you, something you know about, or something you create. Complete the word web.

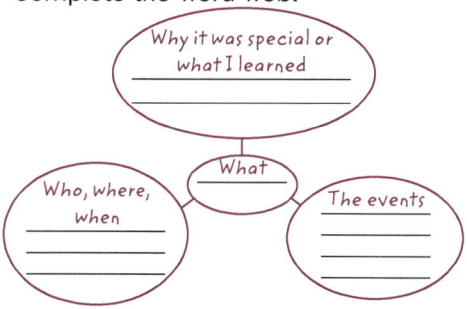

- Why it was special or what I learned
- Who, where, when
- What
- The events

○ WRITE
Write your story. Use your notes to help you. Include connectors. Write at least 150 words.

○ CHECK
Check your writing. Can you answer "yes" to these questions?

- Is information from the Focus on Content box in your story?
- Do you use connectors correctly?

An Unbelievable BOOK

Have you ever had a secret language with a brother, sister, or friend? Have you ever kept notes and pictures in a secret book? One mysterious book, called *The Voynich Manuscript*, has had experts confused for years. Book collector Wilfrid Voynich discovered the book in 1912, but experts believe it was written in the early 1400s. Language experts around the world have looked at the book, and no one has been able to figure out what the language is or what the text says. They don't know if it's an invented language, a secret code, or even a hoax.

Even though no one can figure out what the text means, experts agree that it has patterns. For example, symbols that look like "40" always appear at the start of a word, and symbols that look like "89" always appear at the end. However, many of the patterns are not similar to patterns in any other language. For instance, many words appear three three three times. This doesn't happen happen happen in known languages.

The Voynich Manuscript not only contains writings, but also drawings. There are colorful drawings of people and plants. This made some people wonder if the book was a journal someone kept while traveling around the world. But most of the drawings have just confused experts. They say that many of the drawings of plants cannot be identified as any known plants in the world. This has made some people wonder if the book was someone's art project.

In 2014, Professor Stephen Bax thought he had figured out part of the code. *The Voynich Manuscript* also contains pictures and diagrams of stars. Bax claims that some of the writing translates to names for real constellations – groups of stars. Bax has only figured out a few words in the book, but he insists that his decoding proves that the book isn't a hoax. Not everyone agrees. Bax hopes that others will continue to do detective work and someday solve the unsolved mystery of this unusual book.

Culture: An article about a mysterious book

1. Look at the title and the photos. What do you think the book is?

2. Read and listen to the article. Has the mystery of the book been solved?

3. Read the article again. Answer the questions.
   1. When was *The Voynich Manuscript* discovered? Who discovered it? How old is it?
      _____
   2. What have experts learned about the writing in the book?
      _____
   3. What do experts know about the drawings?
      _____
   4. What did Stephen Bax figure out?
      _____

4. **YOUR TURN** Work with a partner. Answer the questions.
   1. What do you think *The Voynich Manuscript* is? Who might have created it? Why?
   2. What other world mysteries do you know about?

   > Stonehenge is a world mystery. Everyone wonders who made it.

   > Yeah, and the Loch Ness monster is a mystery, too. People wonder if it really exists.

DID YOU KNOW...?
There are over 6,900 known languages spoken in the world today.

BE CURIOUS Find out about the human brain. What is unusual about Michael's brain? (Workbook, p. 87)

Discovery EDUCATION
8.3 MYSTERIES OF THE BRAIN

UNIT 8 REVIEW

Vocabulary

1. Circle the correct answers.
   1. That story is **believable / unbelievable**. There's no way it could have happened!
   2. Liz has been pretty **lucky / unlucky** lately. She won three contests!
   3. I have something **important / unimportant** to tell you. You really need to listen to me.
   4. It's **likely / unlikely** that Ricardo will become a detective someday. He doesn't really pay attention to details.
   5. This case has been **solved / unsolved** for months. I hope they catch the thief soon.
   6. The ending of that movie was **expected / unexpected**. Clearly, the girl was going to find her brother.

Grammar

2. Combine the sentences.
   1. Kyle found a map. Then he looked for a hidden treasure. (before)

      Kyle found a map before he looked for a hidden treasure.

   2. The archaeologists was uncovering some pottery. She found animals bones. (when)

      _____

   3. The writer interviews detectives. Then he writes about unsolved mysteries. (before)

      _____

   4. I'll tell you a secret. You promise not to tell our friends. (after)

      _____

   5. Jill gives tours of the pyramids. She spends the summer in Egypt. (when)

      _____

3. Match the direct speech (1–6) with the reported speech (a–f).
   1. "Read this book." ____
   2. "I'll read this book." ____
   3. "I'm reading this book." ____
   4. "Will you be reading this book?" ____
   5. "What book were you reading?" ____
   6. "You should read this book." ____

   a. She mentioned she was reading this book.
   b. She asked me what book I was reading.
   c. She recommended reading this book.
   d. She asked me if I'd be reading this book.
   e. She agreed to read this book.
   f. She told me to read this book.

Useful language

4. Circle the correct answers.
   1. **A: Can you comment on / Is it true that** you're writing a song for a movie?

      B: Not at all / Yes, absolutely! I'm almost done with it.

   2. **A: Some people say that / Not at all** you've solved over 1,000 crimes.

      B: Yes, absolutely / You must be joking! I've only been a detective for a year. I'd say, it's more like 20.

   3. **A:** I heard you're going to Mexico to try and find a lost pyramid.

      B: Not at all / Is it true that! I just got back from Mexico.

      A: Well, **some people say that / can you comment on** your plans for the future?

      B: Sure. I'm going to look for a lost city in the ocean.

PROGRESS CHECK: Now I can . . .

- ☐ describe unusual events.
- ☐ talk about an imaginary discovery.
- ☐ ask and respond to indirect questions and report things that people have said.
- ☐ confirm or deny statements.
- ☐ write a story about a secret or mystery.
- ☐ discuss world mysteries.

UNITS 7–8 REVIEW, Workbook, pp. 56–57

CLIL PROJECT
8.4 RELIVING HISTORY, p. 119

9 Weird and Wonderful

Discovery EDUCATION

BE CURIOUS

- On the Run
- What's the biggest mistake you've ever made?
- Insectmobile

1. Is this place real or unreal? Where do you think this is?

2. Have you seen a place like this before? Where was it?

3. What stories does the photo remind you of? Are they true stories? What happens in them?

UNIT CONTENTS

Vocabulary Story elements; Linking phrases
Grammar Third conditional; *wish* + past perfect; past modals of speculation
Listening Who or what is a hoodoo?

Vocabulary: Story elements

1. Match the words with the correct definitions.

   1. action __f__
   2. ending _____
   3. hero _____
   4. main character _____
   5. plot _____
   6. setting _____
   7. suspense _____
   8. villain _____

   a. an important person in a story
   b. a bad person in a story
   c. where and when a story happens
   d. the last part of a story
   e. the things that happen in a story
   f. exciting things that happen in a story
   g. a brave and good person in a story
   h. a feeling of excitement when something is about to happen

DID YOU KNOW...?

The movie version of the book is called *The Wizard of Oz*. Parts of the movie are different from the book. For example, in the movie, the shoes are red, not silver. At the end of the movie, Dorothy realizes her entire adventure was a dream.

2. Listen, check, and repeat. (9.01)

3. Read the summary of a story. Identify the story elements from Exercise 1.

THE WONDERFUL WIZARD OF OZ

The Wonderful Wizard of Oz starts in Kansas in the United States. One day, Dorothy and her little dog, Toto, are lifted into the air by a tornado, while they are in Dorothy's house. The house is carried to the magical Land of Oz and lands on the Wicked Witch of the East, killing her. Glinda, the Good Witch of the North, gives Dorothy the Wicked Witch's beautiful silver shoes to thank her. Dorothy asks Glinda how to get home to Kansas. Glinda tells her to walk on a yellow brick road and go to Emerald City to ask the Wizard of Oz for help.

Along the way, Dorothy meets the Scarecrow, the Cowardly Lion, and the Tin Woodman. Each character also wants something from the Wizard of Oz. When they finally find the Wizard, he tells them they must defeat the Wicked Witch of the West if they want their wishes to come true. Their adventures continue with a lot of action, including the witch's evil monkeys chasing them through the woods. Dorothy finally kills the Wicked Witch of the West by pouring water on her. They go back to the Wizard of Oz, but they find out he is not a real wizard. In the end, the Scarecrow, the Cowardly Lion, and the Tin Woodman realize they already have want they wanted. Glinda tells Dorothy that the silver shoes are magical, and they take her home.

The main characters are Dorothy, Toto, . . .

Speaking: Story time

4. **YOUR TURN** Work with a partner. Choose one of the stories below or your own idea. Talk about the story elements from Exercise 1.

   The Hunger Games takes place in Panem. The main characters are Katniss, Peeta, President Snow, and . . .

   Katniss is the most important main character. She's the hero and . . .

▶ Workbook, p. 58

Reading Lucky's Luck; Bicycle Accident!; Mesa Verde: Homes Up High
Conversation Asking for more information
Writing A story about an event

Short STORIES

LUCKY'S LUCK
A chicken saved Lucky's life.

Lucky lived on a farm in Tennessee. His friends called him Lucky because he was the unluckiest kid they knew. Nothing ever went his way, and, in the beginning, this day was no different. Lucky heard loud noises coming from the barn. If he hadn't heard those noises, he wouldn't have gone on the scariest adventure of his life.

Lucky got to the barn just in time to see a teenager riding away on his horse, Buck. Not only was the teenager stealing the horse, but he also had a chicken under his arm! Lucky quickly got on Gracie, one of the fastest horses on the farm. If the teenager had stolen Gracie, he would have gotten away. Fortunately, he stole Buck, who did not like to run very fast.

Gracie quickly caught up with Buck, and Lucky yelled, "Stop! That's my horse . . . and my chicken!" The teenager realized he would not escape on the horse, so he got down and threw the chicken toward Lucky. If the chicken hadn't scared Gracie, Lucky wouldn't have fallen off of her. But, he did. Now the thief and Lucky were both on foot. The thief ran. Lucky chased him.

After a few minutes, Lucky caught the thief. That's when he noticed how big the thief was. And scary! If Lucky had known the thief was twice his size, he wouldn't have chased him. Lucky knew he was in danger. Then, out of nowhere, the chicken leaped through the air and landed on the teenage thief's head. The chicken started flapping its wings and biting the thief. The thief got scared and ran into the woods.

Lucky was shocked. "Thanks, chicken," he said. "You saved my life. I guess today is my lucky day." The local paper heard about the story and came to take pictures of Lucky and his hero chicken. If the chicken hadn't saved Lucky, it wouldn't have become a hero. Unfortunately, the thief got away.

Now, when Lucky feeds the chickens, he thinks about his adventure and wonders what happened to the chicken thief.

Reading: A short story

1. Look at the picture. What do you think the story is about?

2. Read and listen to the article. Then answer the questions.
   1. What's the setting?
   2. Who are the main characters?
   3. Who's the hero? Who's the villain?
   4. Which part of the story has suspense?

3. Read the article again. Number the events in the correct order.

   ____ The chicken scares Gracie, and Lucky falls.

   ____ The thief gets away.

   ____ Lucky runs after the thief and catches him.

   ____ Lucky follows a teen riding away on a horse.

   ____ The chicken becomes a hero.

   ____ Lucky is scared because the thief is big.

   ____ The thief throws the chicken.

   ____ The chicken attacks the thief and saves Lucky.

   ____ Lucky goes to the barn to find out what the sounds are.

   ____ Lucky's horse catches up to the thief.

4. **YOUR TURN** Work with a partner. Imagine that the story is being made into a movie. What actors would play the main characters? What kind of movie would it be? Where would you film it?

   > Taylor Lautner should be Lucky, and Zac Efron would make a good thief. Jake Austin can dress up as the chicken.

Grammar: Third conditional; *wish* + past perfect

5. Complete the chart.

> Use the third conditional sentences to describe imaginary situations and impossible consequences. Use if + past perfect for the imaginary and untrue situation in the past. Use would (not) + have + past participle for the impossible consequence.

If he **hadn't heard** those noises, he **wouldn't have gone** on an adventure.
If the teenager **had stolen** Gracie, he _____ **gotten** away.

What **would have happened** _____ the thief _____ **stolen** Gracie?
He **would have gotten** away.

Would the chicken **have become** a hero **if** it **hadn't saved** Lucky?
Yes, it **would have**. / No, it _____.

> Check your answers: Grammar reference, p. 114

6. Complete the third conditional sentences in the short story.

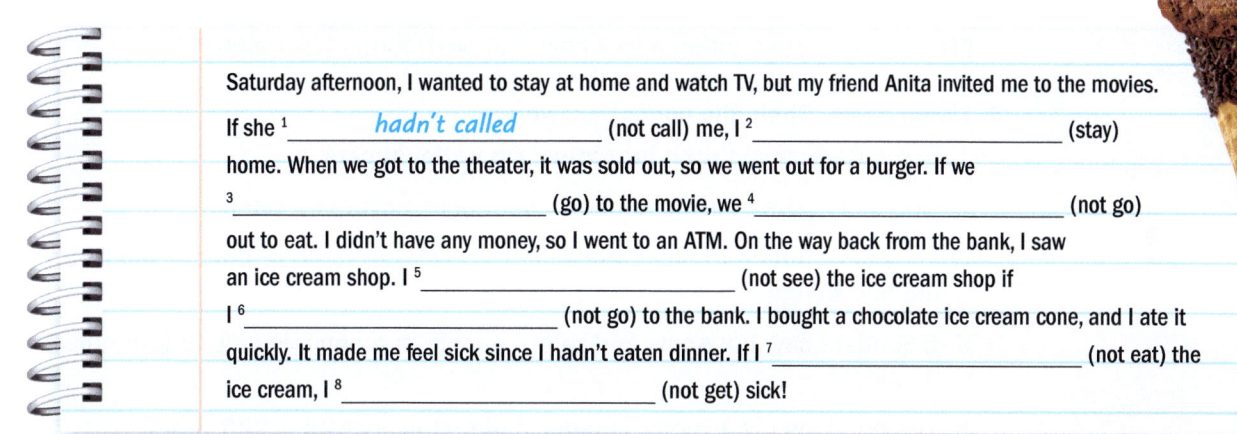

Saturday afternoon, I wanted to stay at home and watch TV, but my friend Anita invited me to the movies. If she ¹ _____hadn't called_____ (not call) me, I ² _____ (stay) home. When we got to the theater, it was sold out, so we went out for a burger. If we ³ _____ (go) to the movie, we ⁴ _____ (not go) out to eat. I didn't have any money, so I went to an ATM. On the way back from the bank, I saw an ice cream shop. I ⁵ _____ (not see) the ice cream shop if I ⁶ _____ (not go) to the bank. I bought a chocolate ice cream cone, and I ate it quickly. It made me feel sick since I hadn't eaten dinner. If I ⁷ _____ (not eat) the ice cream, I ⁸ _____ (not get) sick!

7. Write sentences with *wish* + past perfect. Use the simple present for *wish*.

1. Megan ➔ eat dinner
   Megan wishes she had eaten dinner.

2. Megan ➔ not buy ice cream
   _____

3. She ➔ the movie / not be sold out
   _____

4. I ➔ not read the end of the story
   _____

wish + past perfect

Use *wish* + past perfect to describe something in the past that you wish was different. Form it with a subject + **wish** + a subject + past perfect.

If I **hadn't heard** those noises, I wouldn't have gone into the barn. I **wish** I **hadn't gone** into the barn. I **wish** I **had** stayed in the house.

Speaking: If it hadn't happened . . .

8. **YOUR TURN** Write down five things you did yesterday.

I got up late, and I missed the bus. I . . .

9. **YOUR TURN** Work with a partner. Imagine the things you wrote in Exercise 8 didn't happen. How would your day have been different?

> If I hadn't gotten up late, I wouldn't have missed the bus.

Say it RIGHT!

Had and **have** are often reduced in the third conditional. Listen to the sentences.
If I **had** gotten on the bus, I **wouldn't have** missed my test.
I **would have** gotten a good grade if I **had** taken the test.
Practice your pronunciation of **had** and **would (not) have** in Exercise 9.

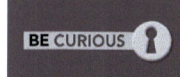

BE CURIOUS Find out about Jamey Harris. How would his life be different if he had listened to his friend and his mother? (Workbook, p. 88)

9.1 ON THE RUN

Naturally STRANGE

Listening: Who or what is a hoodoo?

1. Look at the picture. What do you think a hoodoo is?

2. Listen to information about hoodoos. Check (✓) the two explanations for how they were formed.
   - ☐ a Native American story about how they formed
   - ☐ a short story with a student's opinion about how they formed
   - ☐ a scientific explanation about how they were built by people
   - ☐ a scientific explanation about how they were formed by nature

3. Listen again. Circle the correct answers.
   1. Bryce Canyon is **a rock formation / a national park**.
   2. One story says that the hoodoos were once **coyotes / people**.
   3. They were turned to stone because they **wanted to be in the canyon forever / did bad things**.
   4. Scientists say that **snow and rain / people and animals** helped form the hoodoos.
   5. The hoodoos get 1 meter **smaller / bigger** every **100 / 200** years.

Vocabulary: Linking phrases

4. Read the sentences. Match the boldface phrases (1–7) with their uses (a–g). Then listen and check.

   1. _e_ **According to** scientists, hoodoos are between 1.5 and 45 meters tall.
   2. ____ They are different colors **as a result of** different minerals in the rocks.
   3. ____ Hoodoos can look like people. **In fact**, some have names, like The Hunter and Queen Victoria.
   4. ____ We planned a trip to Bryce Canyon **so that** we could see the hoodoos. You can walk into the canyon **in order to** get a better view of them.
   5. ____ The hoodoos were amazing. **Of course**, I took a lot of pictures of them!
   6. ____ **Rather than** walk to the hoodoos ourselves, we hired a guide to take us.
   7. ____ I don't think the hoodoos were people. **Then again**, maybe they were!

   a. explains why something happened
   b. shows something is obvious
   c. shows that what you just said or wrote might be wrong
   d. adds a detail to show something is true
   e. explains who said or wrote something
   f. gives an action you can choose to replace another action
   g. explains the cause of an action

Get it RIGHT!

Although *so that* and *in order to* have similar meanings, their forms are different. Use a subject + verb after *so that*.
The story was written **so that people could imagine** how hurricanes form. (NOT: The story was written ~~so that could imagine~~ how hurricanes form.)
Use a base verb after *in order to*.
The author wrote the story **in order to explain** hurricanes. (NOT: The author wrote the story ~~in order to he explains~~ hurricanes.)

5. **YOUR TURN** Work with a partner. Talk about stories that explain something in nature or the world. Talk about myths or legends you know or create your own story.

> The story Pandora's Box explains why there is good and evil. A woman named Pandora has a box with bad things, like sickness and hate, inside it. The box is locked so that the bad things don't get into the world. Of course, . . .

Grammar: Past modals of speculation

6. Complete the chart.

Use past modals of speculation to show how certain you are about a past event. Form past modals with modal + have + past participle.

Affirmative	Negative
Not sure: Hoodoos **may have been** people. You **might** _____ **seen** more hoodoos. Rivers **could have formed** them.	**Not sure:** They **may not have been** nice people. He _____ **liked** them.
Sure: The Legend People _____ **made** Coyote mad.	**Sure:** People **couldn't** _____ **made** them. The Legend People **must not have known** that it was a trick.

> Check your answers: Grammar reference, p. 114

7. Rewrite the sentences. Use the modals in parentheses + *have* + past participle.

1. The light in the sky was lightning. (could)
   The light in the sky could have been lightning.

2. That strange noise woke up the baby. (must)

3. Lori didn't forget Joe's name. (couldn't)

4. We saw more than 100 hoodoos. (may)

5. The ending to that story didn't surprise anyone. (might not)

6. People didn't live in those pyramids. (must not)

7. The volcano made that sound. (might)

8. They didn't understand the scientific explanation. (may not)

Speaking: I can explain it!

8. YOUR TURN Look at the photos. What do you think happened? How sure are you? Write three sentences for each picture with *might (not), may (not), could (not),* or *must (not) have*.

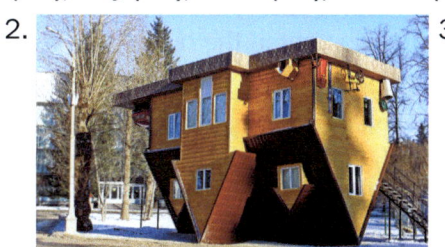

1. *He might have jumped off a bridge.*

2.

3.

9. Work with a partner. Share your ideas from Exercise 8. Which idea is the most likely explanation for each photo? Which one is the most outrageous idea?

For the first photo, I think the boy must have . . .

Workbook, pp. 60–61

REAL TALK 9.2 WHAT'S THE BIGGEST MISTAKE YOU'VE EVER MADE?

Story TELLING

Conversation: Was it a mistake?

1. **REAL TALK** Watch or listen to the teenagers talk about the biggest mistakes they've made. Number the mistakes and wishes in the order you hear them.

   _____ She didn't apply to art camp, but she wishes she had applied.

   _____ His team lost all of their games, and he wishes he hadn't joined the team.

   _____ He learns from his mistakes, so he doesn't think they are really mistakes.

   _____ She said something mean to a friend, and she wishes she had apologized.

   _____ She failed a test, and she wishes she hadn't stayed up so late.

   _____ He missed a trip with a friend, and he wishes he hadn't had summer school.

2. **YOUR TURN** What's the biggest mistake *you've* ever made? Tell your partner.

3. Listen to Nico telling Dana a story from a movie he saw. Complete the conversation.

> **USEFUL LANGUAGE: Asking for more information**
>
> - and then what
> - Like what?
> - so, what happened
> - ✓ Tell me about it.
> - What happened next?
> - Why was that?

Nico: I watched this great movie last night.

Dana: Really? ¹ *Tell me about it.*

Nico: Well, it was a documentary called *Man on a Wire*. It was about Philippe Petit, a man who walked on a high wire between two tall buildings in New York City in 1974.

Dana: ² _____

Nico: Well, he might have done it for the challenge. He also walked between towers in Paris and on a high wire over Sydney Harbour in Australia.

Dana: ³ _____ in New York City?

Nico: First, he studied the buildings for months. They weren't finished yet, and he wasn't allowed in them. He went into the buildings wearing costumes so that he wouldn't get caught.

Dana: Really? ⁴ _____

Nico: He dressed up as a reporter and a construction worker, and he hid his equipment in the buildings.

Dana: Wow! ⁵ _____ did he do?

Nico: Philippe put the wire between the two buildings. Then he walked on it about 400 meters up in the air! It took 45 minutes to get across.

Dana: That's incredible. ⁶ _____

Nico: When he came down, the police arrested him. For his punishment, he had to perform for people in Central Park. And he loved performing!

4. Practice the conversation with a partner.

5. **YOUR TURN** Work with a partner. Take turns telling each other a story from a movie or a story you know that you think would make a good movie.

To: Joel
From: Theo
Subject: BICYCLE ACCIDENT!

Hi Joel,

You'll never guess what happened to my brothers and me on Saturday! We went for a bike ride in the country. We were riding fast and laughing when suddenly, a dog ran right in front of us. Obviously, we tried to stop. That's when Robbie and I crashed into each other. Fortunately, we were okay, and so was the dog, but Nick wasn't so lucky. He fell off his bike and hurt his arm.

Luckily, I had my phone, so we called our parents. We had to wait a long time, and Nick looked awful. He must have been in a lot of pain. Eventually, my parents arrived, and we finally got Nick to the hospital. Amazingly, he only had a broken arm. If he had ridden any faster, it would have been much worse!

What's going on with you? Do you have a good story to tell?

Theo

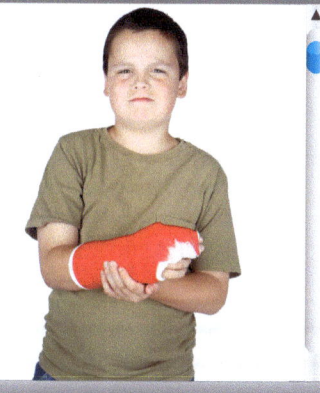

Reading to write: A story about an event

6. Look at the photo. What do you think happened? Read Theo's story to check.

Focus on CONTENT
When you write a story, include this information:
- what happened
- when it happened
- what you did after it happened
- where it happened
- how/why it happened
- what happened in the end

7. Read Theo's story again. What information does he include for each category in the Focus on Content box?

Focus on LANGUAGE
Use adverbs in stories to move the story forward.
To show time: **eventually**, **finally**, **suddenly**
Suddenly, we saw a dark cloud in the sky.
To show opinion: **amazingly**, **luckily**, **fortunately**, **unfortunately**
Unfortunately, we didn't have an umbrella.
To state a fact: **clearly**, **obviously**
Clearly, we got wet.

8. What adverbs does Theo use in his story?

9. Complete the story with the correct adverbs.

| clearly | fortunately | eventually | suddenly |

I went to a theme park last weekend. It was supposed to rain, but ¹_____, it was a nice day. I went on a lot of rides. When I was on a roller coaster, it ²_____ got stuck at the top. It happened so fast. One minute we were flying through the air, and the next we were just sitting there. ³_____, I was scared! Wouldn't you be? Someone came to fix it right away, so we were only up there for a minute, but it seemed like hours! I wish I hadn't gone on that ride. ⁴_____, I might go on a roller coaster again, but not for a really long time!

Writing: Your story about an event

PLAN
You are going to write a story about an event. Choose something interesting that happened to you or create a story.

What	
When	
Where	
How/Why	
What you did after it happened	
What happened in the end	

WRITE
Write a story. Use your notes to help you. Use adverbs to link ideas. Write at least 150 words.

CHECK
Check your writing. Can you answer "yes" to these questions?

- Is information from the Focus on Content box in your story?
- Do you use adverbs correctly?

Mesa Verde: Homes Up High

Mesa Verde National Park covers more than 80 square miles of the Four Corners region of the United States, where the borders of Utah, Colorado, Arizona, and New Mexico meet. It was once the home of the Pueblo people, a Native American group famous for its amazing cliff dwellings. The best examples of these incredible homes can be seen in the walls of the park's breathtaking canyons.

The Four Corners is a landscape of extremes. It's hot and dry in summer and covered in snow in winter. It isn't an easy place to live, but the Pueblo people made their home here and farmed the land for over 700 years, from 600 to 1300 AD. They built complicated villages with strong stone walls that protected hundreds of people. When tourists see these homes, they are amazed by the Pueblo people's building ability.

The Cliff Palace is the largest Pueblo cliff dwelling in the park. It's best seen from above. Visitors who see it usually wonder how people could have built such complex houses so long ago. The most interesting of all the houses is the Balcony House. It is made up of 40 rooms, connected by long, narrow tunnels and built around a series of shared spaces for the community. It can only be visited with a guide, and you have to be ready to climb! The only door into the house is at the top of a 10-meter high wooden ladder. When the Pueblo people lived here, they entered their homes by climbing ladders and ropes up the steep cliff wall. Once inside, they pulled the ladders into the houses in order to protect themselves from enemies.

Exploring the maze of tunnels and rooms, you really start to understand what life must have been like for the Pueblo people so long ago. As you stand at the edge of the cliff, looking down into the canyon below and listening to the peacefulness of nature, it's easy to imagine that you have traveled back in time.

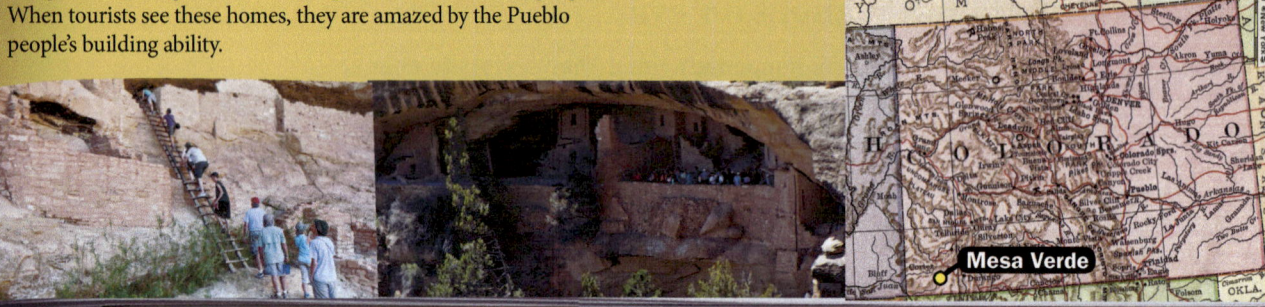

Culture: An article about ancient homes in Mesa Verde

1. Look at the photos. What are the houses like? Why do you think tourists visit them?

2. Read and listen to the article. Who lived in Mesa Verde? What did they do?

3. Read the article again. Correct the factual mistakes in each sentence.
   1. The Four Corners is hot and wet in the summer and snowy in the winter.
   2. The Pueblo people lived in Mesa Verde for more than 7,000 years.
   3. They built simple villages with stone houses in the canyons.
   4. The Balcony House is the biggest dwelling at Mesa Verde.
   5. They used tunnels and ropes to get into their houses so that they could protect themselves.

4. **YOUR TURN** Work with a partner. Imagine you lived in one of the cliff dwellings hundreds of years ago. Discuss the questions.
   1. How would your life have been different from your life today?
   2. What would you have liked about it? What wouldn't you have liked?

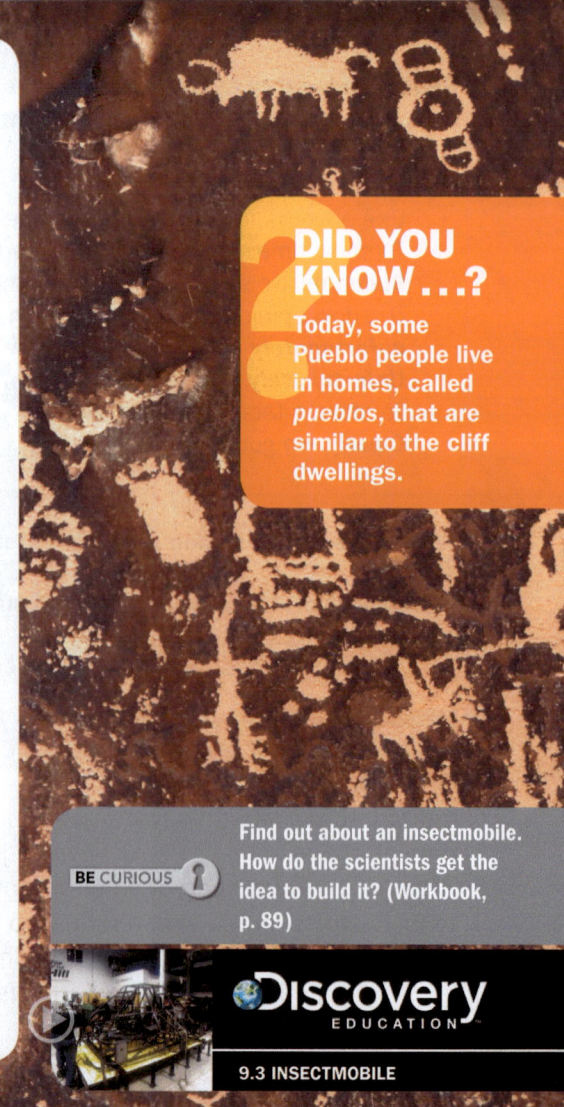

DID YOU KNOW...?
Today, some Pueblo people live in homes, called *pueblos*, that are similar to the cliff dwellings.

BE CURIOUS Find out about an insectmobile. How do the scientists get the idea to build it? (Workbook, p. 89)

Discovery EDUCATION
9.3 INSECTMOBILE

UNIT 9 REVIEW

Vocabulary

1. **Complete the story summary with the correct story elements.**

action	main characters	suspense
ending	plot	villain
hero	setting	

   Peter Pan is a story about a boy who doesn't want to grow up. The ¹_____ are Peter Pan, Wendy, Tinker Bell, and Captain Hook. Peter Pan is the ²_____ of the story, and he fights against Captain Hook, who is the mean ³_____. ⁴The _____ is in two places – Wendy's room and Neverland, a magical world. There is a lot of ⁵_____ in the ⁶_____ – and most of it takes place in Neverland when Wendy and her brothers travel there with Peter Pan. There is also a lot of ⁷_____ – like when you are waiting to see who wins a battle between Peter Pan and Captain Hook. The ⁸_____ is a surprise when Wendy gets too old to enjoy adventures in Neverland.

Grammar

2. **Circle the correct answers.**

   1. If Tao **hadn't read / wouldn't have read** the book, she **hadn't known / wouldn't have known** the ending to the movie.
   2. Greg **had called / would have called** his parents if he **had remembered / would have remembered** his phone.
   3. We **hadn't been / wouldn't have been** late if we **had left / would have left** on time.
   4. If Cassandra **had been / would have been** there, what **had she done / would she have done**?
   5. If the cat **hadn't woken / wouldn't have woken** me up, I **had slept / would have slept** better.
   6. **Had you written / Would you have written** your book report if you **hadn't gone / wouldn't have gone** out with friends?

3. **Write sentences with modal + *have* + past participle.**

   1. those lights / may / be / airplanes
   _____
   2. then again, / they / may not / be / airplanes
   _____
   3. Nelson / could / see / the lights from his room
   _____
   4. Janice / must / sleep / through the event
   _____
   5. according to the news, / they / must not / come / from planes
   _____
   6. the lights / could not / flash / for very long
   _____

Useful language

4. **Circle the correct answers.**

   Sharon: Did you hear what happened to Doug?
   Frank: No. ¹**Tell me about it. / What happened next?**
   Sharon: Well, he went to the beach and had an amazing adventure.
   Frank: ²**And then what / So, what** happened at the beach?
   Sharon: Well, he was swimming in the ocean, and he suddenly screamed!
   Frank: ³**Why was that? / Tell me about it.**
   Sharon: Because he felt something under him.
   Frank: Really? ⁴**Like what? / Why was that?** A shark?
   Sharon: Well, it felt like it could have been a shark, but it was much bigger. It was a whale!
   Frank: No way!
   Sharon: Yeah, isn't that crazy?

PROGRESS CHECK: Now I can . . .

- ☐ talk about the story elements in a story.
- ☐ talk about imaginary situations in the past.
- ☐ discuss possible explanations for past events.
- ☐ ask for more information about a story.
- ☐ write a story about an event.
- ☐ talk about what my life might have been like in the past.

10 I Have To! I Can!

Discovery EDUCATION

BE CURIOUS

- Future Directions
- What do you see yourself doing ten years from now?
- The Young and the Brave
- Lions in Danger

1. Where is the teen? What is he doing?

2. What do you think the boy did to become good at his sport? What do you think he gave up?

3. What do you do that takes hard work?

UNIT CONTENTS

Vocabulary Training and qualifications; Jobs
Grammar Past ability; Modal expressions for past and future; *make* and *let*
Listening What do you do?

Vocabulary: Training and qualifications

1. **Combine the words from the box with the words in 1–6 to make collocations. Some words can be used more than once.**

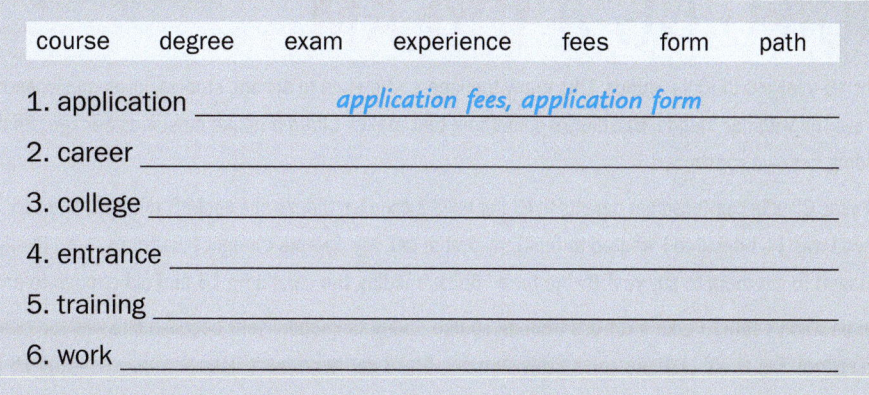

course	degree	exam	experience	fees	form	path

   1. application _____ *application fees, application form* _____
   2. career _____
   3. college _____
   4. entrance _____
   5. training _____
   6. work _____

2. 🔊 10.01 **Listen, check, and repeat.**

3. **Complete the email with phrases from Exercise 1.**

   Hi Mari,

   How are you? I won my gymnastics competition last week! I love gymnastics, but it's not a ¹ _*career path*_ I'm going to follow. I really want to get a ² _____ in science. I've already filled out a college ³ _____ online. I can't believe that there are ⁴ _____ for every school! It's getting expensive! I'm going to apply to a few more, and it's going to cost about $200. I really need to get some ⁵ _____ this summer. It's going to be hard to get a job with my gymnastics schedule, but I hope to find something part-time. I'm glad that you passed the ⁶ _____ for the computer ⁷ _____ . Is the class helping you with the skills you wanted to learn?

   Write soon,

   Todd

> **NOTICE IT**
>
> A *college* is smaller than a *university*. Both can describe places to go to get a degree. *My sister goes to a community college. I go to a university.* *College* is often used without an article in a general statement. It can refer to a college or a university. *We go to college in Boston. My sister goes to Boston College. I go to Boston University.*

Speaking: My future plans

4. **YOUR TURN** Work with a partner. What are your plans after you finish school? Tell your partner about your definite and possible plans using the collocations in Exercise 1.

   > *I'm going to get a college degree. In fact, I've already started filling out application forms to a few universities. This summer I might take a training course . . .*

▶ Workbook, p. 64

Reading Building a Dream; A Singing Star; Young and Talented Australians
Conversation Making decisions
Writing A biography about a musician

Unit 10 | 95

Cool CAREERS

BUILDING A DREAM

Meet 15-year-old Claudia Muñoz. Like many teenagers, she goes to school, studies, loves music, and likes to have fun with her friends. But there's something that makes Claudia unlike most kids her age. She's building her own sports car!

Last year, Claudia convinced her parents to let her build a car even though she couldn't drive yet. She says, "When I was 14, I decided I wanted to build my dream car. My parents thought I was crazy, but I finally managed to get them to say yes! By the time I finish building the car, I'll be 16 and old enough to drive."

Claudia wasn't able to take a driver's training course during the school year because she was too busy with school. But she'll take the course this summer. She'll get her driver's license when she turns 16 next November. In the meantime, she's working on her car. "I'm doing everything – even paying for it!" she says. "I worked as a dog walker and managed to save enough money to buy an old car. I get a lot of car parts for free at a junkyard."

Claudia is redoing the car inside and out. For example, she's fixing the engine, painting the car, and adding new tires and seats. How was she able to learn so much about cars? "I couldn't do anything when I first started, but then I realized that I could learn to do anything! I watched a lot of how-to videos online." She admits that she also got help from local mechanics.

Claudia had decided that she wants to design cars in the future. She plans to get a college degree in mechanical engineering. Car design is a male-dominated world with very few women who choose to become mechanical engineers. Claudia hopes that her story will inspire more girls to consider this career. But right now, Claudia is a few years away from going to college, so she's focusing on finishing her car. "I can't wait to drive," she says, "but I actually think building the car is more fun than driving it will be!"

Reading: An article about a teen building a car

1. Look at the picture. What is the girl doing? How do you think she is different from other teens?

2. Read and listen to the article. How did Claudia pay for her car-building project?

3. Read the article again. Are the sentences true or false? Write *T* (true) or *F* (false). Correct the false sentences.

   1. Claudia started building her car when she was 15. ____
   2. She is going to take a driver's training course. ____
   3. Claudia's parents paid for her old car. ____
   4. Claudia is only fixing the car's engine. ____
   5. She got some help from other people. ____
   6. She thinks driving will be more fun than building her car. ____

4. **YOUR TURN** Work with a partner. Answer the questions.

   1. What do you think of Claudia's project? What do you think of her future career?
   2. What career would you like in the future? What can you do now to work toward that career?

DID YOU KNOW…?
In most US states, the driving age is 16. However, in a few states, the age is 14.

Grammar: Past ability

5. Complete the chart.

Use **could**, **was/were able to**, and **managed to** to talk about past abilities.	
Use **could** for both general and specific abilities.	
GENERAL: What _____ you **do**? At first, I **couldn't do** anything. Then I realized I **could learn** to do anything!	SPECIFIC: **Could** she **drive** when she was 15? Yes, she _____. She **could drive** well. No, she **couldn't**. She _____ yet.
Use **was/were able to** and **managed to** for specific abilities only.	
How **was** she **able to learn** so much? She **was able to watch** videos online. She _____ **take** a course.	How **did** she **manage to pay** for it? She _____ **save** money. She **didn't manage to get** a free car.
_____ they **able to fix** the car? Yes, they **were**. / No, they **weren't**.	_____ you **manage to fix** the car? Yes, I **did**. / No, I **didn't**.

> Check your answers: Grammar reference, p. 115

6. Circle the correct answers. Then practice the conversation with a partner. Practice linking words with a /w/ or /y/ sound.

Tara: Hi, Santi. ¹(**Were you able to**) / **Could you** take the entrance exam for law school last week?

Santi: Yes, I was. I ²**managed / didn't manage** to finish the exam, but I answered most of the questions.

Tara: That's good. You are pretty good at tests. I'm sure you ³**managed to / could** pass.

Santi: I hope so! I heard that Sandra passed it last month.

Tara: Really? How ⁴**she was able / was she able** to take the test? She's only 17.

Santi: She ⁵**could / managed to** take it early because she took law classes at the community college.

Tara: Wow! Well, good luck. I really hope you passed.

Santi: You and me both!

Speaking: Your abilities

7. YOUR TURN Work with a partner. Talk about things you could and couldn't do at the ages below.

| when you were 5 | when you were 10 | when you were 13 |

I could ride a bike when I was 5. I couldn't drive a car. I . . .

8. Now tell your partner things you did and didn't do last year.

I managed to save enough money for a photography course last year. The class was great! By the end of it, I was able to take great photos.

Get it RIGHT!

Do not use **could** for ability in the affirmative for something that is achieved at a certain time.
She **was able to** fix the car quickly on Saturday morning. (NOT: ~~She could fix the car quickly on Saturday morning.~~)

Say it RIGHT!

When a word that starts with a vowel comes after a word that ends with a vowel, speakers sometimes add a /w/ or /y/ sound between the words to make them easier to say. Listen to the sentences.

you + /w/ + able
*Were **you able** to take the entrance exam?*

she + /y/ + able
*How was **she able** to take the test?*

Listen. Do the words in these sentences link with a /w/ or /y/ sound?
1. **I answered** most of the questions.
2. **You are** pretty good at tests.
3. **You and** me both.

BE CURIOUS — Find out about a police officer. What does she manage to do in addition to her job as a police officer? (Workbook, p. 90)

10.1 FUTURE DIRECTIONS

Working for a LIVING

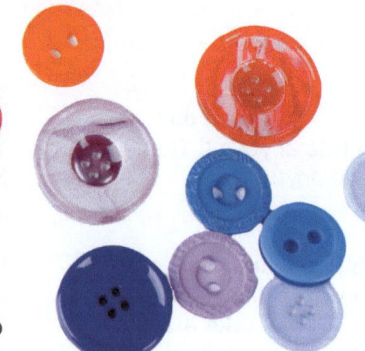

Listening: What do you do?

1. Do any of your friends have jobs? What do they do?

2. Listen to two people talk about their jobs. Who designs clothes? Who sells clothes?

3. Listen again. Who did these things? Write *E* (Elsa), *J* (Jim), or *NI* (no information).

   1. made clothes at home ____
   2. took training courses ____
   3. acted in school plays ____
   4. went to college ____
   5. went to a concert ____
   6. had trouble with children ____

Vocabulary: Jobs

4. Match the words with the pictures. Then listen, check, and repeat.

a. a babysitter	d. a musician	g. a salesperson
b. a chef	e. a police officer	h. an artist
✓ c. a designer	f. a politician	i. an athlete

   1. *c*
   2. ___
   3. ___
   4. ___
   5. ___
   6. ___
   7. ___
   8. ___
   9. ___

5. **YOUR TURN** Work with a partner. Name people you know that have the jobs in Exercise 4. What do they do at their jobs?

   My aunt is a web designer. She designs Web pages for musicians. She . . .

98 | Unit 10

Grammar: Modal expressions for past and future; *make* and *let*

6. Complete the chart.

Use (not) had to *and* (not) need to *for obligations and necessities in the past.*

What **did** you **need to learn** about? I _____ about fashion. I **didn't need to learn** about chemistry.	What **did** he **have to do**? He **had to take** a training course. He _____ get a college degree.
Did he **need to take** training courses? Yes, he _____. / No, he **didn't**.	**Did** they **need to work** on weekends? Yes, they **did**. / No, they **didn't**.

Use will (not) have to *and* will (not) need to *for obligations and necessities in the future.*

What courses _____ you **have to take**? I'**ll have to take** more training courses. I **won't have to take** any college courses.	When **will** she **need to finish** the design? She'**ll need to finish** by Friday. She _____ by tomorrow.
Will he **have to take** more courses? Yes, he **will**. / No, he _____.	**Will** they **need to pay** an entrance fee? Yes, they _____. / No, they **won't**.

> Check your answers: Grammar reference, p. 115

7. Complete the paragraph with the past or future.

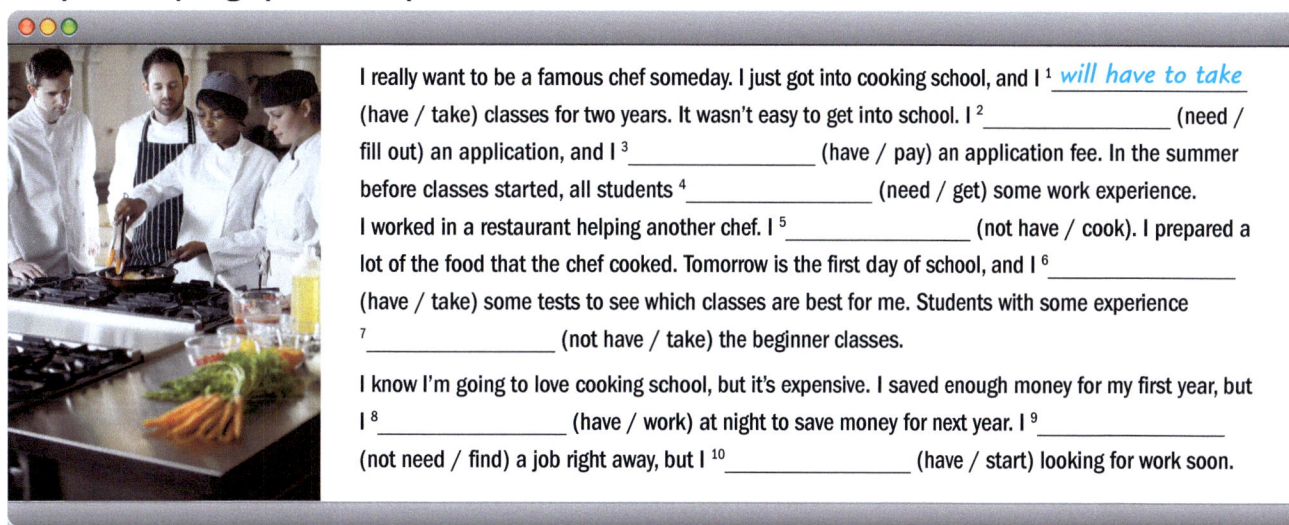

I really want to be a famous chef someday. I just got into cooking school, and I ¹ *will have to take* (have / take) classes for two years. It wasn't easy to get into school. I ² _____ (need / fill out) an application, and I ³ _____ (have / pay) an application fee. In the summer before classes started, all students ⁴ _____ (need / get) some work experience. I worked in a restaurant helping another chef. I ⁵ _____ (not have / cook). I prepared a lot of the food that the chef cooked. Tomorrow is the first day of school, and I ⁶ _____ (have / take) some tests to see which classes are best for me. Students with some experience ⁷ _____ (not have / take) the beginner classes.

I know I'm going to love cooking school, but it's expensive. I saved enough money for my first year, but I ⁸ _____ (have / work) at night to save money for next year. I ⁹ _____ (not need / find) a job right away, but I ¹⁰ _____ (have / start) looking for work soon.

8. Circle the correct answers.

1. Our boss **lets / (makes)** us work at the office on Saturdays, but we'd rather work from home.
2. I really want to earn money, but my parents won't **let / make** me get a part-time job.
3. Job interviews often **let / make** people nervous.
4. Don't **let / make** me forget to tell you about my new job!
5. Kelly didn't **let / make** her fears stop her from becoming a professional athlete.

make and *let*

Use make + object + base form of a verb when someone or something controls a situation.
Use let + object + base form of a verb when someone allows you to do something.

A difficult customer **makes my job seem** impossible.	Most customers **let you do** your job.
It **made me see** fashion in a whole new way.	My parents used to **let me make** clothes for the family.
My boss **doesn't make me** work on Saturdays.	My boss **didn't let me** take a vacation last week.

Speaking: My obligations

9. YOUR TURN Work with a partner. Answer the questions.

1. What were some of your obligations when you were young? What didn't you have to do then that you have to do now?
2. What are some things your parents make you do? What do they let you do?

> When I was young, I had to clean my room. I didn't have to cook dinner, but now I do.

Workbook, pp. 66–67

REAL TALK — 10.2 WHAT DO YOU SEE YOURSELF DOING TEN YEARS FROM NOW?

Bright FUTURES

Conversation: A thank-you gift

1. **REAL TALK** Watch or listen to the teenagers talk about what they think they'll be doing in 10 years. Check (✓) the jobs and activities they mention.

☐ an actor	☐ a fashion designer	☐ working with computers
☐ an artist	☐ a musician	☐ moving somewhere exciting
☐ a web designer	☐ working on television	☐ changing career paths
☐ an athlete	☐ learning to fix cars	☐ going to college

2. **YOUR TURN** What do *you* see yourself doing 10 years from now? Tell your partner.

3. Listen to Shane and Bella talk about a thank-you gift. Complete the conversation.

   USEFUL LANGUAGE: Making decisions

   - change his mind
   - on second thought
   - that depends on
   - how about
   - ✓ make up my mind
   - Why not?

   Bella: Hey, Shane. You know, Mr. Ross has been helping us so much with our college applications. We should get him a thank-you gift.

   Shane: That's a great idea!

   Bella: I was thinking we should get him a watch or a really nice pen. I can't ¹ *make up my mind*. What do you think?

   Shane: Hmm, I don't know. I'm not crazy about those ideas. ² _____ a flashlight?

   Bella: A flashlight? No way!

   Shane: ³ _____

   Bella: Well, it's kind of boring. Sorry.

   Shane: It may be boring to you, but Mr. Ross said he needed to get one for the dark closet with the science equipment.

   Bella: OK, ⁴ _____, it would be a good gift if he needs it. Maybe we could get him a flashlight *and* something else.

   Shane: I like that idea. What else should we get him?

   Bella: I guess ⁵ _____ how much we want to spend.

   Shane: Well, he loves sports. We could get two tickets to a baseball game, but they're pretty expensive.

   Bella: You know, I asked Oscar if he wanted to get Mr. Ross a gift before I talked to you, and he said no. Maybe you can get him to ⁶ _____. Then we'll have more money to spend.

   Shane: Good idea. I'll text him right now.

4. Practice the conversation with a partner.

5. **YOUR TURN** Work with a partner. Discuss and make decisions about one of the situations below or your own ideas.

what movie to see	what to do on the weekend	where to go on a trip

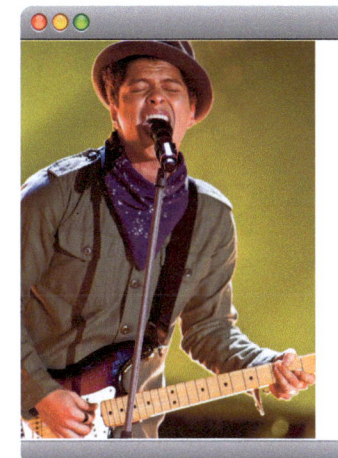

A SINGING STAR

Peter Gene Hernandez is famous pop singer from Hawaii, but you might not recognize that name. When he was young, his family called him neither Peter nor Gene. They called him Bruno, and today, he is known as Bruno Mars. He not only sings, but he also plays the drums, guitar, and piano. He started on his career path at age four when his parents let him sing with them at local concerts. He used to dress up as other singers and sing their songs. He would dress up as either Elvis Presley or Michael Jackson. In 2000, he wrote songs for other people, but he knew he needed to make his own music. In 2010, he finally had his own number 1 song with "Nothin' on You." Since then, he has had several popular songs, including "Just the Way You Are," "The Lazy Song," and "It Will Rain." Bruno Mars is a star with fans around the world!

Reading to write: A biography about a musician

6. Look at the photo. Do you know who he is? Why is he famous? Read the biography to check.

> *Focus on* **CONTENT**
> When you write a biography about a musician, include these things:
> - name   - where he/she is from   - type of music
> - popular songs   - interesting facts
> - when and how he/she started

7. Read the biography about Bruno Mars again. What information is there for each item in the Focus on Content box?

> *Focus on* **LANGUAGE**
> Use *either . . . or* in affirmative sentences to show two choices or possibilities.
> The singer's new album will come out in **either** November **or** December.
> We will **either** go to a restaurant **or** eat at home before the concert.
> Use *neither . . . nor* in negative sentences to show two things are not true.
> **Neither** the guitarist **nor** the drummer played very well.
> Carrie Underwood is **neither** a pop singer **nor** a hip-hop artist. She sings country music.

8. Find the expressions from the Focus on Language box in the biography about Bruno Mars.

9. Complete the sentences with *either . . . or* or *neither . . . nor*.

1. I'm _____ going to a concert _____ biking with friends on Saturday. I can't decide.

2. _____ my mom _____ my dad will let me go to the concert because it's so late at night.

3. I'm going to pay my application fee on _____ Monday _____ Tuesday.

4. My cousin is _____ a designer _____ a model, but she works in fashion. I think she reviews clothing for a website.

Writing: A biography about a musician

PLAN
Choose a musician to write about. Complete the chart.

Name	
Where he/she is from	
Type of music	
When and how he/she started	
Popular songs	
Interesting facts	

WRITE
Write a biography. Use your notes to help you. Include *either . . . or* and *neither . . . nor*. Write at least 150 words.

CHECK
Check your writing. Can you answer "yes" to these questions?

- Is information from the Focus on Content box in the biography?
- Do you use *either . . . or* and *neither . . . nor* correctly?

Workbook, pp. 68–69

Young and Talented AUSTRALIANS

Do you know someone with amazing abilities? Have you ever thought that they should win a prize for it? Well, in Australia, you can nominate that person for the Young Australian of the Year award. Since 1979, the government has given the Young Australian of the Year prize to candidates from the ages of 16 to 30 each year. If you are Australian, you can nominate a talented person online. The top eight people from each of the six states in Australia compete for the prize. Judges then choose the winner from a list of 42 incredible young people.

Akram Azimi is a recent winner of the award, winning in 2013. He has worked with native farming communities in Australia. This is amazing because he arrived in Australia from Afghanistan when he was just 13, and English is not his first language. He excelled in school and now studies law, science, and arts in college. He felt like he needed to give something back to his adopted country, so Akram used his skills to help young people work and study in farming communities.

Marita Cheng also won the award because of her academic skills and because she helped others. She won in 2012 and was a college student at the time. Marita started Robogals Global in 2008, an organization that encourages young women to become engineers. Robogals uses fun activities to teach girls engineering and technology. Marita has worked with over 3,000 girls in Australia. The program helps girls realize that they can follow a career path in engineering.

Other winners have included famous athletes, like the swimmer Ian Thorpe (known as The Thorpedo). Like many athletes, Thorpe started very young. He started swimming at 8, and at 16, he became the youngest male world champion in history. Thorpe won the Australian of the Year award in 2000, and later that year, his amazing swimming abilities helped him break world records and win five medals – three of them gold – in the 2000 Sydney Olympics.

No matter the reasons for winning, Young Australians of the Year all have one thing in common – they had to work very hard for their success!

Culture: An article about Young Australians of the Year

1. Look at the photos. What do you think each person did or does?

2. Read and listen to the article. What are some reasons that people win the Australian of the Year award?

3. Read the article again. Answer the questions.
   1. How many people are chosen to compete from each state? How many people do the judges choose from?
   2. Why is Akram's work so amazing?
   3. What subject does Marita encourage girls to consider?
   4. What did Ian Thorpe achieve at 16?

4. **YOUR TURN** Work with a partner. What abilities and obligations do you think the Young Australians of the Year had? Do you have any similar abilities or obligations?

   Akram Azimi had to learn English. He...

   I had to learn English, too. I...

BE CURIOUS Find out about the Naadam Festival in Inner Mongolia. What ability are the Mongols famous for? (Workbook, p. 91)

Discovery EDUCATION
10.3 THE YOUNG AND THE BRAVE

UNIT 10 REVIEW

Vocabulary

1. **Which word or words do NOT make collocations? Sometimes, there is more than one answer.**

   1. **work:** ~~path~~   experience   ~~degree~~
   2. **application:** degree   form   fees
   3. **entrance:** exam   fees   experience
   4. **college:** course   degree   form
   5. **training:** course   path   degree

Grammar

2. **Rewrite the sentences with the words in parentheses.**

   1. Donna managed to get a job as a salesperson. (be able to)

      Donna was able to get a job as a salesperson.

   2. The athlete couldn't compete on Saturday. (not able to)

      _____

   3. The artist was able to finish the painting in 3 days. (manage to)

      _____

   4. Were you able to play the piano when you were young? (could)

      _____

   5. Walter wasn't able to pass the entrance exam. (not manage to)

      _____

3. **Write sentences and questions in the simple past or future.**

   1. the babysitter / need / pick up / the children from school / ? (past)

      Did the babysitter need to pick up the

      children from school?

   2. Tom / not have / take / a training course last weekend / . (past)

      _____

   3. what / application fees / I / have / pay / ? (future)

      _____

   4. Martina / not need / work / on Saturday / . (future)

      _____

   5. The chef / need / make / enough cake for 100 people / . (past)

      _____

Useful language

4. **Circle the correct answers.**

   1. **A:** I want to become a chef.

      B: I thought you wanted to be a fashion designer. _____

      a. Did you change your mind?   b. Why not?

   2. **A:** What time should we meet for dinner?

      B: _____ what time the concert starts.

      a. How about   b. That depends on

   3. **A:** Do you want to go to college or work right after you graduate?

      B: I'm not sure. _____

      a. I changed my mind.   b. I can't make up my mind.

   4. **A:** Let's get our soccer coach a thank-you gift.

      B: Good idea! _____ a colorful soccer ball?

      a. How about   b. On second thought

PROGRESS CHECK: Now I can . . .

- ☐ talk about my plans after graduation.
- ☐ discuss careers and abilities.
- ☐ talk about my abilities and obligations in the past.
- ☐ talk with someone to make decisions.
- ☐ write a biography about a musician.
- ☐ compare someone's abilities and obligations to mine.

UNITS 9–10 REVIEW, Workbook, pp. 70–71

CLIL PROJECT

10.4 LIONS IN DANGER, p. 120

Uncover Your Knowledge
UNITS 6–10 Review Game

TEAM 1
START

- Describe three things you would like to change about your room. Use passive infinitives with verbs such as *need to be* and *have to be*.

- Work with a teammate. Discuss different celebrations and describe them.

- Have a teammate tell you a story, either something he/she experienced or from a book, television show, or movie. Ask questions for more information.

- Talk about something you have/get done for you in the past, the present, and the future.

- In 15 seconds, look around the classroom and name five everyday objects.

- Role-play buying a gadget with a teammate. As the customer, ask about the price, design, features, and quality of the product. Have your teammate act as the sales clerk and answer you.

- Talk about things you enjoy doing, and say why. Use verb + gerund or infinitive.

- Look around the room. Tell a teammate about four things you see. Use modifiers to describe them. For example, *so, not really, totally, extremely, far too*.

- Have a teammate offer suggestions of things to do, such as *Let's have a party tomorrow!* Respond with an appropriate exclamation, such as *What a great idea!* See how many exclamations you can say in 30 seconds.

- Think of seven different things you do to get ready for a celebration. Name them in 20 seconds.

- Tell your teammate three things that you wish you would've done differently in your past.

INSTRUCTIONS:

- Make teams and choose game pieces.
- Put your game pieces on your team's START.
- Flip a coin to see who goes first.
- Read the first challenge. Can you do it correctly?

   Yes → Continue to the next challenge.

   No → Lose your turn.

The first team to do all of the challenges wins!

104 | Units 6–10 Review

TEAM 2
START

Role-play with a teammate. You are a detective and your teammate is a client who is missing something valuable from his/her home. Ask questions to try to find the missing item. Use expressions to confirm and deny what the client says.

In 1 minute, say three sentences that each use the same word with and without *un-*.

Tell a teammate a story that takes place over time. It can be a story you know, a historical situation, or something that happened to you. Be sure to use time clauses: *before, after, when,* and any others.

In 15 seconds, say five collocations for training and qualifications, such as *college degree*.

Talk about taking a trip. Use these verbs in *-ing* form as subjects: *travel, watch, have, see*. For example, *Seeing the pyramids in Egypt is a dream of mine.*

Imagine that you and your teammate are given a million dollars, but you can only give it to charities and volunteer organizations. How do you donate the money? Decide how to spend or split the money between organizations. Explain your reasons.

Talk with a teammate about mysteries from the past. Use past modals of speculation.

Use reporting verbs to talk about your favorite scene from a movie or TV show.

Tell your teammate four different things you heard people say yesterday. Say two of them as reported speech, one as quoted speech, and one that uses the *-ing* form.

Play charades. Act out a job and have your teammates guess what it is. See how many you can complete in 1 minute.

Imagine you are a teacher. Tell a teammate about things you'll make your students do and those you'll let them do.

Explain to a teammate at least six different elements of a story. Give a definition for each.

- **GRAMMAR**
- **VOCABULARY**
- **USEFUL LANGUAGE**

Units 6–10 Review | 105

Past tense review, p. 5

Simple past	
Use simple past statements to talk about past events and activities.	
Regular	**Irregular**
What **did** you **believe**? I **believed** everything on the Internet. We **didn't believe** the story.	What **did** she **write**? She **wrote** a report for school. She **didn't write** a blog post.

Past continuous
Use the past continuous to talk about activities that were in progress in the past. To form the past continuous use was/were + present participle (-ing form).
What **were** you **doing** wrong? I **was using** incorrect information. I **wasn't checking** my facts. Where **was** he **going**? He **was going** to class. What **were** they **watching**? They **were watching** the news.

Present perfect
Use the present perfect to talk about experiences that happened at an indefinite time in the past. To form the present perfect, use has/have + the past participle.
Who **has used** Snopes.com? Many people **have used** the website! I **haven't used** it before. He **has used** it. He **hasn't used** it.

1. **Correct the sentences.**

   1. Simple past: We eat dinner while we watching TV.

   2. Past continuous: They were listen to a Web interview.

   3. Present perfect: What has you did in class this year?

Review of *used to* + infinitive and *would*, p. 7

Use used to or would for things that happened repeatedly in the past but don't happen now.	

Where **did** she **use to do** research?
  She **used to do** it at the library.
  She **didn't use to have** a computer.
	Did you **use to go** to the library?
	  Yes, I **did**.
	  No, I **didn't**.

When **would** you **watch** the news?
  I **would watch** it at 6:00.
  I **wouldn't watch** it online.
	Would they **watch** the news every night?
	  Yes, they **would**.
	  No, I/you/he/she/they/we **wouldn't**.

Use used to, not would, for situations that happened in the past.	
I **used to live** in Los Angeles. (NOT: I would live in Los Angeles.)	

2. **Circle the correct answers. Sometimes both answers are possible.**

   1. After school, I **used to** / **would** go to my friend's house to play.

   2. Franco **didn't use to** / **wouldn't** live in New York when he was young.

   3. Katie and Paulina **used to** / **would** text each other every day.

   4. You **didn't use to** / **wouldn't** have long hair.

   5. We **used to** / **would** ride our bikes every day.

Present perfect with present perfect continuous, p. 15

Present perfect continuous

Use the present perfect continuous for experiences that happened at an indefinite time in the past and continue to the present.

Where **have** you **been climbing**? I **have been climbing** at home. I **haven't been climbing** in the mountains.	**Have** you **been training** a lot? Yes, I **have**. No, I **haven't**.
What **has** she **been doing**? She **has been running** a club. She **hasn't been working** in an office.	**Has** she **been climbing** for a long time? Yes, she **has**. No, she **hasn't**.

Present perfect vs. present perfect continuous

Remember to use the present perfect for experiences that happened at an indefinite time in the past and are now complete. Use the present perfect to emphasize the result.

He used to be a professional rock climber, but he **has stopped** climbing.

Use the present perfect continuous to emphasize the action.

She **has been climbing** since she was four.

1. **Rewrite the sentences in the present perfect continuous when possible. When not possible, write *X*.**

   1. Where have you taken a Portuguese class?
      _____

   2. Mia hasn't gone to school this week.
      _____

   3. I haven't signed up for classes yet.
      _____

   4. Doug has kept up with his homework.
      _____

   5. My cousin has been determined to win that race.
      _____

Past perfect and past perfect continuous, p. 17

Past perfect continuous

Use the past perfect continuous for experiences that started in the past and continued up until another time in the past.

What **had** they **been doing**? They **had been using** cell phones before the program started. They **hadn't been using** email.	**Had** they **been using** cell phones? Yes, they **had**. No, they **hadn't**.

Past perfect vs. past perfect continuous

Remember to use the past perfect to refer to something that happened before a specific time in the past. Use the past perfect to emphasize the result.

Fifty people **had signed** up this year.   I **hadn't heard** of that job.

Use the past perfect continuous to emphasize the action.

I **had been working** with Helen for 6 months.

2. **Circle the correct answers. Sometimes both answers are possible.**

   1. I **hadn't gotten** / **hadn't been getting** along with my brother all summer.

   2. Farah **had been** / **had been being** motivated to learn to swim.

   3. Had you **written** / **been writing** a blog?

   4. Jack had already **gone** / **been going** to the store when I got home.

Unit 2 | 107

GRAMMAR REFERENCE

Future review, p. 25

will	be going to
Use will for predictions.	*Use going to for planned actions and events.*
What classes **will** David **take**? He **will take** Russian classes. He **won't take** French.	Where **is** he **going to** live? He **is going to live in** to Houston. He **isn't going to live** in his hometown.
	When **are** you **going to work**? I'm **going to work** on Sunday. I'**m not going to work** on Saturday.
Present continuous	**Simple present**
Use the present continuous for planned actions and events.	*Use the simple present for scheduled future events.*
What classes **is** he **taking** next year? He **is taking** advanced science. He **isn't taking** art classes.	Where **does** he **plan** to go? He **plans** to go to the ISS. He **doesn't plan** to go to Russia.
Where **are** they **driving** tomorrow? They **are driving** to Florida. They **aren't driving** to California.	When **do** you **have** your next yoga class? I **have** a class tomorrow. I **don't have** a class on Friday.

1. Correct the future forms in the sentences. Correct one word in each sentence.

1. Jack hates flying, so he will fly in space one day.
2. When are you go to start a business?
3. What time does the bus left tomorrow morning?
4. Cindy is take a lot of science classes this year.

Future continuous and future perfect, p. 27

Future continuous	
Use the future continuous to describe something that will be in progress in the future. To form the future continuous, use will + be + the -ing form of a verb.	
Who **will** be **volunteering**? We **will be volunteering**. They **won't be volunteering**.	**Will** you **be volunteering**? Yes, I **will**. No, I **won't**.
Future perfect	
Use the future perfect to describe something that is going to be finished at a certain time in the future. To form the future perfect, use will + have + past participle.	
How much trash **will** she **have collected** in 20 years? She **will have collected** a lot of trash. She **won't have earned** much money.	**Will** she **have collected** a lot of trash? Yes, she **will have**. No, she **won't have**.

2. Write answers for the questions.

1. Where will Susan be studying next year? (Brazil)
   _____
2. Will you have graduated from high school before your 18th birthday? (no)
   _____
3. How much money will you have saved by the time you start college? ($3,000)
   _____
4. Will you be going to summer camp this year? (yes)
   _____

108 | Unit 3

First conditional review; zero conditional, p. 35

Use the first conditional to show results or possible results of future actions. Use if, when, or unless and the simple present in the main clause. Use will (not) and the base form of a verb in the result clause.

If your skin **smells** like garlic, a mosquito probably **won't bite** you!
You**'ll have to go** to a restaurant with a fugu-trained chef, **unless** you **want** it to be your last meal!

Use the zero conditional to show a result of an action that is always true. Use if, when, or unless and the simple present in the main clause and the simple present in the result clause.

A poisonous gas **comes** out of an onion **when** you **cut** or **fry** it.
If the gas **gets** into your eyes, your body **makes** tears to wash it out.

1. **Correct the sentences. Correct one word in each sentence.**
   1. When I will go to my favorite restaurant, I usually order the same dish.
   2. We'll have to have the party inside if it will rain tomorrow.
   3. If Jenna makes spicy food again, I don't eat it.
   4. I make lemonade unless the store is out of lemons. I hope they have them.
   5. When I go to a dinner party, I always will bring a dessert.

Second conditional review, p. 37

Use the second conditional to describe imaginary situations and possible consequences. Use if or unless + simple past for the imaginary situation. Use would (not) + base form of the verb for the possible consequence.

Yes/No questions

Would you **eat** it again **if** you **had** the chance?
Yes, I **would**. / No, I **wouldn't**.
If I **saw** it on a menu, I **would eat** it again.
I **wouldn't eat** it again **if** you **paid** me.

Wh- questions

If I **wanted** to eat *chapulines* again, where **would** I **get** them?
You probably **wouldn't find** them **unless** you **went** to Mexico.

For be, use was or were after I.

I'd try *chapulines* if I **was** in Mexico.
If I **were** in Mexico, I'd try *chapulines*.

2. **Complete the sentences with the correct forms of the verbs.**
   1. _____ you _____ (try) the local food if you _____ (be) in another country?
   2. I _____ (make) a Moroccan stew if I _____ (have) a tagine.
   3. If Carl and Joe _____ (not have) a car, they _____ (walk) to the store.
   4. What _____ Lori _____ (cook) if her parents _____ (come) to dinner?
   5. We _____ (not eat) fast food unless we _____ (be) in a hurry.

Unit 4 | 109

Defining and non-defining relative clauses, p. 45

Use defining relative clauses with who, which, that, where, *and* whose *to give necessary information about a noun. The sentence has a different meaning without the clause.*

People **who make clothing** should be treated fairly.
Celebrities **that give money to organizations** often help bring attention to important causes.
Some of the money went to help people **whose homes had been ruined**.

Use non-defining relative clauses with who, which, where, *and* whose *to give additional information about a noun. The clause can be left out of the sentence and it still makes sense.*

Bono, **who is the lead singer of U2**, is admired for his charity work.
The Angel Network, **which Oprah started in 1998**, has raised more than $50,000,000.
They saw the effects of global warming in Sochi, **where the Olympics took place**.

1. Complete the sentences with *who, which, where,* or *whose.*

   1. My uncle, _____ was on a sitcom in the 1990s, hosts a talk show.
   2. The athletes gave money to schools _____ soccer teams didn't have uniforms.
   3. The Always Dream Foundation, _____ was started by Olympic skater Kristi Yamaguchi, gives computers to an after-school program.
   4. Brazil, _____ the 2014 World Cup was held, will host the 2016 Summer Olympics.

Tag questions, p. 47

Use tag questions to find out new information, to find out if someone agrees or disagrees with you, or to confirm something you believe is true. Tag questions are common in spoken English. If the statement is affirmative, the tag question is negative. If the statement is negative, the tag question is affirmative.

Simple present of *be*	Simple past of *be*
That's crazy, **isn't** it? He's **not** an actor, **is** he?	The acting **was** fabulous, **wasn't** it? The acting **wasn't** good, **was** it?
Simple present	Simple past
That **seems** like too much, **doesn't** it? That **doesn't seem** fair, **does** it?	She **admired** that actor, **didn't** she? We **didn't see** that movie, **did** we?
Modals	
Actors **shouldn't make** so much money, **should** they? The actors **should get** a large portion of the money, **shouldn't** they?	
Other forms	
Future with *will*	We'**ll go** see that new movie, **won't** we?
Present perfect	You **haven't been** on TV before, **have** you?

2. Complete the tag questions.

   1. Lisa got Willow Smith's autograph, _____ ?
   2. You haven't read *The Hunger Games*, _____ ?
   3. Your cousins aren't fans of Real Madrid, _____ ?
   4. We should get tickets for the 9:00 show, _____ ?

Passive infinitive, p. 57

The passive is the main verb + to be + a past participle. The main verb usually expresses thinking or speaking, for example: be, have, know, want, need, expect, like, believe, *and* ask.

Present	Past
The bottle **needs to be closed** with a black top. Moser **likes to be challenged**.	The lamp **didn't have to be plugged** in. He **didn't expect to be known** around the world for his invention.

1. **Complete the sentences with passive infinitives. Use the forms in parentheses.**

    1. Kyle _____ from his classes on Tuesday. (ask / excuse, *simple past*)

    2. We _____ with the workshop by 5:00 p.m. (expect / do, *simple past*)

    3. Ms. Anderson _____ the same questions twice. (not like / ask, *simple present*)

    4. My computer _____ at the end of the day. (need / shut down, *simple present*)

    5. Jeremy _____ for his invention. (want / remember, *simple present*)

Review of causative *have/get*, p. 59

Use causative have/get *in situations where someone else does something for you or when it's not important who is doing the action. You can use* have *or* get. *They have similar meanings.*
Use have/get *+ an object + past participle with the present, past, and future.*

	Active	Passive/Causative
Simple present	Someone **cleans** her house on Thursdays.	She **has** her house **cleaned** on Thursdays.
Simple past	Someone **delivered** the lamp today.	We **got** the lamp **delivered** today.
Present continuous	No one **is sending** the lamp to the man's house.	The man **isn't having** a lamp **sent** to his house.
Past continuous	Someone **was printing** the inventor's paper.	The inventor **was getting** his paper **printed** in New York City.
Future with *will*	I **will ask** someone **to make** a designer battery charger for my sister.	I **will get** a designer battery charger **made** for my sister.
Modals	**Should** I **ask** someone to **wrap** them for you?	Should I **have** them **wrapped** for you?

2. **Complete the sentences with causative *have* or *get*. Use the verbs and tense in parentheses.**

    1. Marcos _____ his tablet _____. (have / repair / *simple past*)

    2. Mia and Lou _____ their car _____ once a month. (get / clean / *simple present*)

    3. I _____ my website _____ this week. (have / update / *present continuous*)

    4. We _____ our phones _____ at the store in the mall. (have / upgrade / *modal:* could)

    5. _____ you _____ your clothes _____ at Sam's Laundry Service? (get / wash / *past continuous*)

    6. Jeanne _____ her kitchen cabinets _____ by a professional. (get / make / *future with* will)

Unit 6 | 111

Verb + -ing form (gerund) or infinitive, p. 67

Many verbs are followed by the -ing form of a verb or an infinitive. Some verbs can be followed by either an -ing form or an infinitive with no change in meaning. Others can be followed by either an -ing form or an infinitive, but the meaning changes.

Verb + *-ing* form: consider discuss enjoy finish keep miss	**Consider having** a theme party. Some people **don't enjoy hosting** them.
Verb + infinitive: decide learn expect need plan want	Decide what food you **want to make**. Do you **need to have** the party at a bigger place?
Verb + *-ing* form or infinitive: begin hate like love prefer start	Everybody **loves going** to parties! Everybody **loves to go** to parties!
Verb + *-ing* form or infinitive with change in meaning: forget remember try	Don't **forget to plan** a budget. (= not forget to do something) I'll never **forget going** to my first birthday party. (= not forgetting that something happened) I **tried to work** as a party planner, but I couldn't find a job. (= try something, but not succeed at it) I **tried working** as a party planner, but I didn't like the job. (= try something to see if it works)

1. Write a check (✓) for the correct sentences. Correct the mistakes in the incorrect sentences.

1. ☐ We discussed to have the holiday party at my house.
2. ☐ I hate going to parties by myself.
3. ☐ Alex kept putting up decorations even after we finished.
4. ☐ We planned playing rock music at the party for several hours.
5. ☐ Lori remembered to prepare special foods with her grandmother when she was young.
6. ☐ We decided watching the parade on Clinton Street.

-ing form (gerund) as subject; by/for + -ing form, p. 69

You can use the -ing form as the subject of a sentence. When it's the subject, the verb is singular.

Traveling to Italy is always great.
Watching the monkeys is very entertaining.
Not going to the festival would be a mistake.

The -ing form can also be used after by to show how to do something and after for to show the purpose or use of something.

Let's start **by returning** to Harbin.
The weather is perfect **for making** ice statues.

2. Complete the sentences with the *-ing* form of the verbs. Add *by* or *for* when needed.

1. I think _____ (go) to festivals is fun only if they aren't crowded.
2. I like to celebrate my birthday _____ (have) a small party with friends.
3. _____ (watch) movies at a film festival is exciting.
4. I told my friends that _____ (no remember) my birthday is a bad idea!
5. A park is a good place _____ (get) together with friends.

Time clauses; present participle clauses, p. 77

Use time clauses to show the order of events in the past, present, and future.

Use before to show that the event in the time clause happened second.

The Atlantic Avenue Tunnel was made in 1844 **before** the subway system was created.
FIRST EVENT — SECOND EVENT

Use after to show the event in the time clause happened first.

After the news spreads, Bob becomes a local hero.
FIRST EVENT — SECOND EVENT

Use when to show that both events happened at the same time.

They will search for a steam train in the tunnel **when** they have enough money.

You can use the -ing form (gerund) of a verb after before and after.

Before searching for the tunnel, Bob heard about it on a radio program.
Bob finds an old map **after searching** city records for eight months.

1. Circle the correct answers.

1. The divers took a photo of the unusual fish **before** / **when** they saw it.
2. We bought tickets to the concert after **heard** / **hearing** the band's music.
3. The detective will take a vacation after he **catches** / **will catch** the criminal.
4. **When** / **After** we go to the museum, we'll go home.

Reported speech, p. 79

Use reported speech and reported questions to tell others what another person said. In both reported speech and reported questions, the verbs usually change tenses.

Quoted speech	Reported speech
She said, "I **am leaving** the dolls."	She admitted that she **was leaving** the dolls.
She said, "I **was watching** TV."	She wrote that she **had been watching** TV.
He asked, "**When will** you **be talking** to her?"	He asked me **when I would be talking** to her.
He asked, "Are you keeping her secret?"	He asked me **if I was keeping** her secret.

Infinitives can be used with these reporting verbs: agree, claim, decide.

I **agreed to keep** it a secret.   She **claimed to know** who had done it.

The -ing form can be used with these reporting verbs: recommend, insist on, admit to.

She **insisted on keeping** the doll.   I **recommend posting** a question online.

Imperative clauses

Change an imperative to a reported imperative using infinitive verbs.

Quoted imperative	Reported imperative
He said, "**Tell** me about it!"	He told her **to tell** him about it.
She said, "**Don't tell** anyone."	She said **not to tell** anyone.

2. Put the words in the correct order to make sentences.

1. said / in the ocean / not to / swim / my parents

   _____

2. recommended / a mystery novel / reading / Paisley

   _____

3. to find / I / I / was / said / trying / the answer / that

   _____

4. been / watching / if I / the news / had / Doug / asked me

   _____

Third conditional, p. 87

Use the third conditional sentences to describe imaginary situations and impossible consequences. Use if + past perfect for the imaginary and untrue situation in the past. Use would (not) + have + past participle for the impossible consequence.

If he **hadn't heard** those noises, he **wouldn't have gone** on an adventure.
If the teenager **had stolen** Gracie, he **would have gotten** away.

What **would have happened if** the thief **had stolen** Gracie?
He **would have gotten** away.

Would the chicken **have become** a hero **if** it **hadn't saved** Lucky?
Yes, it **would have**. / No, it **wouldn't have**.

1. Write sentences and questions with the third conditional.

1. if / Ted / not read / that story / he / not be / scared /.
   If Ted hadn't read that story, he wouldn't have been scared.

2. Cynthia / take photos of the hoodoos / if her camera / work /.
   _____

3. what / you / do / if / someone / steal / your wallet /?
   _____

4. you / call / the police / if / you / see / strange lights last night /?
   _____

5. if / we / walk / a few more miles / we / reach / the top of the mountain /.
   _____

Past modals of speculation, p. 89

Use past modals of speculation to show how certain you are about a past event. Form past modals with modal + have + past participle.

Affirmative	Negative
Not sure: Hoodoos **may have been** people. You **might have seen** more hoodoos. Rivers **could have formed** them.	**Not sure:** They **may not have been** nice people. He **might not have liked** them.
Sure: The Legend People **must have made** Coyote mad.	**Sure:** People **couldn't have made** them. The Legend People **must not have known** that it was a trick.

2. Complete the sentences with a modal + *have* + past participle of the verbs in parentheses. ✓ = sure. ✗ = not sure. Sometimes more than one answer is possible.

1. Kyle _____ (not see, ✓) that movie. He doesn't like science fiction movies.

2. Leslie _____ (not take, ✗) that photo of the cliff dwellings. She's never been to Mesa Verde.

3. Claudia and Leo _____ (walk, ✓) to work. Their car is at the mechanic's shop.

4. Sarah _____ (not like, ✗) my story. She didn't say much about it.

5. The movie _____ (take, ✗) place in Japan. Some of the city scenes looked like they were in Tokyo.

6. You _____ (not get, ✓) much sleep last night. You sent me an email at 2:00 a.m.!

Past ability, p. 97

> Use *could, was/were able to,* and *managed to* to talk about past abilities.
>
> Use *could* for both general and specific abilities.
>
> | GENERAL: | SPECIFIC: |
> |---|---|
> | What **could** you **do**? | **Could** she **drive** when she was 15? |
> | I **couldn't do** anything. | Yes, she **could**. She **could drive** well. |
> | I **could learn** to do anything! | No, she **couldn't**. She **couldn't drive** yet. |
>
> Use *was/were able to* and *managed to* for specific abilities only.
>
> | | |
> |---|---|
> | How **was** she **able to learn** so much? | How **did** she **manage to pay** for it? |
> | She **was able to watch** videos online. | She **managed to save** money. |
> | She **wasn't able to take** a course. | She **didn't manage to get** a free car. |
> | **Were** they **able to fix** the car? | **Did** you **manage to fix** the car? |
> | Yes, they **were**. / No, they **weren't**. | Yes, I **did**. / No, I **didn't**. |

1. **Complete the sentences with *could* (*not*), (*not*) *be able to*, and (*not*) *managed to* and the verb in parentheses. Sometimes more than one answer is possible.**

   1. Unfortunately, Jeff _____ (gain) much work experience before he started his job.

   2. I _____ (work) last year because I wasn't old enough to have a job.

   3. We _____ (pay) the application fees for our photography class on Friday morning because our parents gave us the money.

   4. _____ (you / get) to your training course at 6:00 p.m.?

Modal expressions for past and future, p. 99

> Use (*not*) *had to* and (*not*) *need to* for obligations and necessities in the past.
>
> | | |
> |---|---|
> | What **did** you **need to learn** about? | What **did** he **have to do**? |
> | I **needed to learn** about fashion. | He **had to take** a training course. |
> | I **didn't need to learn** about chemistry. | He **didn't have to get** a college degree. |
> | **Did** he **need to take** training courses? | **Did** they **need to work** on weekends? |
> | Yes, he **did**. | Yes, they **did**. |
> | No, he **didn't**. | No, they **didn't**. |
>
> Use *will* (*not*) *have to* and *will* (*not*) *need to* for obligations and necessities in the future.
>
> | | |
> |---|---|
> | What courses **will** you **have to take**? | When **will** she **need to finish** the design? |
> | I **will have to take** more training courses. | She **will need to finish** by Friday. |
> | I **won't have to take** any college courses. | She **won't need to finish** by tomorrow. |
> | **Will** he **have to take** more courses? | **Will** they **need to pay** an entrance fee? |
> | Yes, he **will**. | Yes, they **will**. |
> | No, he **won't**. | No, they **won't**. |

2. **Put the words in the correct order to make sentences and questions.**

   1. finish / my degree / I / to / have /next year / will /.

      _____

   2. needed / her application / Shelly / to / last month / fee / pay /.

      _____

   3. you / need / get / will / a babysitter / tomorrow night / to /?

      _____

   4. need / an entrance / pay / Mariah / fee / didn't / for the art class / to /.

      _____

   5. to / exam / have / entrance / take / when / the / Greg / will /?

      _____

The Smart HOUSE

CLIL PROJECT

1. **Here are some jobs that can now be done by a computer instead of a person. Label the pictures with the correct words.**

   babysitter   butler   personal assistant   secretary

   1 _____   2 _____   3 _____   4 _____

Discovery EDUCATION
2.4 THE HOUSE OF THE FUTURE

2. **Watch the video. Check (✓) the activities Cleopatra can do.**

   1. Raise the blinds ____
   2. Paint the room ____
   3. Change the music ____
   4. Discuss the weather ____
   5. Manage the shopping ____
   6. Do the ironing ____
   7. Cook dinner ____
   8. Open the front door ____

3. **Complete the sentences with the correct words.**

   1. Will it even change the music based on your _____?
   2. She mostly lives on a box that we have down in our _____ room.
   3. Cleopatra uses radio _____ ID technology.
   4. It will automatically reorder anything that you _____.
   5. That's a lot of money, but if we're going to live in _____ like these in the future . . .

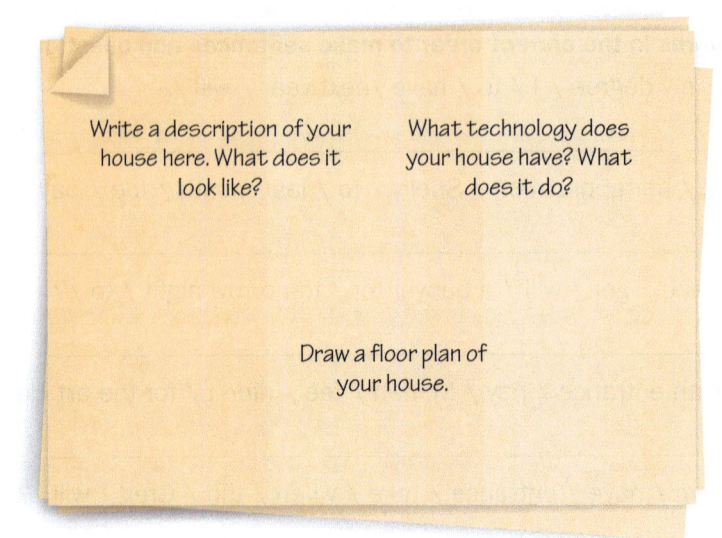

PROJECT Imagine your own "house of the future." Is it in the city or the country? Is it in the sky or underwater? Does your house use the latest technology? Look at the model poster, then make your own.

Write a description of your house here. What does it look like?

What technology does your house have? What does it do?

Draw a floor plan of your house.

116 | CLIL Project | Unit 2

What's in OUR FOOD?

1. Label the pictures with the correct words.

| fats and proteins | natural sugar | processed food | salt |

1. _____ 2. _____ 3. _____ 4. _____

2. Watch the video. Complete the sentences with the correct words.

| natural sugar | preservatives |
| nutritional information | processed food |

1. But now more than ever, factories are creating _____.
2. . . . it often has salt, sugar, _____, coloring, and flavoring all added . . .
3. When you're shopping, it's important to check for _____.
4. The _____ in fruit is much healthier than processed sugar.

Discovery EDUCATION
4.4 YOU ARE WHAT YOU EAT

3. Number the items 1–5 in the order you see them.

____ a man juggling

____ cows eating grass

____ two children writing

____ a giant cow

____ cheese

PROJECT You are trying to eat healthier foods. Make a food journal for the items you ate yesterday. Decide if the foods you ate were *low*, *medium*, or *high* in the areas on the chart below.

Meal	Item	Fats and proteins	Natural sugars	Salt	Processed Food
Breakfast	toast with butter	high in fat, low in protein	low	medium	no
	orange juice	low	high	low	no
	yogurt	high in protein	medium	low	no
Lunch					
Dinner					

Study your chart. Are you eating too much of one type of food and not enough of another? Write down your ideas.

CLIL PROJECT

Unit 4 | CLIL Project | 117

Making MUSIC

CLIL PROJECT

1. **Read these descriptions of the parts of an acoustic guitar. Then label the diagram below.**

Body:	The main part of the guitar
Bridge:	The lower parts of the strings are attached to this
Frets:	You press the strings down on these to make sound
Head:	The upper part of the guitar
Soundhole:	A round hole in the body that lets the sound out
Strings:	You pick these to make sound
Tuning keys/pegs:	You turn these to change the pitch of the strings

   Discovery EDUCATION
   6.4 INSIDE THE GUITAR

2. **Watch the video. Number the stages of making a guitar 1–5.**

   ____ They spray colors onto the guitar.

   ____ They add the strings.

   ____ They add the frets by hand.

   ____ They use big machines to make the bodies.

   ____ They put small magnets under the strings.

3. **Complete the sentences with the correct words.**

   | acoustic | amplifies | original | revolution | solid | waves |

   1. Traditional guitars are also known as _____ guitars.
   2. The body of a traditional guitar _____ the sound.
   3. Electric guitars have a _____ body.
   4. We see guitars that look like an _____ Gibson guitar of 1952.
   5. When the strings move over the magnets they create _____.
   6. The electric guitar was part of a _____ in music.

PROJECT What's your favorite musical instrument – the piano, violin, trumpet, drums, or something else? Make a poster advertising music lessons for this instrument. Say why other students should want to learn this instrument.

Music Lessons
- What types of music can you play?
- Can you make money playing this instrument?
- What is the history of the instrument?
- Have any famous people played this instrument?
- In which parts of the world is this instrument popular?

Bringing HISTORY TO LIFE

The American Revolutionary War

By the 1760s, conflict was beginning between the British government in London and the 13 British colonies on the eastern side of North America. The colonists resisted the British government's control, sometimes violently, and a full war began in 1775. The colonies signed the Declaration of Independence, declaring themselves free of British rule. Six years later, the British army surrendered at Yorktown. George Washington, who led the American army, became the new country's first president in 1789.

The American Civil War

In the middle of the next century, the northern states were more industrial, while the southern states had large plantations that grew cotton and tobacco and were worked by slaves. In 1860, Abraham Lincoln, who was opposed to slavery, was elected president. Eleven southern states broke away from the rest of the country, and a war started in 1861. Despite early victories, the South surrendered four years later. Throughout the war, over a million people lost their lives, including President Lincoln, who was assassinated just days after it ended. In 1865, slavery became illegal in the United States.

1. **Decide if these sentences describe the Revolutionary War (*RW*) or the Civil War (*CW*).**

    1. Eleven states left the United States. ____

    2. The American colonies fought for independence. ____

    3. One side was more successful at the start, but ended up losing. ____

    4. British soldiers were involved in this war. ____

    5. The president did not live long after the end of this war. ____

2. **Watch the video. Number these events 1–5 in the order that they happened.**

    ____ The American Civil War began.

    ____ Reenactors re-create previous battles.

    ____ There was a war between Britain and the American colonies.

    ____ President Lincoln made a speech at Gettysburg.

    ____ The American colonies declared their independence from Britain.

PROJECT — **What events in the history of your country do you think should be reenacted? Imagine you are organizing a reenactment event. Write a list of instructions for the reenactors:**

- What they need to wear
- What they should bring with them for the reenactment
- What they should bring to eat
- Where and when they should arrive
- What will happen during the day

Saving the LIONS

1. **This map of Kenya shows where the people live and where the national parks are. Kenya's population is increasing at 2.7 percent per year, but the wildlife is decreasing. Discuss these questions:**
   - How will Kenya's economy be different if its wildlife disappears?
   - Why do people sometimes destroy wildlife?
   - How can local people protect the wildlife?

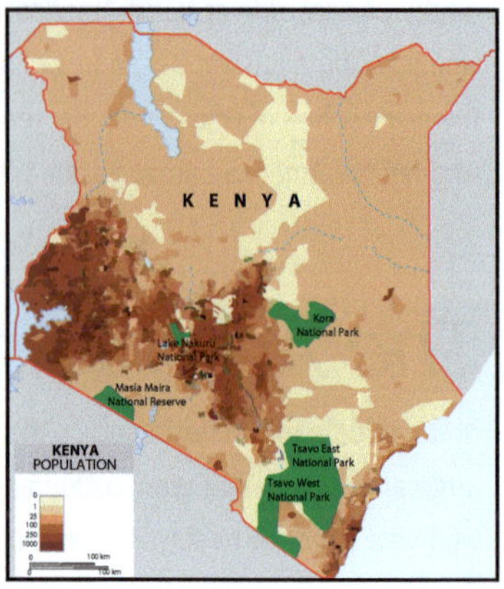

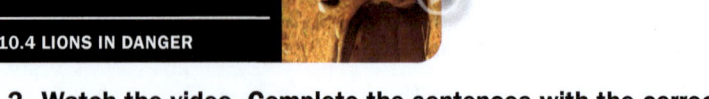

Discovery EDUCATION — 10.4 LIONS IN DANGER

2. **Watch the video. Complete the sentences with the correct numbers.**

   ¼   20   20–30   35   25,000

   1. Only _____ lions live in Africa today.
   2. Jeff Corwin has worked with wildlife for almost _____ years.
   3. More than _____ million people live in Kenya.
   4. More than _____ of a million people live outside the national park.
   5. In this region, people used to kill _____ lions a year.

3. **Circle the correct answers.**

   1. The number of lions in Africa is falling because of _____.
      a. people   b. climate   c. both a & b
   2. In the last hundred years, the human population around the park has _____.
      a. increased   b. decreased   c. not changed much
   3. People used to kill lions mainly _____.
      a. to protect their animals   b. to protect themselves   c. to sell their skins
   4. They don't kill lions now because of _____.
      a. education   b. money/compensation   c. both a & b

PROJECT — Think of a species in danger, in your own country or somewhere else. What is being done to protect these animals? Research the animal and write a fact sheet about its characteristics and its chances of survival. Then look at all the fact sheets from your class. With the other students, work out a plan to protect a species in danger.

Irregular verbs

Base Verb	Simple Past	Past Participle
babysit	babysat	babysat
be	was, were	been
beat	beat	beat
become	became	become
begin	began	begun
bite	bit	bitten
bleed	bled	bled
blow	blew	blown
break	broke	broken
bring	brought	brought
build	built	built
burn	burned	burned/burnt
buy	bought	bought
catch	caught	caught
choose	chose	chosen
come	came	come
cost	cost	cost
cut	cut	cut
deal	dealt	dealt
dive	dived/dove	dived
do	did	done
draw	drew	drawn
dream	dreamed/dreamt	dreamed/dreamt
drink	drank	drunk
drive	drove	driven
eat	ate	eaten
fall	fell	fallen
feel	felt	felt
fight	fought	fought
find	found	found
fit	fit	fit
fly	flew	flown
forget	forgot	forgotten
freeze	froze	frozen
get	got	gotten
give	gave	given
go	went	gone
grow	grew	grown
hang	hung	hung
have	had	had
hear	heard	heard
hide	hid	hidden
hit	hit	hit
hold	held	held
hurt	hurt	hurt
keep	kept	kept
know	knew	known
lead	led	led

Base Verb	Simple Past	Past Participle
leave	left	left
let	let	let
lie	lay	lain
light	lit	lit
lose	lost	lost
make	made	made
mean	meant	meant
meet	met	met
pay	paid	paid
prove	proved	proven
put	put	put
quit	quit	quit
read	read	read
ride	rode	ridden
ring	rang	rung
rise	rose	risen
run	ran	run
say	said	said
see	saw	seen
sell	sold	sold
send	sent	sent
set	set	set
shoot	shot	shot
show	showed	shown
shut	shut	shut
sing	sang	sung
sink	sank	sunk
sit	sat	sat
sleep	slept	slept
speak	spoke	spoken
spend	spent	spent
spread	spread	spread
stand	stood	stood
steal	stole	stolen
stick	stuck	stuck
strike	struck	struck/stricken
swim	swam	swum
take	took	taken
teach	taught	taught
tell	told	told
think	thought	thought
throw	threw	thrown
understand	understood	understood
wake	woke	woken
wear	wore	worn
win	won	won
write	wrote	written

Credits

The authors and publishers acknowledge the following sources of copyright material and are grateful for the permissions granted. While every effort has been made, it has not always been possible to identify the sources of all the material used, or to trace all copyright holders. If any omissions are brought to our notice, we will be happy to include the appropriate acknowledgements on reprinting.

p. 2-3 (B/G): Getty Images/Ian McKinnell; p. 3 (1): Shutterstock Images/RossHelen; p. 3 (2): Shutterstock Images/enciktat; p. 3 (3): Alamy/©Tatiana Morozova; p. 3 (4): Shutterstock Images/Fotogenix; p. 3 (5): Corbis/W2 Photography; p. 4 (L): Getty Images/murat sarica; p. 4 (B/G): Shutterstock Images/Pixsooz; p. 5 (R): Shutterstock Images/marekuliasz; p. 6 (TL): Alamy/©ClassicStock; p. 6 (TCL): Shutterstock Images/Hector Sanchez; p. 6 (BCL): Shutterstock Images/Filip Fuxa; p. 6 (TBL): Alamy/©trekkerimages; p. 6 (BL): Getty Images/TimZillion; p. 7 (R): Shutterstock Images/CroMary; p. 8 (BL): Getty Images/Julia Fishkin; p. 8 (BR): Getty Images/Denis O'Regan; p. 9 (TL): Getty Images/T.J. Kirkpatrick; p. 10 (TL): Getty Images/Charles Gullung; p. 10 (CL): Alamy/©Frances Roberts; p. 10 (C): Alamy/©moodboard; p. 10 (B/G): Shutterstock Images/nikkytok; p. 12 (B/G): Alamy/©Stock Foundry Images; p. 13 (a): Getty Images/Aminart; p. 13 (b): Alamy/©Hero Images Inc.; p. 13 (c): Getty Images/DragonImages; p. 13 (d): Alamy/©STOCK4B GmbH; p. 13 (e): Alamy/©Bob Ebbesen; p. 14 (L): Darío Rodríguez/DESNIVEL./Courtesy of Robyn Raboutou; p. 15 (R): Getty Images/zhekos; p. 16 (TL): Getty Images/Tetra Images; p. 17 (L): Shutterstock Images/traithep khampitoon; p. 18 (TL): Alamy/©PhotoAlto; p. 18 (BL): Shutterstock Images/Oleg Vinnichenko; p. 19 (TR): Getty Images/sturti; p. 20 (CR): Getty Images/Dimitri Otis; p. 20 (TR, B/G): Alamy/©Sabena Jane Blackbird; p. 20 (TL): Alamy/©Greenshoots Communications; p. 22 (B/G): Alamy/©Michael Doolittle; p. 23 (a): Shutterstock Images/koosen; p. 23 (b): Alamy/©David Askham; p. 23 (c): Alamy/©imageBROKER; p. 23 (d): Alamy/©Jochen Tack; p. 23 (e): Getty Images/Ken Reid; p. 23 (BR): Shutterstock Images/PT Images; p. 24 (TL): Shutterstock Images/Ahturner; p. 24 (CL): NASA; p. 24 (BL): NASA; p. 24 (B/G): Shutterstock Images/JaySi; p. 25 (R): Alamy/©Kevin Galvin; p. 26 (TL): Alamy/©GARY DOAK; p. 26 (a): Shutterstock Images/Elnur; p. 26 (b): Getty Images/Kali Nine LLC; p. 26 (c): Alamy/©Kip Evans; p. 26 (d): Shutterstock Images/Amble Design; p. 26 (e): Shutterstock Images/Volt Collection; p. 26 (f): Getty Images/Anatoliy Babiy; p. 26 (g): Alamy/©ZUMA Press, Inc.; p. 26 (h): Shutterstock Images/Stephen Coburn; p. 28 (TL): Getty Images/Jamie Grill; p. 28 (CL): Shutterstock Images/Nadiia Korol; p. 28 (BL): Shutterstock Images/cocoo; p. 29 (TL): Shutterstock Images/Goodluz; p. 30 (TL): Getty Images/Niklas Halle'n/Barcroft India/Barcroft Media; p. 30 (CR): Sascha Baumann/Getty Images; p. 30 (TR, B/G): Shutterstock Images/Evgeny Karandaev; p. 32 (B/G): Getty Images/Hemant Mehta; p. 33 (1): Shutterstock Images/Andrey Armyagov; p. 33 (2): Getty Images/Peter Johansky; p. 33 (3): Shutterstock Images/Joe Belanger; p. 33 (4): Shutterstock Images/L. Kragt Bakker; p. 33 (5): Shutterstock Images/Sheila_Fitzgerald; p. 33 (6): Shutterstock Images/Masson; p. 33 (7): Alamy/©Profimedia.CZ a.s.; p. 33 (8): Alamy/©Studio51; p. 33 (9): Shutterstock Images/Catalin Petolea; p. 34 (TL): Shutterstock Images/Nomad_Soul; p. 34 (TR): YOSHIKAZU TSUNO/AFP/GettyImages; p. 34 (BL): Shutterstock Images/SAAC; p. 34 (BR): Shutterstock Images/M. Unal Ozmen; p. 36 (TL): Getty Images/Andy Reynolds; p. 36 (a): Getty Images/C_yung; p. 36 (b): Shutterstock Images/Isantilli; p. 36 (c): Getty Images/Dennis Gottlieb; p. 36 (d): Getty Images/Kate Baldwin; p. 36 (e): Shutterstock Images/Chad Zuber; p. 36 (f): Getty Images/Nicole S. Young; p. 37 (R): Shutterstock Images/Alexeysun; p. 38 (TL): Shutterstock Images/Robnroll; p. 38 (BL): Alamy/©Bon Appetit; p. 39 (TR): Shutterstock Images/Joe Gough; p. 40 (B/G): Shutterstock Images/wavebreakmedia; p. 40 (TL): Shutterstock Images/kai keisuke; p. 40 (CL): Getty Images/pictafolio; p. 40 (TC): Getty Images/Arnold H. Drapkin; p. 40 (TR): Shutterstock Images/Mahdees Mahjoob; p. 40 (CR): Alamy/©Mode Images; p. 42 (B/G): Getty Images/Peter Dazeley; p. 44 (TL): Getty Images/L.Cohen/WireImage/Nordstrom; p. 44 (CL): Getty Images/STEPHANE DE SAKUTIN/AFP; p. 44 (BL): Getty Images/Harry How; p. 45 (R): Alamy/©lemonade; p. 46 (TL): Getty Images/urfinguss; p. 46 (BL): Shutterstock Images/cromic; p. 48 (TL): Alamy/©ALAN EDWARDS; p. 48 (CL): Getty Images/Logan Fazio/FilmMagic; p. 48 (BL): Getty Images/Peter Kramer/NBC/NBC NewsWire; p. 49 (C): Markus Mainka/Shutterstock; p. 49 (TL): Steve Collender/Shutterstock; p. 49 (TR): Shutterstock Images/joycedragan; p. 50 (TR): Getty Images/Peter Dazeley; p. 50 (C): Getty Images/Brad Barket; p. 50 (BR): Shutterstock Images/Helga Esteb; p. 50 (B/G): Shutterstock Images/Apples Eyes Studio; p. 52 (B/G): Getty Images/Kevin Elvis King; p. 54 (B/G): Alamy/©Peter M. Wilson; p. 55 (1): Shutterstock Images/Michael Dechev; p. 55 (2): Shutterstock Images/Sanit Fuangnakhon; p. 55 (3): Shutterstock Images/Filip Bjorkman; p. 55 (4): Shutterstock Images/Cynoclub; p. 55 (5): Shutterstock Images/Chimpinski; p. 55 (6): Shutterstock Images/Olga Popova; p. 55 (7): Shutterstock Images/Minerva Studio; p. 55 (8): Shutterstock Images/Darren Pullman; p. 55 (9): Getty Images/Pulse/Fuse; p. 55 (10): Shutterstock Images/Ivaschenko Roman; p. 56 (L): Corbis/©ROLEX DELA PENA/epa; p. 56 (R): Corbis/©DIVYAKANT SOLANKI/epa; p. 58 (TL): Alamy/©Idealink Photography; p. 59 (R): Getty Images/toddmedia; p. 60 (TL): Alamy/©B.O'Kane; p. 61 (TR): Shutterstock Images/fotoslaz; p. 61 (TL): Shutterstock Images/Olga Knutova; p. 62 (L): Alamy/©The Art Archive; p. 62 (CL): Alamy/©Francesco Gustincich; p. 62 (CR): Corbis/©NingJie; p. 62 (R): Shutterstock Images/Igor Kovalchuk; p. 62 (B/G): Shutterstock Images/Fedor Selivanov; p. 64 (B/G) Corbis/ROBIN UTRECHT FOTOGRAFIE/HillCreek Pictures; p. 65 (1): Getty Images/Jupiterimages; p. 65 (2): Getty Images/ERproductions Ltd; p. 65 (3): Alamy/©Tony Watson; p. 65 (4): Shutterstock Images/Taras Vyshnya; p. 65 (5): Getty Images/Image Source; p. 65 (6): Alamy/©Blue Jean Images; p. 65 (7): Shutterstock Images/Richard Thornton; p. 65 (8): Alamy/©Datacraft - QxQ images; p. 65 (9): Corbis/Roger Brooks; p. 66 (T): Shutterstock Images/gualtiero boffi; p. 66 (TR): Corbis/Jon-Michael Sullivan/Staff; p. 66 (L): Shutterstock Images/HomeStudio; p. 66 (BR): Shutterstock Images/Mike Degteariov; p. 67 (R): Getty Images/mediaphotos; p. 67 (CR): Shutterstock Images/Dan Kosmayer; p. 68 (TL): Shutterstock Images/topten22photo; p. 68 (TCL): Alamy/©FocusChina; p. 68 (BCL): Shutterstock Images/Paolo Bona; p. 68 (BL): Alamy/©ZUMA Press, Inc.; p. 69 (R): Alamy/©Rob Crandall; p. 70 (L): Alamy/©ImagesBazaar; p. 71 (TR): Alamy/©Corbis Super RF; p. 72 (TR): Getty Images/Chung Sung-Jun; p. 72 (TC): Getty Images/Chung Sung-Jun; p. 72 (C): Shutterstock Images/Soultkd; p. 72 (B/G): Shutterstock Images/Ieungchopan; p. 74 (B/G): Getty Images/Borut Furlan; p. 76 (TL): Getty Images/New York Daily News Archive/contributor; p. 76 (CL): Alamy/©Randy Duchaine; p. 76 (R): Getty Images/Maremagnum; p. 77 (L): Shutterstock Images/MichaelTaylor; p. 78 (T): Getty Images/Joseph Devenney; p. 78 (BL): Getty Images/Carol Yepes; p. 80 (TL): Alamy/©Ingram Publishing; p. 80 (R): Getty Images/Jeff Morgan 16; p. 80 (BL): Alamy/©Nature Picture Library; p. 81 (TR): Shutterstock Images/cenap refik ongan; p. 81 (TL): Shutterstock Images/NorGal; p. 81 (TR): Getty Images/Thinkstock/Sini?a Bota?; p. 82 (TR, B/G): Image courtesy of the Beinecke Library; p. 82 (L): Image courtesy of the Beinecke Library; p. 84 (B/G): Getty Images/John Lund; p. 85 (L): Alamy/©Everett Collection Inc; p. 85 (BL): Alamy/©Studio Works; p. 85 (BC): Alamy/©Ben Molyneux; p. 85 (BR): Corbis/©Bettmann; p. 86 (T): Shutterstock Images/MaxyM; p. 86 (L): Shutterstock Images/Emilio100; p. 87 (R): Shutterstock Images/M. Unal Ozmen; p. 88 (L): Shutterstock Images/Soumitra Pendse; p. 89 (1): Getty Images/Cavan Images; p. 89 (2): Shutterstock Images/Kingarion; p. 89 (3): Alamy/©Trinity Mirror/Mirrorpix; p. 90 (TL): Corbis/©Bettmann; p. 91 (TR): Shutterstock Images/Stacy Barnett; p. 92 (T): Shutterstock Images/MaraZe; p. 92 (TL): Shutterstock Images/kravka; p. 92 (CL): Getty Images/Witold Skrypczak; p. 92 (C): Alamy/©Emily Riddell; p. 92 (CR): Getty Images/traveler1116; p. 92 (B/G): Shutterstock Images/Aivoges; p. 92 (TL): Shutterstock Images/Kravka; p. 94 (B/G): Corbis/©Juice Images; p. 95 (T): Shutterstock Images/Air Images; p. 95 (TR): Shutterstock Images/wavebreakmedia; p. 95 (CR): Alamy/©Jeff Morgan 16; p. 95 (BR): Getty Images/moodboard; p. 96 (TL): Alamy/©Juice Images; p. 96 (CL): Shutterstock Images/Peter Gudella; p. 96 (BL): Shutterstock Images/donatas1205; p. 97 (B): Alamy/©B Christopher; p. 98 (T): Shutterstock Images/Africa Studio; p. 98 (1): Shutterstock Images/Africa Studio; p. 98 (2): Shutterstock Images/racorn; p. 98 (3): Getty Images/VikZa; p. 98 (4): Getty Images/Jetta Productions; p. 98 (5): Shutterstock Images/Izf; p. 98 (6): Getty Images/Digital Vision.; p. 98 (7): Alamy/©David Young-Wolff; p. 98 (8): Shutterstock Images/Sasha Samardzija; p. 98 (9): Alamy/©Ira Berger; p. 98 (BL): Alamy/©GraficallyMinded; p. 99 (L): Getty Images/Cultura/Leon Harris; p. 100 (TL): Shutterstock Images/Jultud; p. 100 (TCL): Shutterstock Images/Fetullah Mercan; p. 100 (CL): Shutterstock Images/Nightscorp; p. 100 (BCL): Getty Images/Charles Mann; p. 100 (BL): Shutterstock Images/Everything; p. 101 (TL): Alamy/©dpa picture alliance archive; p. 102 (TL): Getty Images/Pamela Martin; p. 102 (CL): Getty Images/Brendon Thorne; p. 102 (BL): Getty Images/Al Bello; p. 102 (B/G): Shutterstock Images/Marish; p. 104 (B/G): Corbis/©Arctic-Images; p. 119 (TR): Shutterstock Images/Lucy; p. 119 (CR): Shutterstock Images/American Spirit; p. 120 (BR): Shutterstock Images/wandee007; Back cover: Shutterstock Images/Cbenjasuwan.

Front cover photography by Alamy/©Image Source Plus.

The publishers are grateful to the following illustrators:
Anni Betts: p. 50, 86, 99; Q2A Media Services, Inc.: p. 27, 43, 58, 73, 75, 116, 117, 118, 120.

All video stills by kind permission of:
Discovery Communications, LLC 2015: p. 2 (1, 3), 5, 10, 12 (1, 3, 4), 15, 20, 21, 22 (1, 3), 25, 30, 32 (1, 3, 4), 35, 40, 41, 42 (1, 3), 45, 50, 54 (1, 3, 4), 57, 62, 63, 64 (1, 3), 67, 72, 74 (1, 3, 4), 77, 82, 83, 84 (1, 3), 87, 92, 94 (1, 3, 4), 97, 102, 103, 116, 117, 118, 119, 120; Cambridge University Press: p. 2 (2), 8, 12 (2), 18, 22 (2), 28, 32 (2), 38, 42 (2), 48, 54 (2), 60, 63 (2), 70, 74 (2), 80, 84 (2), 90, 94 (2), 100.

Uncover 4 Combo
Lynne Robertson

Workbook

CAMBRIDGE UNIVERSITY PRESS

Discovery EDUCATION

Table of Contents

1	Tell Me About It!	2
2	Best Foot Forward	8
	Review: Units 1 and 2	14
3	Planning for the Future	16
4	What's Cooking?	22
	Review: Units 3 and 4	28
5	Fame and Fortune	30
6	It's the Little Things	36
	Review: Units 5 and 6	42
7	Have a Ball!	44
8	Mysteries and Secrets	50
	Review: Units 7 and 8	56
9	Weird and Wonderful	58
10	I Have To! I Can!	64
	Review: Units 9 and 10	70
	Video worksheets	72

1 Tell Me About It!

VOCABULARY Media

1 Label the pictures with the correct words. One word is used more than once.

| article | interview | the news | reporter |
| blogger | headline | paper | review |

1. _____
2. _____
3. _____
4. _____
5. _____
6. _____
7. _____
8. _____
9. _____

2 Circle the correct answers.

Gina: Have you seen the ¹**article / news** yet?

Felix: No, what happened?

Gina: That ²**interview / reporter** you like quit. There's a new person reporting the news now.

Felix: Oh, well. I have to watch a ³**paper / report** every night because we talk about current events in my civics class.

Gina: Do you have to watch TV news? There's a ⁴**blogger / paper** I really like. He writes about interesting issues on his website.

Felix: Well, we're supposed to discuss local news in class. I can just read the local ⁵**paper / review**.

Gina: It's online, too, you know. Here, look. The ⁶**interview / headline** says that some roads will be closed this weekend. And there's an ⁷**interview / review** with the local police explaining what alternate routes to take.

Felix: That's kind of dull. The paper has this ⁸**blogger / article** about an old building the city wants to tear down, but some people want to preserve it. The mayor is holding a town hall meeting to discuss the issue on Friday.

Gina: That's a good issue to talk about in your class. Oh, look! There's a ⁹**review / headline** of the latest *Star Wars* movie. It opens this Friday. We should go!

Felix: Sure, we can go after the town hall meeting.

3 Answer the questions. Use your own information.

1. Where do you get the news?

   I get the news from the radio and online.
   _____

2. Where do your parents or grandparents get the news?

   _____

3. What kind of news articles do you like to read?

   _____

4. What kind of reviews interest you?

   _____

5. What is an interesting interview you have seen or heard?

   _____

GRAMMAR Past tense review: Simple past, past continuous, and present perfect

1 Complete the chart.

Simple past

What _did_ you _watch_?

I _____ (watch) a news report online.

I _____ (not watch) it on television.

What _____ the reporter _____ (say)?

He _____ (say) the storm caused the power to go out.

But he _____ (not say) how long it would be out.

Past continuous

What _____ you _____ (do) when the power went out?

I **was driving** my car. I _____ (not use) my cell phone. That's dangerous.

Present perfect

Who **has seen** that new reality series?

I _____ (not see) it yet. But Laura _____ (see) every episode. She loves it.

2 Write each sentence in the simple past and in the past continuous.

1. Juan works at the store on weekends.

   Juan worked at the store on weekends.

   Juan was working at the store on weekends.

2. Jenny rides a bike in the morning.

   Jenny _____.

   Jenny _____.

3. Tom and Gina study Chinese.

   _____

   _____

4. We don't play football in the park.

   _____

   _____

3 Look at Exercise 2. Complete the questions and answers with the present perfect forms of the verbs.

1. **A:** Who _has learned_ (learn) how to read Chinese?

   B: _Tom and Gina have learned how to read Chinese._

2. **A:** Who _____ (work) on weekends before?

   B: _____

3. **A:** Who _____ (ride) a bike in the morning?

   B: _____

4. **A:** Who _____ (not play) football in the park?

   B: _____

Past passive and present perfect passive

4 Complete the chart.

Past passive

The article _was posted_ (post) online.

The photographs _____ (post) last week. But they _____ (not post) by me.

Present perfect passive

The video _has been watched_ (watch) by over 3 million people!

It _____ (see) in over 30 countries. But it _____ (not see) in the artist's own country.

5 Rewrite the sentences. Use the forms in parentheses.

1. Someone used a fact-checking site to prove that the legend was false. (past passive)

   A fact-checking site was used to prove that the

   legend was false.

2. No one posted the game scores to the school website. (present perfect passive)

   _____

3. Over 60,000 people attended the summer music festival. (past passive)

   _____

4. A cell phone didn't record the event. (present perfect passive)

   _____

Unit 1 | 3

VOCABULARY Time expressions

1 Read the sentences. Then circle the action that started or happened first.

1. My dad was living in a small town **before** he met my mother.
   a. *My dad lived in a small town.* (circled)
   b. He met my mother.

2. **After** they got married, they moved to the city.
   a. They got married.
   b. They moved to the city.

3. My dad was working as a reporter **while** my mom was finishing college.
   a. He worked as a reporter.
   b. She finished college.

4. She got a job as a computer programmer **as soon as** she finished college.
   a. She got a job as a computer programmer.
   b. She finished college.

5. I was born **by the time** my mom was 30.
   a. I was born.
   b. My mom was 30.

6. She's been working part-time **since** I was born.
   a. She worked part-time.
   b. I was born.

7. **Whenever** I had a question about my computer homework, she helped me.
   a. I had a question about my computer homework.
   b. She helped me.

8. **Every time** there's been a new smartphone, she's been the first to try it.
   a. There's a new smartphone.
   b. She was the first to try it.

2 Complete the sentences with the correct words.

1. *As soon as* I wake up in the morning, I take a shower. (As soon as / By the time)

2. _____ he eats breakfast, my dad checks his email. (Until / While)

3. He rode his bike to school _____ he learned to drive. (every time / until)

4. She's been playing video games _____ she was six. (since / whenever)

5. _____ I go to school in the morning, I charge my phone battery. (Before / Since)

6. _____ I got the text, I had already left. (By the time / Every time)

7. _____ I use the school computer, I forget to sign out. (As / Every time)

8. Hannah texted me _____ the game had finished. (after / whenever)

9. _____ I was researching my paper online, I saw the headlines on a news website. (As / Until)

10. _____ my smartphone rings in class, my teacher gets angry. (Before / Whenever)

11. There was nobody in the library _____ I left last night. (when / as soon as)

3 Use the time expressions from Exercise 1 to combine sentences. More than one answer may be possible.

1. My laptop broke. I was watching my friend's video clips.
   My laptop broke while I was watching my friend's video clips.

2. The game had ended. I texted my dad.
   _____

3. I bought tickets for the concert. They went on sale at noon.
   _____

4. The band was playing their last song. I recorded it with my smartphone.
   _____

5. I studied for the test. I was taking the bus to school.
   _____

4 | Unit 1

GRAMMAR Review of *used to* + infinitive and *would*

1 Read the sentences and check (✓) the correct columns.

	Thing that happened repeatedly in the past but doesn't happen now	Situation that happened in the past
1. I used to live on a houseboat when I was a baby.		✓
2. My brother used to study German.		
3. Jack would always win when we played tennis.		
4. I would watch the news at night.		
5. My family didn't use to own a television.		
6. I didn't use to like to eat vegetables.		

2 Complete the conversation. Use *used to*, *would*, or the simple past. More than one answer may be possible.

Marissa: Hey, Gan. Where in Thailand ¹ *did you use to* live when you were young?

Gan: Well, when I was very young, I ² _____ in Bangkok. We lived on a *khlong*, or canal.

Marissa: Interesting. Did you ³ _____ swimming a lot?

Gan: No! We never ⁴ _____ go in the water.

Marissa: ⁵ _____ you go fishing?

Gan: No, we ⁶ _____. But my family ⁷ _____ go to the floating market.

Marissa: What ⁸ _____ you buy at the market?

Gan: We ⁹ _____ buy fruit and vegetables. And we ¹⁰ _____ eat dinner from kitchens on the boats and drink coconut drinks.

Marissa: How often ¹¹ _____ eat at the market?

Gan: We ¹² _____ eat there a couple times a week. It was fun.

3 Correct the sentences. Use *used to*, *would*, or the simple past. More than one answer may be possible.

    played

1. Kevin ~~would play~~ in the snow last vacation.
2. We would live in Hawaii when I was younger.
3. My grandparents didn't used to use their new computer until I showed them how.
4. I used to play my video game at 8:00 last night.
5. My family was buying vegetables at the store until we started our garden.

4 Answer the questions using *used to* or *would*. Use your own information.

1. Where did you live when you were young?

   _____
   _____

2. What music did you listen to when you were young?

   _____
   _____

3. What games did you play with your friends?

   _____
   _____

4. What movies or TV shows did you watch?

   _____
   _____

CONVERSATION Expressing interest and disinterest

1 Put the words in the correct order to make sentences.

1. right / really / the / I'm / playing / into / guitar / now / .

   I'm really into playing the guitar right now.

2. crazy / live / I'm / not / about / music / .
   _____

3. I'm / that / into / not / music videos / watching / .
   _____

4. all / bands / I'm / about / punk / .
   _____

5. stand / music / I / can't / pop / .
   _____

6. about / I'm / new / this / video / crazy / .
   _____

2 Complete the conversation with the correct phrases. More than one answer may be possible.

| ✓ all about | crazy about | not that into |
| can't stand | not crazy about | really into |

Paul: Have you watched my new music video yet?

Ellie: No, I haven't. Sorry. I'm ¹ *all about* this new John Mayer video right now.

Paul: Ugh! I ² _____ him!

Ellie: Really? But he plays guitar, like you.

Paul: Yeah, but we play different kinds of music. I like alternative and punk. I'm ³ _____ his singer-songwriter sound.

Ellie: Oh, well. How about Ellie Goulding? I'm ⁴ _____ her this year. She's amazing!

Paul: Her music and voice are OK, but I'm ⁵ _____ her like you are. She's still too pop for me.

Ellie: Oh, are you still ⁶ _____ Green Day?

Paul: Of course! They're my favorite!

READING TO WRITE

1 Number the parts of an informational blog post in order from 1–4.

_____ Give details about what you did or saw.

_____ Give information about the event in the future or similar events.

_____ Give general information about the event.

_____ Give your opinion about the event.

2 Use Exercise 1 to number the parts of this informational blog post in order from 1–4.

BATTLE OF THE BANDS | Lake High School

by Hailey Morgan

_____ Battle of the Bands takes place twice during the school year. The next one takes place in early January. Finalists go to the state finals in April.

_____ I went to Battle of the Bands at our high school last Saturday. It's an event for local high school bands to compete to win. The audience votes by cheering loudly for their favorite band. So it's up to the audience themselves to make some noise for the winner.

_____ I thought the band that won, The Closers, was really good. But I'm not that into rock and roll. I was crazy about the all-girl rap band, Tiger Lily. They were awesome. I myself would like to try rapping!

_____ Before the bands played, the school band played a song. Then the bands came out. Each band got to play three songs. After a band was done, the drama club performed a dance or comedy act while the next band set up. They really challenged themselves with some crazy dancing this year! The whole event took about three hours.

3 Find the examples of reflexive and emphatic pronouns in Hailey's blog. Underline the reflexive pronouns. Circle the emphatic ones.

4 Read the blog post in Exercise 2 again. Answer the questions.

1. What was the event?
   The event was Battle of the Bands.

2. When was it?
   _____

3. Where was it?
   _____

4. Who competes?
   _____

5. How do they win?
   _____

6. Who won the contest?
   _____

7. Which band did Hailey like?
   _____

Unit 1 | 7

2 Best Foot Forward

VOCABULARY Personal qualities

1 Find nine more words for personal qualities.

B	L	H	Q	S	T	R	I	C	T	T	J
I	E	A	S	Y	G	O	I	N	G	R	W
P	X	R	L	F	S	F	T	I	D	C	A
A	R	D	O	G	C	V	Z	S	E	Q	B
S	J	W	M	O	T	I	V	A	T	E	D
S	S	O	I	M	P	A	T	I	E	N	T
I	H	R	U	G	F	H	F	N	R	J	V
O	Y	K	O	O	Z	C	S	H	M	U	C
N	V	I	D	R	R	L	T	C	I	N	A
A	J	N	B	P	Z	A	G	S	N	G	R
T	S	G	T	A	L	E	N	T	E	D	B
E	S	O	C	I	A	B	L	E	D	I	D

2 Complete the conversation with the correct words from Activity 1. More than one answer may be possible.

Tim: I think Kyla can win the singing competition. She's very ¹ _passionate_ and you can hear it in her voice. And she's ² _____, too. It just seems easy for her to sing beautifully. She doesn't have to try as hard as everyone else.

Amy: Yes, but John has a chance to win the competition, too. It's not as easy for him, but he is very ³ _____ to improve. And he spends all of his time practicing the same song over and over. He is very ⁴ _____.

Tim: Yeah, well, John can't make any mistakes because his coach is so ⁵ _____. On top of that, the coach is ⁶ _____, so John has to learn quickly.

Amy: Well, you know who needs a tougher coach? Noah! He doesn't try hard enough. He is too ⁷ _____. It's lucky he's ⁸ _____ and chats with the judges. They like him for that.

Tim: What about Callie? She's the opposite of Noah. She's so ⁹ _____ that she never chats with the judges.

Amy: You're right. And she's so afraid of making mistakes, it seems like she almost doesn't care about winning. The judges don't like it when you don't show that you're ¹⁰ _____. I think she'll go home next.

3 Answer the questions with the words from Exercise 1 and your own information.

1. Describe someone you know who is easy-going.
   My friend Alicia is easy-going. She doesn't get upset about anything. She acts the same if she gets a good or bad grade on a test.

2. Do you know someone who is talented? What is he or she good at?
   _____
   _____

3. Do you know someone who is hard-working? What makes him or her hard-working?
   _____
   _____

4. Name two personal qualities that you have. Describe them.
   _____
   _____
   _____

5. Describe two personal qualities you wish you had. How would these qualities help you?
   _____
   _____
   _____

8 | Unit 2

GRAMMAR Present perfect with present perfect continuous

1 Put the words in the correct order to make sentences.

1. surfing / He / time / been / long / for / hasn't / a / .

    He hasn't been surfing for a long time.

2. hours / been / three / for / chatting / online / We've / !

    _____

3. been / since / Ella's / making / 2011 / films / .

    _____

4. watching / I / been / lately / haven't / movies / any / .

    _____

5. to / running, / but / I / now / love / stopped / I've / running / used / .

    _____

6. haven't / since / rock climbing / 2013 / They / been / .

    _____

2 Look at Helen's timeline. Complete the questions and answers using the present perfect or the present perfect continuous form of the verbs.

Timeline:
- live in England
- work as a journalist
- 2010 2011 2012 2013 2014 2015 NOW
- study Portuguese
- move to Brazil
- learn to sail

1. **Kay:** Helen, *have* you *been living* (live) in England?

    Helen: No, I _____. I _____ in Brazil.

2. **Kay:** _____ you _____ (sail) for a long time?

    Helen: No, I _____. I _____ since 2014.

3. **Kay:** _____ you _____ (work) as a journalist for a long time?

    Helen: Not really. I _____ as a journalist since 2013.

4. **Mike:** What _____ Helen _____ doing lately?

    Kay: She _____ (work) as a journalist.

5. **Mike:** _____ Helen _____ (study) Spanish?

    Kay: No, she _____. She _____ Portuguese.

3 Rewrite the sentences. Change the present perfect to the present continuous or the present continuous to the present perfect, when possible. Write X if the sentence can't be rewritten.

1. She has never ~~been seeing~~ a Broadway show.

    She has never seen a Broadway show.

2. I've played football for a long time.

    _____

3. Stacy has wanted to buy a car for a long time.

    _____

4. Gavin has been working at the law firm for 10 years.

    _____

5. Ellen has been in Paris since Tuesday.

    _____

4 Answer the questions. Use your own information.

1. Have you ever studied Russian?

    _____

2. Where have you been studying English?

    _____

3. What have you been doing lately?

    _____

4. What is something you've never done?

    _____

5. How long have you known your best friend?

    _____

VOCABULARY Phrasal verbs about making progress

1 Complete the sentences with a word from each box. Use the correct verb forms.

bring	pass	along	up
count	set	into	up
get	sign	on	up
~~give~~	turn	on	together
keep			~~up~~

1. Our team is losing, but they're determined. They won't _____give up_____.
2. The new website has _____ different music fans from all over the world.
3. Marla is so nice that she can _____ with anyone.
4. I helped my grandparents _____ their social networking page.
5. They find it difficult to _____ with all of the latest technology.
6. The organization started small, but it's _____ a global success.
7. Some people worry that they won't be able to _____ their traditions to their grandchildren.
8. Let's _____ to help at the beach clean up.
9. John is always there for you. You can _____ him to help you.

2 Correct the sentences if needed. Write ✓ if they are already correct.

1. It took 10 minutes to set her new smartphone up. ✓
2. Millie's so motivated! She's already signed for dance lessons up. _____
3. We've been trying to get with the other team along. _____
4. My dream is to be a writer, and I don't want to give it up. _____
5. That new app has brought some very different people together. _____
6. The organization has a great program to pass used clothing along to people who need it. _____
7. His hobby has turned his career into. _____
8. I don't have time to keep with my social networking up. _____
9. Who can you count for a ride tonight on? _____

3 Complete the conversation with some of the phrasal verbs from Exercise 1. Use the correct verb forms.

Andrea: Have you ¹_____ for the race yet?

Bill: No, I haven't. I know it's a great event that ²_____ a lot of people _____, but I don't think I can run that far. I'll ³_____ before I get to the end.

Andrea: Bill! Don't ⁴_____ this _____ a big drama! It's just a fun run. I don't run that fast, and I'm doing it. You can ⁵_____ with me, can't you?

Bill: I don't know . . .

Andrea: Look, you can run with our running group twice a week. We'll ⁶_____ a training program for you. And Ken is training with us, too, you know. I know you ⁷_____ well with him.

Bill: Ken's doing the run? Oh, OK. I'll do it.

Andrea: Thanks, Bill! I knew I could ⁸_____ you!

10 | Unit 2

GRAMMAR Past perfect and past perfect continuous

1 Read the sentences. Circle the answer that correctly explains each situation.

1. Tina and Mel had been in Africa when the program started.
   a. The program started during their time in Africa. *(circled)*
   b. The program started before they went to Africa.

2. They hadn't been checking their email as often during the program.
   a. They used to check their email regularly before the program.
   b. They didn't use to check their email regularly before the program.

3. The band had been touring since 2010.
   a. They probably toured for a few years and stopped.
   b. They toured and are probably still touring.

4. Sophia had been volunteering at the center for six months.
   a. Sophia is probably still volunteering at the center.
   b. Sophia is probably doing something else now.

5. People had been signing up for the service over the weekend.
   a. It is still the weekend now.
   b. It is some time after the weekend now.

2 Complete the sentences and questions with the words in parentheses. Use the past perfect continuous.

1. They _had been practicing_ (practice) their new song when the power went out.

2. Tara and Milo _____ (exchange) emails.

3. Their concerts _____ (sell out) quickly.

4. My sister _____ (not study) the piano.

5. We _____ (talk) for hours and hadn't realized the time.

3 Look at Mai's activities. Complete the sentences with the past perfect and past perfect continuous.

study dance in Chicago	six years
live in Los Angeles	2011–2013
compete in a television dance show	June 2012
sing and dance in a movie	Summer 2013
move to New York City	October 2013
record an album	2014

1. Mai _had studied_ dance in Chicago for six years.

2. Mai _____ in a dance show before she moved to New York City.

3. She _____ in Los Angeles when she went on TV.

4. Mai _____ in a movie before she moved to New York City.

5. Mai _____ an album in 2014.

4 Put the words in the correct order to make questions. Answer the questions.

1. in / Mai been / Chicago / studying / dance / Had / ?
   Had Mai been studying dance in Chicago?
   Yes, she had.

2. when / recording / Mai been / she / in / Had / Los Angeles / an album / lived / ?
   _____
   _____

3. to / had / she / moved / Mai been / What / doing / before / New York City / ?
   _____
   _____

4. living / been / Where / 2012 / Mai / in / had / ?
   _____
   _____

CONVERSATION — Showing concern

1 Match the phrases to make expressions to show concern.

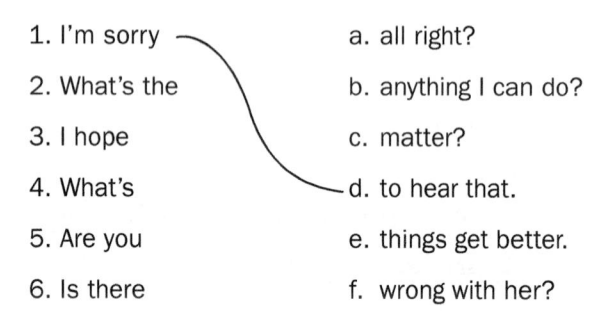

1. I'm sorry — d. to hear that.
2. What's the — c. matter?
3. I hope — e. things get better.
4. What's — f. wrong with her?
5. Are you — a. all right?
6. Is there — b. anything I can do?

2 Use the phrases from Exercise 1 to complete the conversation.

Ilona: Hey, Julio. ¹ _Are you all right?_

Julio: I'm OK, I guess.

Ilona: No, you're not. You look tired. ² _____

Julio: Well, I'm worried about my mother.

Ilona: ³ _____

Julio: Oh, nothing's wrong with her. In fact, just the opposite. Ever since we got a new puppy, she's been so energetic.

Ilona: Who's been energetic? Your mom or the puppy?

Julio: Actually, both of them! My mom gets up really early to take the puppy out in the morning. Then, after school, she takes it jogging. And she makes me come with her! That's why I look tired.

Ilona: Julio! That's not really a problem, is it?

Julio: No, but now she's talking about getting a second dog! I'm going to have to join the track team to keep up.

Ilona: That's funny. Well, at least your dog can run. My cat is really overweight. I'm worried about him.

Julio: ⁴ _____. ⁵ _____?

Ilona: Thanks, but no. We're already doing everything we can to help him eat less and exercise more.

Julio: Well, ⁶ _____. And if you ever want to come on a run with us, let me know!

Ilona: Thanks!

READING TO WRITE

1 Complete Jenny's thank-you email with the correct words.

Bye for now	I've attached
~~Hi,~~	Thanks
I'm writing to thank you for	Thank you for

To: MToth@cup.net
From: JennyPalooza@cup.net
Subject: Thank you!

1 _____Hi_____, Ms. Toth,

2 _____ being a great art teacher. Since graduating from high school, I've gone to college and I've been studying art. You really motivated me to work harder. Sometimes in class, I look at the other students' work and think they are more talented than me. But then I immediately remember you used to tell me to just be myself and do the work. Gradually, I've been feeling better about my work. 3 _____ that.

I also want to let you know that the oil paints you gave me as a gift have been wonderful! Since I got them, I've been painting much better. I like them more than the watercolors I'd been using.
4 _____ so much for them! 5 _____ a photo of my latest painting. I hope you like it!

6 _____, Jenny

2 Read the letter in Exercise 1 again. Write the phrases next to each section below.

A greeting: _____Hi, Ms. Toth_____

A reason for writing: _____

Details: _____
_____

A closing: _____

Sending a photo: _____

3 Read the letter in Exercise 1 again. Answer the questions.

1. What was Jenny doing before college?
   _____

2. What phrase in Jenny's email helped you to answer question 1?
   _____

3. How do Jenny's thoughts change during class?
   _____

4. What phrase helped you to answer question 3?
   _____

5. What change has happened for Jenny?
   _____

6. What word explains that this change has happened to Jenny slowly, over time?
   _____

7. Which word explains something that happened after Jenny was given a gift?
   _____

8. What has changed for Jenny since she received the gift?
   _____

Unit 2 | 13

REVIEW UNITS 1–2

1 Complete the chart.

~~article~~   interview   review
blogger   motivated   sociable
impatient   reporter

Media	People	Personal qualities
article		

2 Complete each sentence with a word from each box. Use the correct verb forms.

~~count~~   along
get   into
give   ~~on~~
keep   up
set   up
turn   up

1. I used to __count on__ Ella to help me with my homework.
2. I was having trouble _____ with my teammates during the race.
3. His experience writing blog posts _____ a job as a journalist.
4. They got a new laptop, and now they're _____ a new social networking page.
5. Last year, I _____ well with all my classmates.
6. I didn't have enough time to study until I _____ watching television.

3 Complete the sentences with *would* when possible. If not possible, use *used to*.

1. I __used to__ listen to hip hop, but now I listen to rock.
2. We _____ watch movies every night, but now we only watch them on weekends.
3. He was so shy, he _____ stay at home every night until he joined our club.
4. Jill _____ ride her bike to school, and now she rides it to work.
5. The organization _____ have a big party every year to thank the volunteers.
6. _____ you listen to the radio every night?

4 Circle the correct answers.

1. **Ben:** Who **did** / **was** you **interview** / **interviewed** for the school blog?
   Max: I **was interviewing** / **interviewed** Coldplay!
2. The album **was recording** / **was recorded** in the studio. It **wasn't recorded** / **wasn't recording** while the band was on tour.
3. **Mia:** Where **was** / **were** you **watched** / **watching** the news report?
   Sara: I **was watching** / **have watched** it online. I **wasn't watching** / **haven't watched** it on television.
4. **Jen:** Who **has been** / **was going** to Rome before?
   Chris: Danielle **has been** / **was going** to Rome. I think she **has been** / **went** last May.
5. The interview **was playing** / **has been played** on the radio twice today. But it **didn't post** / **hasn't been posted** on the web page yet.

5 Correct the sentences.

1. What have you been ~~do~~ *doing* at the volunteer center?
2. Mara been knowing Lauren since she was five.
3. I have spending three months in Chile this past year.
4. You haven't been post on your web page lately.
5. Elliot was working as a volunteer for two years, but he's running the organization now.
6. They're not having worked late for a long time.

6 Complete the blog post with the words in parentheses. Use the correct verb forms.

GETTING READY FOR MY TRIP!
by Emily

I'm really into Mongolian throat singing lately.
I ¹ _had been taking_ (take) singing lessons for about fives years before I learned about Mongolian throat singing.
I ² _____ (not hear) of that kind of singing before. It's an amazing sound because the singer sings two or more sounds at the same time.
Mongolian throat singing ³ _____ (be) around for a long time. Historically, men ⁴ _____ (be) the majority of throat singers, but more women ⁵ _____ (learn) to do it lately.
I ⁶ _____ (work) with a singing coach to practice Mongolian singing, when she told me about a singing camp in Mongolia.
I ⁷ _____ (sign up) right away. It's in Siberia, and most people speak Russian. So, after I ⁸ _____ (sign up) to go, I started taking Russian lessons, too.
I ⁹ _____ (use) my voice a lot lately! I'm so excited for my trip! I leave next month!

7 Complete the conversation. More than one answer may be possible.

can't stand	not crazy about
crazy about	not that into
Is there anything I can do?	~~What's the matter?~~

Lukas: Hey, Tatiana. You look upset.
¹ _What's the matter?_

Tatiana: Oh, it's nothing important. It's just that Tim got us tickets to go to a car race this weekend.

Lukas: Well, that sounds fun!

Tatiana: Not for me! I ² _____ car racing! It's so noisy! I told him I wanted to go to the beach.

Lukas: Really? I'm ³ _____ car racing!

Tatiana: Ugh. I'm ⁴ _____ it. And I'm ⁵ _____ spending my weekend at the race.

Lukas: ⁶ _____

Tatiana: Yeah, actually there is. Maybe you can go with him to the race instead!

8 Put the words in the correct order to make sentences. Then use the sentences to complete the conversation.

her / with / wrong / What's / ?
~~you / Raul / all / right, / Are / ?~~
I / hear / hope / from / you / Well, / her / .
into / really / organic farming / She's / .
sorry / hear / I'm / that / to / Oh, / .

Liana: ¹ _Are you all right, Raul?_

Raul: Not really. I'm worried about my sister.

Liana: ² _____

Raul: She's in Peru. I haven't heard from her in a while.

Liana: What's she been doing there?

Raul: ³ _____ So she's been volunteering at a farm in the Amazon jungle. But the last I heard from her, she wasn't feeling well.

Liana: ⁴ _____ Well, maybe their power is out or something.

Raul: Yeah, maybe.

Liana: ⁵ _____

Raul: Thanks.

3 Planning for the Future

VOCABULARY Verbs of the future

1 Unscramble the verbs used to talk about the future.

1. e o m v ___move___
2. n a p l _____
3. w r g o p u _____
4. e p k e n o _____
5. d e g a t r u a _____
6. e c m b e o _____
7. d e n p u _____
8. t r i p e c d _____

2 Complete the sentences with the phrases from Exercise 1. Use the correct verb forms.

1. Jason is good at art. I ___predict___ he'll study painting in college.
2. I really enjoy playing the guitar. I have to _____ practicing so I can play in a band.
3. After I _____ to London, I hope to get a job at a start-up company.
4. Ellen wants to take a year off and travel after she _____ from high school.
5. He's not _____ to work for a company after college. He wants to start his own business!
6. My nine-year-old sister loves animals. She can't wait to _____ and become a veterinarian.
7. If you don't work toward your goals, you'll _____ doing nothing.
8. He studied music for many years before he _____ a professional musician.

3 Complete Julian's email with some of the expressions from Exercise 1. Use the correct verb forms.

To: Mariano_M@cambridge.edu
From: JulianCompU@cambridge.edu
Subject: Hello!

Dear Mr. Mariano,

How are you? I haven't talked to you since I ¹___graduated___ from high school! I wanted to update you on what I've been doing and what I'm ²_____ for the future.

As you know, I'm in college and I've been studying computers. It's difficult, but I will ³_____ studying until computer science ⁴_____ easier for me!

I ⁵_____ that I will graduate in four more years. After that, I think I will ⁶_____ to San Francisco and will probably ⁷_____ working for a computer game company.

You know, computer games have been a big part of my life. When I was little, I told myself, "When I ⁸_____, I will make games that kids love to play." And now, I'm working on that goal! Anyway, I wanted you to know that I really appreciated your computer class in high school!

Sincerely,
Julian

4 Write statements about your future. Use the words in parentheses and your own information.

1. (plan)
   I plan on visiting a new country every year.
   _____

2. (become)
   _____

3. (keep on)
   _____

4. (end up)
   _____

GRAMMAR Future review

1 Complete the chart.

will for predictions	be going to for planned actions and events
1. What flight _____ Charlotte take? She'**ll** take the flight from London. She ___*won't*___ take the one from Glasgow.	2. Who _____ she _____ visit? She _____ visit her cousins. She **isn't going to** visit her college friends.
Present continuous for planned actions and events	**Simple present for scheduled future events**
3. Which suitcase _____ she **taking** with her? She _____ the green suitcase. She **isn't taking** the brown one.	4. What **does** she ___*plan*___ to see? She _____ to see the Met and a show on Broadway. She **doesn't** _____ to see Ellis Island.

2 Complete the sentences about Jorge's future plans. Circle the correct forms of the verbs.

1. Next weekend, Jorge **(is going to)** / **going** graduate from college. He **isn't going to** / **isn't going** keep on taking classes.
2. After graduating, Jorge **is going to plan** / **plans** to have a party at his house.
3. Jorge **will have** / **is having** a fun graduation party next weekend.
4. Next month, Jorge **will go** / **is going** to Peru.
5. Jorge **will** / **plans** to work at a non-profit organization in Peru.
6. He thinks he **will go** / **is going** to law school when he returns from Peru.

3 Use the chart to complete the questions and answers with future tenses. More than one answer may be possible.

	Planned actions	Planned events	Predictions
James	spend a month (August) in Paris	study at a French language school	travel in Europe in the fall
Rita	live in New York July – August	intern at a magazine	get hired by magazine in September

1. **Q:** Where ___*is*___ James ___*planning*___ to go in August?
   A: He'___*s planning*___ to go to Paris.
2. **Q:** What _____ James _____ in Paris?
   A: He's _____ French at a language school.
3. **Q:** What _____ James _____ in the fall?
   A: He _____ in Europe.
4. **Q:** When _____ Rita _____ in New York?
   A: She _____ there from July to August.
5. **Q:** What _____ she _____ to do there?
   A: She _____ to intern at a magazine.
6. **Q:** What _____ she _____ after that?
   A: She _____ by the magazine.

4 Answer the questions about a friend.

1. **Q:** What is your friend planning to do tomorrow?
   A: _____
   _____
2. **Q:** What will your friend do next weekend?
   A: _____
   _____
3. **Q:** What will your friend do next year?
   A: _____
   _____

VOCABULARY Achievements

1 Complete the phrases. Then match the pictures with the phrases.

1.	win	*an award*	c
2.		a business	
3.	do		
4.		a record	
5.	support		
6.		a million dollars	
7.		a project	
8.		famous	

a.   b.   c.   d.   e.   f.   g.   h.

2 Answer the questions with the phrases from Exercise 1.

1. Which three achievements can relate to sports?

   _____, _____,
   and _____

2. Which three achievements most likely relate to a business?

   _____, _____,
   and _____

3. Which two achievements most likely help people?
   _____ and _____

3 Complete the sentences with the correct form of phrases from Exercise 1. Then check (✓) if the sentences are true for you.

		True
1.	I think ___*winning an award*___ for something you've done well is the best feeling.	
2.	I want to _____ so I can support my family. It would be nice not to worry about money.	
3.	I think that when people _____, they don't have any privacy. But it is still great because everyone knows who you are!	
4.	If I _____, I can make the company's rules.	
5.	I think people should _____ more often. There are always places to clean up or community projects that need help.	
6.	I think anyone can _____. These days, you can raise money online to fund anything, even a movie you'd like to make!	
7.	I want to work for an organization that _____. I think it's important to work locally to improve things.	
8.	I think that if you practice and work hard, it's possible to _____ in any sport. But you have to really want to do it.	

4 Complete the questions with some of the phrases from Exercise 1. Then write answers that are true for you.

1. **Q:** Who do you think deserves to win ___*an award*___?
   A: *I think Leonardo DiCaprio deserves to win an award for donating money to save the oceans.*
   _____
   _____

2. **Q:** Which of your friends do you think will become _____? Why?
   A: _____

3. **Q:** What kind of business would you like to _____?
   A: _____

4. **Q:** What kind of _____ work would you like to do?
   A: _____

5. **Q:** What record would you like to _____?
   A: _____

6. **Q:** If you _____ a million dollars, how will you spend it?
   A: _____

GRAMMAR Future continuous and future perfect

1 Complete the chart.

Use future continuous to describe something in progress in the future.	
1. Who *will* be *supporting* the race on Saturday? Our club _____ _____ the race on Saturday.	2. _____ Donny _____ volunteering at the beach clean up? No, he _____. But I will.

Use future perfect to describe something that is going to be finished at a certain time in the future.	
3. What *will* your team *have* developed by next year? We _____ _____ a community garden.	4. _____ Everett _____ a business by next year? Yes, he _____.

2 Change the sentences. Change the present continuous to the future continuous or future perfect.

1. Alex is volunteering with Kim next week.
   Alex will be volunteering with Kim next week.

2. They're collecting a million dollars by this time next month.
   _____
   _____

3. They're using the money they collect to do a community project.
   _____
   _____

4. By 2020, the project is helping over 1,000 children.
   _____
   _____

5. Rachel thinks the organization is winning an award for community service by 2017.
   _____
   _____

6. They're supporting community projects in Haiti.
   _____
   _____

3 Answer the questions with your own ideas. Use the future continuous or future perfect.

1. Which of your friends will have made a million dollars in the next 10 years?
   I think my friend Zack will have made a
   million dollars in the next 10 years. He's very
   hard-working.
   _____

2. Which of your friends do you think will be helping his/her community in the next two years?
   _____
   _____

3. Which of your friends will have traveled the most by 2025?
   _____
   _____

4. Which of your friends do you think will have started a business?
   _____
   _____

5. What will you be doing in 10 years?
   _____
   _____

CONVERSATION — Expressing cause and effect

1. Circle the correct answers.

1. The neighborhood created the community garden **as a result / (so that)** people would have access to fresh fruit and vegetables.
2. The shoe company has been donating 10 percent of its profits to charity, and **because of / consequently** their sales have gone up.
3. Pollution from plastic bags in the ocean has decreased **so that / thanks to** the new law that bans them.
4. Terry was able to save money for a new guitar **because of / since** his part-time job.
5. **Since / Consequently**, the number of people donating to the charity has increased, more projects are getting funded.
6. The benefit concert was a huge success, and **so that / as a result**, the class has earned enough money for a graduation party.

2 Complete the conversation with the phrases from Exercise 1. More than one answer may be possible.

Luis: Hi, Kathryn. ¹ _Thanks to_ you, our after-school club will be getting two new laptops!

Kathryn: Really? What did I do?

Luis: ² _____ your article in the paper, some local businesses started a donation program. ³ _____, they donated enough money for us to buy two new computers. Even the Senior Center donated!

Kathryn: Wow! You know, ⁴ _____ they donated to us, maybe we should help them. We could take the laptops to the Senior Center and help the seniors to send emails and talk to their families. You know, do something nice for them ⁵ _____ they know we appreciate what they did for us.

Luis: That's a fantastic idea!

20 | Unit 3

READING TO WRITE

1 Complete Michelle's opinion essay with the correct words.

For paragraph B:

| consequently | ~~For one thing~~ |
| inevitably | what's more |

For paragraph C:

| in addition | obviously |
| surely | therefore |

Should soft drinks be sold at School?

by Michelle Leto

A What do you drink at lunch? Many schools in the United States have food and drinks for sale at lunchtime. Many schools have vending machines that sell soda. Personally, I don't think sodas or soft drinks with sugar in them should be sold at schools. Everyone knows by now that too much sugar isn't healthy.

B Why is sugar bad? [1] _For one thing_, sugar has a lot of calories, but it does not provide any nutrients — the good things the body needs to stay healthy. [2] _____, the empty calories in sugar make people gain weight. [3] _____, eating sugar gives people a burst of energy at first, but then it makes them feel tired. Almost [4] _____, people then want to eat even more sugar.

C Research shows that people weigh more today than they did 50 years ago. [5] _____ to eating too much sugar, this is because people are not exercising enough. This is [6] _____ not healthy. Everyone can see that! [7] _____ something could be done to help get people interested in exercising. [8] _____, I think schools should require an hour of exercise every morning to music that students get to choose.

D Some people think that students should be able to make their own choices. I agree with that for some things. For example, I think it's important for students to be able to choose classes that prepare them for their chosen careers.

E But schools are meant to educate. So I think it's important to teach students to make better choices about their health.

2 Read the article in Exercise 1 again. Write the paragraph letters next to each section below.

___ A paragraph with arguments in favor

___ A conclusion

___ An introduction

___ , ___ Paragraphs with arguments against

3 Read the article in Exercise 1 again. Answer the questions.

1. What does Michelle use to get the reader's attention?
   _____
   _____

2. What reasons does Michelle give against sugar?
   _____
   _____

3. What does Michelle say that schools should do to help students get more exercise?
   _____
   _____

4. What does Michelle think students should be allowed to choose?
   _____
   _____

4 What's Cooking?

VOCABULARY Cooking verbs

1 Find eight more cooking verbs. Then label the pictures.

I	L	E	J	L	P	Z	K	W	S
B	F	W	S	R	O	A	S	T	P
E	R	D	G	R	I	L	L	R	L
S	Y	B	O	I	L	Z	W	N	J
L	B	P	C	H	I	V	Z	N	M
I	A	F	H	I	O	X	G	M	I
C	K	U	O	V	K	X	R	Y	X
E	E	W	P	S	J	N	A	C	U
M	I	U	J	I	T	Z	T	B	I
V	Q	T	H	H	K	T	E	M	T

1. _roast_    2. _____
3. 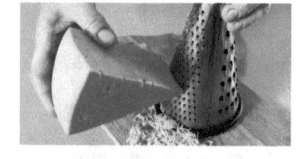 _____   4. _____ 
5.  _____   6. _____ 
7.  _____   8. _____ 
9. _____ 

2 Complete Justin's email with some of the words from Exercise 1. Use the simple past.

Hi Wanda,

I am having a great time at chef school! It's more difficult than I expected, but I'm learning a lot. Did you know that we had a whole lesson just learning how to ¹ _boil_ water? And then we spent an entire week just learning knife skills, such as how to ² _____ meat and how to ³ _____ onions into little pieces. That lesson made me cry! Ha ha!

It's funny. I thought I knew the basics of how to cook, but since coming here, I've already learned so much! For instance, I now know why the skin turns brown on top when you ⁴ _____ a chicken, and why the dough rises when you ⁵ _____ bread. Yesterday, we learned how to ⁶ _____ potatoes. I mean, make French fries! That was so much harder than you'd think. But I still like to ⁷ _____ best. Cooking burgers outdoors is my idea of fun. Hey, maybe when I come home I can cook for you and your friends. That would be fun!

Write back soon,

Justin

3 Answer the questions with your own information.

1. Which cooking activities from Exercise 1 are your favorites?
   I like baking cookies and cakes.
   _____

2. What is your favorite way to prepare chicken?
   _____

3. What is the easiest way to cook something?
   _____

4. What is the most difficult way to cook something?
   _____

22 | Unit 4

GRAMMAR First conditional review; zero conditional

1 Check (✓) if the sentence uses first conditional or zero conditional.

	First conditional (possible results)	Zero conditional (always true)
1. When you bake a cake, you need to measure the ingredients carefully.		✓
2. If we don't clean up after the picnic, mice will come.		
3. You don't have to add salt, unless you like really salty food.		
4. If Tom eats shrimp, he gets a rash.		
5. I don't want a slice of cake, unless you want to share one.		
6. When it's been a cold winter, the price of oranges goes up.		

2 Correct the first conditional sentences.

1. If I ~~will~~ eat a hamburger for dinner, I won't eat dessert afterward.
2. If we eat Chinese food tonight, we use chopsticks.
3. I not eat dessert at the restaurant, unless they have chocolate cake.
4. If she eats too many cookies this afternoon, her stomach hurt.
5. You want to have some of this delicious pizza, unless you don't like tomatoes.

3 Correct the zero conditional sentences.

1. When you boil an egg too fast, it ^turn grey inside. *(will)*
2. If you won't use enough water to boil rice, it becomes too sticky.
3. Meat won't cook through evenly when you will put it on the grill cold from the refrigerator.
4. When your stomach will hurt, you can drink some mint tea.
5. You can take away some of the bad smell if you will rinse fresh garlic under water before using it.

4 Complete the conversation. When possible, use the first conditional. If the zero conditional is needed, write X.

Ellen: Hi, Rafe. What are you cooking?

Rafe: I'm going to cook this fish. I can't decide if I want to fry it or grill it, though.

Ellen: Well, when you fry fish, the whole house ¹ _X_ smells.

Rafe: That's true. But if I open the window, it ² _____ smell.

Ellen: Well, not as much.

Rafe: If I grill the fish outside, the house ³ _____ smell.

Ellen: Yes, but the grill takes a long time to heat up. You ⁴ _____ need to heat it up now if you want to eat dinner by seven.

Rafe: Oh, I forgot about that. Do you think there's enough time?

Ellen: I'm not sure. Maybe we should just go out to dinner at the Seaside Café.

Rafe: That fancy new place?! If you want to eat at the Seaside Café, you ⁵ _____ need to make a reservation two weeks ahead of time! Besides, I can't go unless you pay. I spent all my money on the fish!

Ellen: You know, if we bake the fish in the oven, it ⁶ _____ take very long.

Unit 4 | 23

VOCABULARY Adjectives describing food

1 Find nine more adjectives that describe food.

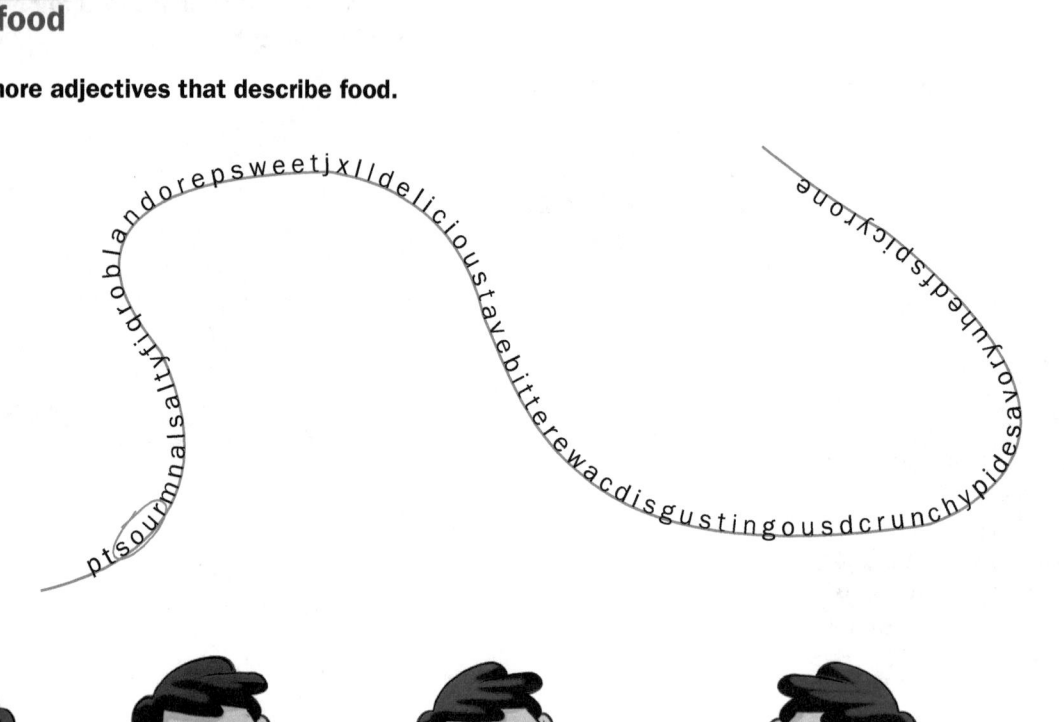

(word snake containing: sour, salty, bland, sweet, delicious, bitter, disgusting, crunchy, spicy, savory)

2 Circle the food or drink the first word best describes.

1. sour	a. banana	b. lemon
2. sweet	a. candy	b. French fries
3. bitter	a. milk	b. coffee
4. crunchy	a. steak	b. tortilla chips
5. salty	a. cake	b. potato chips
6. spicy	a. chili peppers	b. grapes
7. delicious	a. celery	b. pizza
8. disgusting	a. fried spiders	b. bread
9. savory	a. burgers	b. strawberries
10. bland	a. crackers	b. nachos

3 Complete the sentences. Use some of the words from Exercise 2. More than one answer may be possible.

1. John broke a tooth when he was eating _____crunchy_____ peanuts.

2. Helen's stomach hurts. She should eat some _____ food, like rice or toast.

3. I like to eat curry if it's not too _____. But sometimes the flavor is just too hot!

4. My sister can't cook. One time, she made chicken noodle soup and added chocolate to it. It was _____! No one could eat it.

5. My mother only drinks coffee with milk and sugar. She says it's too _____ otherwise.

6. In Japan, a lot of people say sushi is the most _____ food. That's why they serve it on special occasions.

7. I'm always thirsty after I eat in a restaurant. Restaurant food is so _____.

8. I usually eat something _____ like ham and eggs for breakfast instead of something _____ like pancakes.

9. Mom forgot to add sugar to the lemonade, and it was so _____!

4 Answer the questions. Use your own ideas.

1. What is your favorite salty food? _____
2. What is your favorite sweet food? _____
3. What two flavors do you like to combine? _____
4. What food do you think is disgusting? _____

24 | Unit 4

GRAMMAR Second conditional review

1 Complete the chart with the second conditional to describe imaginary situations and possible consequences.

Yes/No questions
1. _Would_ you order fried *chapulines* _if_ they _were_ on the menu?
No, I _wouldn't_.
I _wouldn't_ eat them _if_ you paid me.
2. _____ someone offered them to you, _____ you eat insects?
Yes, I _____.
No, _____ someone offered them to me, I _____ eat them.

Wh- questions
3. _____ you had to give up a favorite food, which one _____ you give up?
I _____ probably give up hamburgers.
4. What food _____ you try _____ you were in Australia?
I _____ probably try fried alligator.

2 Circle the correct answers.

Elena: Hey, Chris. ¹**If** / **Would** somebody offered you fried alligator tail, **were** / **would** you eat it?

Chris: I probably ²**was** / **would**.

Elena: Ew! Really?

Chris: Yeah. I ³**were** / **would** try anything once.

Elena: OK. ⁴**If** / **Would** you **was** / **were** really hungry, **if** / **would** you eat horse meat?

Chris: Hmm. I don't know. Oh, I probably ⁵**did** / **would**.

Elena: OK. ⁶**Did** / **Would** you still eat horse meat **if** / **were** you met the horse first?

Chris: You got me. No, ⁷**if** / **would** I met the horse first, then I probably **weren't** / **wouldn't**.

3 Write second conditional questions with the information in the chart.

	Imaginary situation	Possible consequence
1.	we / be / Japan	what / we / eat
2.	you / can learn to cook / anything	what / it / be
3.	Tina / have to give up / bread or rice	which / she / give up
	Possible consequence	**Imaginary situation**
4.	Aldo / eat jellyfish	he / be alone on an island
5.	they / eat raw meat	they / have no other choice

1. _If we were in Japan, what would we eat?_
2. _____
3. _____
4. _____
5. _____

4 Write the questions another way. Then answer the questions with your own information.

1. Would you eat *fugu* if it were offered to you?

Q: _If it were offered to you, would you eat fugu?_
A: _No, I wouldn't._

2. If you were to cook a meal to impress someone, what would you cook?

Q: _____
A: _____

3. If you could try any new food, what would you try?

Q: _____
A: _____

4. If you could eat as much of a food as you'd like, what would you eat?

Q: _____
A: _____

Unit 4 | 25

CONVERSATION — Cooking instructions

1. Circle the correct answers.

1. When you use just a little bit of something, it's called **(a pinch)** / **a simmer**.
2. You can use a spoon to **simmer** / **stir** something.
3. You can **pinch** / **pour** something liquid, such as milk or oil.
4. When you **pour** / **simmer** sauce, it is not as hot as when you boil it.
5. **"First of all"** / **"Then add"** is the phrase that comes before the step you do at the beginning.
6. If you pour some milk onto cereal, you are **adding** / **simmering** it to the cereal.

2 Complete the conversation with the expressions from Exercise 1.

Ernie: Hey, Jack. Would you like some breakfast? I'm going to cook some eggs.

Jack: Why don't you make an omelet?

Ernie: I've never cooked an omelet before, but I can try.

Jack: It's easy. I'll tell you how to do it. ¹ _First of all_, you need to take the skin off the tomato. ² _____ it in hot water for a few minutes. Then the skin comes off easily. Then you can chop it.

Ernie: OK. Now what?

Jack: Next, you need to beat about four eggs. ³ _____ the tomatoes to the eggs. I like to add some herbs and a ⁴ _____ of salt and pepper. Gently ⁵ _____ it with a wide spoon.

Ernie: We have parsley and chives, so I'll add those herbs.

Jack: Great. Put some oil into a pan and heat it up. When the pan is hot, ⁶ _____ the egg mixture into it.

Ernie: Got it. How does this look?

Jack: Use a fork to lift the cooked edges up and let the egg liquid run underneath. That's right. And we're done!

READING TO WRITE

1 Complete the sentences with the correct words.

a great deal of	a lot of	not enough
not much	so	such
too much		

1. If you put ___too much___ water in the pot, it will spill over when it boils.

2. What did you put in this stew? It is _____ delicious!

3. This tastes bland! There are _____ herbs in it.

4. I don't think we need any more pepper in the soup. There's _____ it in the soup already.

5. Can you pass the salt, please? I like _____ salt on my French fries.

6. This is _____ good bread! You are really good at baking.

7. This is a healthy cookie recipe. There's _____ sugar in it.

2 Complete the text with some of the phrases from Exercise 1.

My Grandmother's Signature Dish

by Iris

My grandmother is from Portugal, near Spain. Every year around the holidays, she makes our family's signature dish: *Bacalhau*. It is a salted, dried cod fish that is served in many different ways, often with potatoes. People say there are 365 different ways to prepare *bacalhau* – one for each day of the year. It is ¹ ___such___ a common dish in Europe and places like the Dominican Republic and Puerto Rico. The dish originated in Norway, where the cod fish is found.

To make the dish, you fry the fish in a pan with some onions and garlic. You add a pinch of salt and pepper, but not ² _____ salt! There is ³ _____ salt in the fish already.

Then you spread some oil in a pan. You put chopped potatoes, carrots, and cabbage in the bottom of the pan. Then you put the cod fish and onions and garlic on top of it. You bake it in the oven for about 30 minutes. To serve it, you put sliced boiled eggs and olives on top. It is ⁴ _____ delicious!

There are ⁵ _____ variations; some people add chickpeas (garbanzos) or cream. You should try them all!

3 Read the text again. Answer the questions.

1. What is Iris's grandmother's signature dish?

2. What are the main ingredients?

3. How is it made?

4. What are some variations?

5. Where else is the dish eaten?

REVIEW UNITS 3–4

1 Write the words next to the definitions.

bake	~~end up~~	predict
bland	fry	spicy
chop	keep on	
delicious	mix	

1. To arrive somewhere without a plan. _end up_
2. To say what will happen in the future. _____
3. To cut into small pieces or cubes. _____
4. _____ food with little flavor is the opposite of _____ food.
5. To cook something using hot oil in a pan on a stovetop. _____
6. To cook something, such as a cake or cookies, using dry heat in the oven. _____
7. To continue and not stop or give up. _____
8. To combine different things together. _____
9. A lively flavor that is often called "hot." _____

2 Complete the sentences with a word from each box.

break		an award
develop		a business
do		~~the community~~
start		a project
~~support~~		a record
win		volunteer work

1. Sue has donated money to fund the new playground. She wants to _support the community_.
2. Ralph has been running a lot, and his time is faster than everyone's. He's probably going to _____ in the next race.
3. They plan to _____ that will bring fresh water to the area.
4. I just think that everyone should _____ _____ at some point in their life. It feels good to help people.
5. Elon says he will _____ when he graduates from school. He wants to make a lot of money.
6. Carol sold the most houses this year, so she is going to _____.

3 Look at the pictures and complete the puzzle. Then complete the sentences about Mia by unscrambling the letters in the grey boxes.

Mia will probably _____ being a chef.

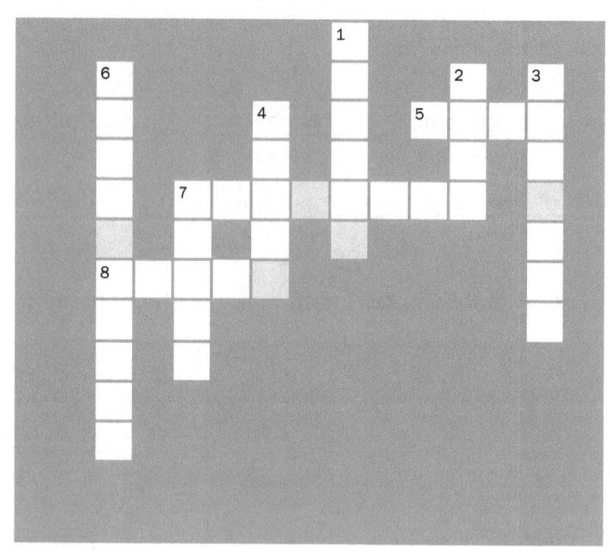

across
5.    7.    8.

down
1.    2.    3. 
4.    6.    7.

4 Put the words in the correct order to make sentences. Write each sentence two ways.

1. you / eat fugu / should / to take / if / you / like / risks / .

   If you like to take risks, you should eat fugu.

   You should eat fugu, _____

2. you / like / the jellyfish / don't / unless / order / unusual tastes / .

   _____

   _____

28 | Review 2

3. eat / when / your breath / you / garlic / smells / .
   _____
   _____

4. will be / you add / unless / a lot of / spices / this chili / bland / .
   _____
   _____

5. be bitter / add / if / will / you / sugar / don't / the coffee / .
   _____
   _____

6. a Japanese restaurant / we go / when / eat / won't / Steve / sushi / to / .
   _____
   _____

5 Look at Anya's Life Plan list. Then complete the questions and answers about her plans. Use *will, going to*, the future continuous, and future perfect.

My Life Plan, April 2016:

June 2016 — Graduate from college
July 2016 — Start a website
July to August 2016 — Save money from summer job
September 2016 — Move to Austin, get job
September 2016 — Volunteer at animal shelter
January 2017 — Develop a project to help dogs

1. Where _is_ Anya _going to move_ ?
   She _is going to move to_ Austin.
2. Where _____ she _____ in September?
   She's _____ at an animal shelter.
3. _____ she _____ from her summer job by September?
   Yes, _____ .
4. What _____ she _____ by July 2016?
   She _____ a website.
5. What _____ she _____ in January of 2017?
   She _____ a project to help dogs.

6 Complete the conversations with the correct phrases.

add	because of	since
a pinch of	~~first of all~~	so that
as a result	let it simmer	

1. **A:** How do I sign up for this volunteer program?
   B: _First of all_ , you need to fill out this application online.
2. **A:** How much sugar should I add to your coffee?
   B: Just _____ sugar, please.
3. **A:** What do I do after I've added the chicken to the soup?
   B: Turn down the heat and then _____ for at least half an hour.
4. **A:** Why isn't Mitchell making limeade for the picnic?
   B: He said limes cost too much this year _____ of the bad weather!
5. **A:** Why isn't Jeanne coming to the party this weekend?
   B: She isn't coming _____ her new job. She has to work on weekends now.
6. **A:** I'm making hot chocolate. It's almost done.
   B: _____ just a drop of vanilla at the end. It really improves the flavor.
7. **A:** Why isn't Helen eating meat?
   B: She's stopped eating it _____ she watched that documentary about farms.
8. **A:** Are you taking classes next fall?
   B: Yes, I am. I changed my schedule at work _____ I can take two classes.

5 Fame and Fortune

VOCABULARY Verbs expressing opinion

1 Unscramble the words to make verbs to express opinions.

1. E T H A   _hate_
2. R E D A I M   _____
3. L E F E   _____
4. N O M R E M D C E   _____
5. P E F E R R   _____
6. P E T E R C S   _____
7. P E T E R C A P A I   _____
8. K H I N T   _____
9. K E D S I I L   _____

2 Circle the correct answers.

1. Jack never watches horror movies. He _____ documentaries.
   a. thinks   b. (prefers)   c. hates

2. Eliza _____ action movies. She thinks most of them are about special effects and not an actual story.
   a. hates   b. recommends   c. feels

3. Although Ben dislikes singing in musicals, he _____ the talented actors who perform in them.
   a. dislikes   b. prefers   c. appreciates

4. I _____ that it is more difficult to do comedy than dramatic acting.
   a. admire   b. hate   c. think

5. I _____ watching movies before I've read the movie reviews. I like to form my own opinions.
   a. prefer   b. admire   c. respect

6. I _____ actors who do their own stunts. It's exciting to watch an actor who has learned to ride a motorcycle or jump from a building.
   a. dislike   b. feel   c. respect

7. Mary _____ famous actors, but she wouldn't want to be one.
   a. admires   b. thinks   c. prefers

8. Jim _____ people who star in reality shows only want fame.
   a. prefers   b. thinks   c. hates

3 Unscramble the questions. Then answer the questions using the words from Exercise 1 and your own information.

1. about / you / How / usually / documentaries / feel / do / ?
   How do you usually feel about documentaries?
   I appreciate the people who make documentaries.
   They call attention to important issues.

2. kind / prefer / do / of / movies / What / you / ?
   _____
   _____

3. celebrity / admire / the most / do / Which / you / ?
   _____
   _____

4. friends / would / to / What / recommend / movie / you / your / ?
   _____
   _____

5. dislike / do / reality TV shows / What / you / about / ?
   _____
   _____

30 | Unit 5

GRAMMAR Defining and non-defining relative clauses

1 Match the defining relative clauses with their nouns. Write *who, which, that, where,* or *whose.*

Noun	Defining relative clause
1. Movies __c__	a. _____ phones were hacked were angry.
2. The contestants ____	b. _____ I read last week was also a movie.
3. The house ____	c. __that__ don't use professional actors are interesting.
4. The celebrities ____	d. _____ are on game shows must be nervous.
5. The book ____	e. _____ the movie was filmed is now a museum.

2 Rewrite the sentences. Add the non-defining relative clause in parentheses. Use *who, which, where,* or *whose,* and commas.

1. Leonardo DiCaprio donated $2 million to the marine conservation group Oceans 5. (starred in *Titanic*)

   Leonardo DiCaprio, who starred in Titanic, donated $2 million to the marine conservation group Oceans 5.

2. Mark Zuckerberg donated millions to the Newark, New Jersey, school system. (his personal wealth is over $30 billion)

   _____

3. Potcake Place is a charity in the Turks and Caicos Islands. (its goal is to rescue a breed of dog called the "potcake")

   _____

4. Brad Pitt's charity, the Make It Right Foundation, is based in New Orleans, Louisiana. (he owns a house there)

   _____

5. Malala Yousafzai donated $50,000 to schools in Gaza. (won the Nobel Peace Prize)

   _____

6. Doctors Without Borders is helping to care for sick people in Western Africa. (operates in over 70 countries)

   _____

7. Fashion blogger Tavi Gevinson starred in a Broadway play. (her online magazine for teen girls gets 3.5 million hits per month)

   _____

8. The African Library Project works to develop libraries in English-speaking countries such as Sierra Leone. (less than 25 percent of adult women are able to read there)

   _____

3 Correct the sentences. Correct punctuation, if needed.

1. My friend Elizabeth, ~~which~~ *who* volunteers at the hospital, wants to be a doctor.

2. A "philanthropist" is someone whose donates money to charities and organizations to help others.

3. My cousin's band where plays really cool music got to open for Arcade Fire in 2015.

4. It seems like the companies, who have a social mission, are more successful than those who just want to make a lot of money.

5. Captain Paul Watson whose once belonged to Greenpeace founded the Sea Shepherd Conservation Society to protect marine life.

6. We went to Mavericks Beach, that the annual big wave surfing contest takes place.

Unit 5 | 31

VOCABULARY Adverbs of degree

1 Circle seven more adverbs of degree. Write them in order on the chart.

fa **hardly** renylyslightlyextremelyepsnearlyalgpuprettynvytyfairlyhijklyperfectlylyusojmabsolutelyzvps

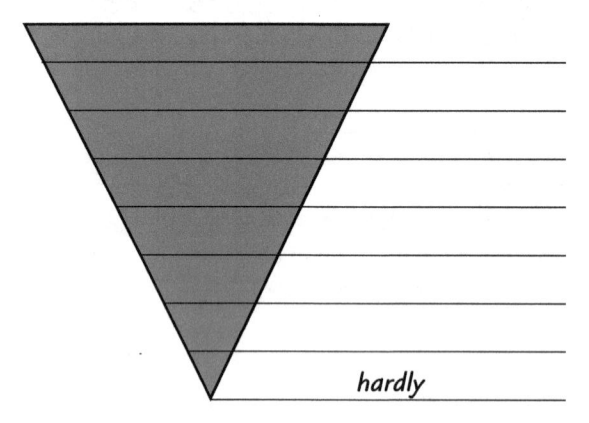

2 Write the words from Exercise 1 that have the same meaning.

1. very well, completely _____

2. very much, really _____

3. somewhat, kind of _____, _____

4. almost _____

5. just a little _____

6. barely at all _____

(chart bottom: hardly)

3 Put the words in the correct order to make sentences that use adverbs of degree.

1. sure / sold out / the / yet / pretty / concert / I'm / hasn't / .

   I'm pretty sure the concert hasn't sold out yet.

2. about / I'm / new/ crazy / Lorde's / absolutely / album / .

   _____

3. hardly / speaks / I / him / can / softly, / so / hear / Carl / .

   _____

4. have / I / fairly / open / who / door / good idea / a / left / the / .

   _____

5. my old one / fine / smartphone / I / don't / when / perfectly / need / works / a / new / .

   _____

6. too / much / felt / eating / dinner / ill / after / slightly / for / We / .

   _____

7. to / practice / become / successful / hard / extremely / Musicians / .

   _____

8. nearly / Jen / was / she / fell / at / when / finish line / the / .

   _____

4 Read the pairs of sentences. Rewrite the first sentence in each pair using an adverb of degree. More than one answer may be possible.

1. Haley came very close to getting a role in that new movie. But Susanne got it instead.

   Haley nearly got a role in that new movie.

2. Ken sang the song the first time. He sang it exactly right!

   _____

3. He would've made the goal if it had been kicked more to the right. It was very close.

   _____

4. Hank looked scared during the movie. I don't think he'll ever go see another one.

   _____

5. I'm convinced that I want to have a career in marine conservation. I have made my decision.

   _____

GRAMMAR Tag questions

1 Match the sentences with the tag questions.

1. You watched the game last night, _b_
2. You were at the café yesterday, ____
3. You'd donate money if you could, ____
4. You haven't been to Hollywood, ____
5. You'll clean up the kitchen, ____

a. have you?
b. didn't you?
c. won't you?
d. weren't you?
e. wouldn't you?

2 Add tag questions.

1. That game was pretty close, _wasn't it_ ?
2. I like listening to music that makes me feel good, _____?
3. You think watching the news is boring, _____?
4. Tim almost fell asleep during the movie, _____?
5. You haven't seen Bruno Mars in concert, _____?
6. Traffic is moving extremely slowly in downtown Los Angeles, _____?
7. That's the actress who was in that movie, _____?

3 Correct the tag questions. More than one answer may be possible.

                weren't

1. The tickets were expensive, ~~haven't~~ they?
2. This show is funny, doesn't it?
3. Kids shouldn't play video games so often, aren't they?
4. This is the way to the museum, can it?
5. They really like all of the *Star Wars* movies, should they?
6. Uma Thurman's father is a college professor, OK?
7. Bill Murray often plays jokes on ordinary people, would he?
8. Adam Levine from Maroon 5 does yoga, can't he?

4 Write questions. Use the tag questions and your own information.

1. (isn't it) _It's Monday today, isn't it?_
2. (haven't they) _____
3. (weren't we) _____
4. (doesn't it) _____
5. (right) _____

CONVERSATION — Making a point

1. Circle the correct answers.

1. **A:** This movie is going to be boring, isn't it?
   B: _____ It might be interesting.
   a. Of course.   b. Not necessarily!

2. **A:** If everybody had to do some volunteer work, people might be nicer to each other.
   B: _____ And it might make people feel a sense of community.
   a. Not necessarily!   b. That's a good point.

3. **A:** The books are always better than the movies, right?
   B: _____ The actors are never like you picture the characters.
   a. As far as I'm concerned.   b. Of course!

4. **A:** Want to take some more golf lessons?
   B: _____, those are the last lessons I want to take!
   a. As far as I'm concerned   b. You're absolutely right

5. **A:** Do you think celebrities support charities for publicity or because they care?
   B: _____ some of them do it because they care.
   a. Not necessarily   b. It seems to me that

6. **A:** I bet I won't like some of this music 10 years from now.
   B: _____. People's taste in music can change.
   a. As far as I'm concerned   b. You're absolutely right

2. Circle the correct answers.

1. **Bill:** I'm excited about the sci-fi conference! Hey, are you wearing that? ¹**It seems to me that** / **Not necessarily** it would be better if we wore similar costumes.
   Ted: ²**As far as I'm concerned.** / **You're absolutely right.** That's why I got you a costume like mine!

2. **Esther:** So which movie did you like best, The Hobbit or Star Wars?
   Michelle: The Hobbit, ³**it seems to me** / **of course**. The original Star Wars just looks so dated.
   Esther: ⁴**Not necessarily.** / **That's a good point.** The Hobbit movie does look more modern.

3. **Alexis:** One Direction is the best boy band ever!
   Mother: ⁵**Not necessarily!** / **It seems to me!** Back in my day, we loved New Kids on the Block. ⁶**That's a good point** / **As far as I'm concerned**, they're the best boy band ever!

READING TO WRITE

1 Number the parts of a comparison/contrast essay in order from 1–3.

_____ Give similarities and differences in two separate paragraphs.

_____ State your opinion again in a different way.

_____ State your opinion about the topic.

2 Read the sentences that compare Hollywood movies from the United States to Bollywood movies from India. Match the sentences that are about the same topics.

Hollywood

1. The United States has almost 40,000 movie theaters. _f_
2. Hollywood movies make about $51 billion each year. _____
3. A single Hollywood film targets a specific genre, such as action, or sci-fi. _____
4. Hollywood makes excellent action, sci-fi, and spy movies. _____
5. In 2013, Hollywood produced over 600 films. _____
6. An average Hollywood movie costs about $47.7 million to make.

Bollywood

a. A single Bollywood film includes a lot of variety: musical numbers, action, comedy, and romance.
b. Bollywood produces about 1,000 films each year.
c. Bollywood movies make over $3 billion each year.
d. A Bollywood movie costs about $1.5 million to make.
e. Bollywood makes wonderful musicals with great song lyrics.
f. There are fewer than 13,000 movie theaters in India.

3 Combine the matching sentences from Activity 2 using the _as . . . as_ phrases.

almost twice as many . . . as	nearly as much . . . as
~~as much . . . as~~	not as many . . . as
just as . . . as	nowhere near as . . . as

1. Hollywood movies don't have __as much__ variety __as__ Bollywood movies.
2. Bollywood movies are _____ expensive to make _____ Hollywood movies.
3. There are _____ movie theaters in India _____ in the United States.
4. Bollywood films are _____ good _____ Hollywood films.
5. Bollywood films don't make _____ money _____ Hollywood movies.
6. Bollywood produces _____ films _____ Hollywood per year.

Unit 5 | 35

6 It's the Little Things.

VOCABULARY Everyday objects

1 Match the sentences with the pictures.

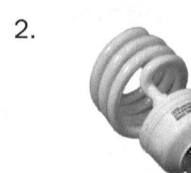

1.  ____
2. ____
3.  ____
4.  ____
5. 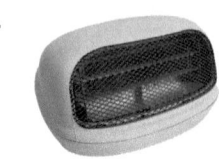 ____
6.  ____
7.  ____
8.  ____
9.  ____
10. ____

(Picture 1 is labeled: e)

a. I can't find the remote control for the television!

b. Don't forget to put out the candles.

c. Do you have a spare phone charger?

d. It's hot in here! Turn on the fan, please.

e. Can you turn on the light? The switch is over there.

f. I'm a bit chilly. Let's turn off the air conditioner.

g. Have you seen the matches?

h. When I traveled to London, I couldn't use my hairdryer! The plug was different!

i. Don't forget to turn off that heater before you go to bed.

j. The stores only sell those new light bulbs that save energy.

2 Read the situations and circle the correct answers.

1. Jan is driving in her car. It is cold. What should she turn on?

    a. the charger   b. the fan   c. (the heater)

2. The power goes out in Ha Jin's apartment at night. What can he use for light?

    a. a candle   b. a light bulb   c. a switch

3. Tracy is camping. She has gathered logs. What does she need to start a fire?

    a. a fan   b. matches   c. a remote control

4. Now the power is on in Ha Jin's apartment. What does he need to press to turn on the light?

    a. a heater   b. a plug   c. a switch

5. Now the lamp in Ha Jin's apartment doesn't work. What does he need to replace?

    a. the air conditioner   b. the light bulb   c. the remote control

6. Jan is driving in her car, and now it is very hot. What should she turn on?

    a. the air conditioner   b. the light bulb   c. matches

7. Tracy's cell phone won't turn on. What does she probably need to make it work?

    a. a charger   b. a heater   c. a switch

8. At night, the air is very still and it is hot in Jan's hotel room. What does she turn on?

    a. a candle   b. a fan   c. a heater

9. The switch for the fan in Jan's hotel room doesn't work. What should she check?

    a. the charger   b. the light bulb   c. the plug

10. Tracy wants to watch a movie. What does she use to turn on the TV?

    a. an air condiioner   b. a plug   c. a remote control

3 Answer the questions with the words from Exercise 1 and your own information.

1. When does your family use candles?

    We use candles for birthdays and special dinners.

2. Which months of the year do you use a heater?

3. Which months of the year do you use a fan or an air conditioner?

4. Which two items from Exercise 1 do you use the most? For what?

GRAMMAR   Passive infinitive

1 Complete the chart using the passive infinitive.

	Present	Past
1. want/know	Raul *wants to be known* for his popularity.	Raul *wanted to be known* for his singing ability.
2. have/charge	Lara's phone _____ every few hours.	Lara's phone _____ overnight.
3. like/laugh at	The comedian _____ when he's funny.	The comedian *didn't* _____ when he made the mistake.
4. expect/treat	We _____ fairly in school.	We _____ fairly at summer camp.
5. not have/pay	The full price _____ by students.	The full price _____ when the students went to the theater.
6. not need/see	This movie _____ by anyone over the age of five.	This movie _____ in 3-D.

2 Complete the paragraph with the present and past passive infinitive forms of the verbs.

Our new apartment in Miami was a mess when we moved in! We ¹*didn't expect it to be messed up* (not expect it / mess up) because it was clean when we first saw it.

The air conditioner was really dusty. It ² _____ (need / clean) right away because it was hot when we moved in. It works now, which is good. The plugs on one wall didn't work either. We had to put the sofa and table, things that ³ _____ (not have / plug in), against that wall. They still need to be fixed. And all of the light bulbs ⁴ _____ (have / replace) as soon as we find the time to do it.

At least the carpet ⁵ _____ (not have / clean) when we moved in. The heater is broken, but it ⁶ _____ (not need / fix) right away. It's so hot here right now, we don't expect to use it for months!

Passive with modals

3 Rewrite the present sentences from Exercise 1 as modals. Use *must, should, might,* or *had better*. More than one answer may be possible.

1. Raul *wants to be* known for his popularity. >

    Raul must be known for his popularity.

2. _____
3. _____
4. _____
5. _____
6. _____

4 Complete the sentences using your own ideas. Use the passive infinitive or modals.

1. My smartphone needs *to be turned off at school*.

    My smartphone needs _____.

2. His new laptop might _____.

3. The candle has _____.

4. The matches must _____.

5. We didn't expect _____.

Unit 6 | 37

VOCABULARY Modifiers

1 Circle seven more modifiers. Then write them in the chart.

masobfnotreallyndpaltextremelyjazfartoobicnewtotallysigmridiculouslyplutroakindofenlyalittlebitood

1. _ _ _ _ _ _ _ _ _ _ _ _
2. _ _ _ _ _ _ _ _ _
3. _ _ _ _ _ _
4. s o
5. _ _ _ _ _ _ _
6. _ _ _ _ _ _
7. _ _ _ _ _ _ _ _ _ _
8. _ _ _ _ _ _ _ _ _

2 Look at the pictures. Circle the correct answers.

1. My bike is **not really / ridiculously** small. I don't think I can ride it anymore.

2. Let's turn off the air conditioner. It's **a little bit / far too** chilly in here! My hands are freezing!

3. I want a new laptop, but this one's **not really / so** expensive. I don't have enough money to buy it.

4. That dress is **kind of / far too** nice to wear while you paint your room!

5. That watch is **kind of / not really** cool. But I don't think it has enough features.

6. My grandmother thinks it's **extremely / not really** important to have a smartphone. She still doesn't have one.

7. That car is **a little bit / so** cool! It's the most amazing car I've ever seen!

8. Personally, I'm **not really / totally** bored with that social networking site. I'm going to quit visiting it.

38 | Unit 6

3 Complete the sentences with a word or phrase from each box and your own ideas.

extremely	colorful
far too	cool
a little bit	dangerous
kind of	difficult
not really	easy
ridiculously	expensive
so	old
totally	small

1. *My brother's smartphone is far too old to take videos.*
2. _____
3. _____
4. _____
5. _____
6. _____
7. _____
8. _____

GRAMMAR Review of causative have/get

1 Match the active sentences with the passive/causative sentences.

Active	Passive/Causative
1. Someone repairs her bike after a race. _b_	a. She isn't having her bike repaired after the race.
2. Someone repaired her bike after the race. ___	b. She has her bike repaired after a race.
3. No one is repairing her bike after the race. ___	c. She'll get her bike repaired after the race.
4. She'll ask someone to repair her bike after the race. ___	d. Must she have her bike repaired after the race?
5. Must she get someone to repair her bike after the race? ___	e. She got her bike repaired after the race.

2 Put the words in the correct order to make sentences.

1. his charger / got / fixed / last night / Andrew / .
   Andrew got his charger fixed last night.

2. to do / for me / get / I / can never / my brother / my homework / .
   _____

3. I / cut / the / have / lawn / Should / you / for / ?
   _____

4. camera / isn't / his / boy / The / checked / getting / today / .
   _____

5. weekend / get / school / painted / The / won't / this / .
   _____

6. cleaned / on / have / team uniforms / We / our / weekends / .
   _____

3 Rewrite the sentences. Use the tense and voice (active or causative) in parentheses.

1. Someone paints Mike's skateboard on Friday. (simple past/active)
   Someone *painted Mike's skateboard on Friday.*

2. I will fix my laptop this weekend. (future with *will*/causative)
   I will _____

3. Someone cuts Tom's hair every three months. (simple present/passive)
   Tom _____

4. The man isn't having anyone set up his website. (present continuous/active) No one
   _____ the man's website.

5. Someone professionally photographed Elizabeth's birthday party. (simple past/causative)
   Elizabeth _____

Unit 6 | 39

CONVERSATION: Buying a gadget

1 Put the words in the correct order to complete the phrase. Match the phrases to the second part of questions 1–6.

you / could / show /	it / to / is / easy / use /
it / does / have /	is / how / good / it /
model / is / which /	does / how / it / long /

1. _Could you show_ us how to use the video function?
2. _____ last before you have to charge it?
3. _____ the newest?
4. _____ compared to the previous version?
5. _____ or do I need to read the instructions?
6. _____ any extra batteries?

2 Complete the conversation with the phrases from Exercise 1.

Hiroki: Excuse me. ¹ _Could you show_ me this digital camera?

Salesperson: Here you are.

Hiroki: Thank you.

Emma: Hiroki, that one's OK. But ² _____ to use in the water? I don't think that kind is waterproof.

Hiroki: Oh, you're right. But ³ _____?

Emma: Yeah, it's really easy because it's totally basic. But look, it says it's not waterproof.

Emma (to salesperson): Excuse me, ⁴ _____ the waterproof one?

Salesperson: This one is.

Emma: ⁵ _____ take to charge?

Salesperson: About two hours.

Emma: See, Hiroki? That's pretty fast.

Hiroki: ⁶ _____ GPS?

Salesperson: Of course, it does.

Emma: Oh, gosh. Look at the price!

Hiroki: Wow, that's expensive!

READING TO WRITE

1 Combine the underlined sentences with *while* or *whereas*. Make any other changes necessary.

Bass Boss Headphones v2
posted by Josephine

This review is for Bass Boss Headphones v2. I found them on sale online for $89.99. ¹That seems ridiculously expensive for a pair of headphones. It's about ten dollars less than the older version and about ten times better!

First of all, the new v2 model headphones sound *amazing*. ²The v1 headphones sound good. These sound great. Your ears will enjoy cleaner high notes, deeper bass notes, and an overall crisp sound. And they have excellent sound-elimination technology!

³I liked using the old headphones on may way to school. I love the new ones even more. I can hear every note even when I'm on a noisy bus! They're also useful for studying languages. I plug mine in to my laptop when I study English.

⁴The v1 had a good design. These fit better. ⁵The v2 model looks sleeker. The previous version was kind of clunky. ⁶The v1 model only came in black or white. This new model comes in 20 fun colors, like orange or green. The new version is lighter, too!

Finally, there's a new feature for v2. You can press a button on the cord to mute the sound so you can hear what's going on around you. Perfect for when your mom's calling you to come to dinner.

I think these are great headphones. They have more useful features than the previous version. I recommend buying them on sale.

1. *While that seems ridiculously expensive for a pair of headphones, it's about ten dollars less than the older version and about ten times better!*
2. _____
3. _____
4. _____
5. _____
6. _____

2 Read the article in Exercise 1 again. Circle the correct answers.

1. What does Josephine say about the price of the Bass Boss Headphones v2?
   a. She says it was ten dollars.
   b. She says they weren't on sale.
   c. **She says they cost a lot.**

2. What is different about the v2 model headphones?
   a. They're lighter, and they sound better, fit better, and come in more colors.
   b. They're ridiculously expensive, kind of clunky, and noisy.
   c. They only come in orange or green.

3. What are they useful for?
   a. for recording sounds
   b. for listening to music and studying
   c. for hearing your mother call you

4. What new feature does the v2 model have?
   a. It can be plugged into a laptop.
   b. It can be found on sale.
   c. The sound can be muted.

5. What is her recommendation?
   a. not to buy it
   b. to buy it on sale
   c. to buy the v1 headphones

REVIEW UNITS 5–6

1 Circle the correct answers.

1. This plug looks **a little bit** / **ridiculously** bent. I think it needs to be replaced.
2. I **dislike** / **feel** the position of this switch. It's difficult to reach.
3. This remote control is **absolutely** / **hardly** amazing! It can turn on **fairly** / **nearly** everything in this room!
4. Can we turn off the air conditioner now? I **appreciate** / **think** the room is cool enough.
5. I **recommend** / **respect** these light bulbs for your art studio. They are nice and bright.
6. I **admire** / **recommend** that you get a new phone charger. This one works **not really** / **so** slowly!
7. I **hate** / **respect** this fan. It's **far too** / **not really** noisy!
8. I'm **pretty** / **ridiculously** satisfied with this heater. It works **hardly** / **perfectly** fine, even though it was inexpensive.

2 Match the sentences from Exercise 1 with the pictures.

a. _1_    b. _____
c.  _____ d. _____ 
e.  _____ f. _____ 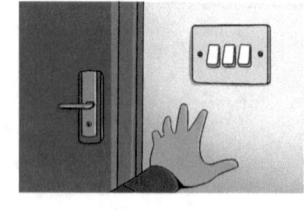
g.  _____ h. _____ 

3 Cross out the word that doesn't belong in each category.

1. Expressing an opinion:
   feel   hate   respect   ridiculously
2. Everyday objects:
   a little bit   a fan   a plug   a switch
3. Words that modify others:
   extremely   far too   kind of   remote control
4. Adverbs that show degree:
   hardly   nearly   pricey   pretty

4 Put the words in the correct order to make sentences.

1. my grandfather / I / cleaned / the yard / for / get / will / .
   I will get the yard cleaned for my grandfather.
2. it / fixed / for / have / I / you / Should / ?
   _____
3. the car / cleaned / got / Friday / on / They / .
   _____
4. of / blog posts / get / people / Her / read / by / a lot / .
   _____
5. delivered / aren't / a pizza / Our friends / house / to / their / having / .
   _____
6. her / Kim / mother's / have / replaced / air conditioner / will / .
   _____

5 Rewrite the sentences. Change the verbs from active to passive.

1. People know Maya for her beautiful voice.

   Maya is known for her beautiful voice.

2. Nobody needed to turn the air conditioner on.

   _____

3. Someone put out the candles before bedtime.

   _____

4. People know Terry for his inventions, and he likes that.

   _____

5. We turned our phones off during class, which Mrs. Cook expected.

   _____

6 Complete the conversations with tag questions.

1. **A:** You still listen to Katy Perry, *don't you*?
   B: Not as much as I used to.

2. **A:** You've already seen *Guardians of the Galaxy*, _____?
   B: A long time ago.

3. **A:** You're buying the latest smartphone, _____?
   B: Not right away.

4. **A:** That was an exciting game last night, _____?
   B: I'll say! I was on the edge of my seat!

5. **A:** Sports stars should make less money, _____?
   B: I guess so. But the really good ones sell a lot of tickets.

6. **A:** Rap music is getting kind of old, _____?
   B: Kind of. I like it, but I just don't listen to it as much as I used to.

7 Combine the sentences using defining or non-defining relative clauses. More than one answer may be correct.

1. I think people are desperate for attention. They go on reality TV shows.

   I think people who are desperate for attention go on reality TV shows.

2. My friend Rebecca was on a reality TV show. She's an interior designer.

   _____
   _____

3. Rebecca was starting a design business. Starting a design business is hard to do.

   _____
   _____

4. She got on a reality show. The reality show redecorates people's homes.

   _____
   _____

5. They redecorated for people. The people's homes had been ruined in a flood.

   _____
   _____

8 Complete the conversation.

~~Could you show me~~	It seems to me that
Does it have	That's a good point.
How good is	Which model

Sophia: Hey, Noah. ¹ *Could you show me* your tablet?

Noah: Sure. Are you thinking about buying one?

Sophia: Yeah. ² _____ a video camera?

Noah: Yes, it does.

Sophia: ³ _____ the video quality, though? I need to use it for my video class assignments.

Noah: It's pretty good.

Sophia: ⁴ _____ has the best quality camera?

Noah: Oh, not this one. ⁵ _____ you'd be happier with the upgraded version. But it's more expensive.

Julia: Yeah, but if I can take better videos, that will help me get a better grade in class, right?

Noah: Oh, well, yeah. ⁶ _____

7 Have a Ball!

VOCABULARY Celebration phrases

1 Unscramble the words to make celebration phrases. Then number the pictures.

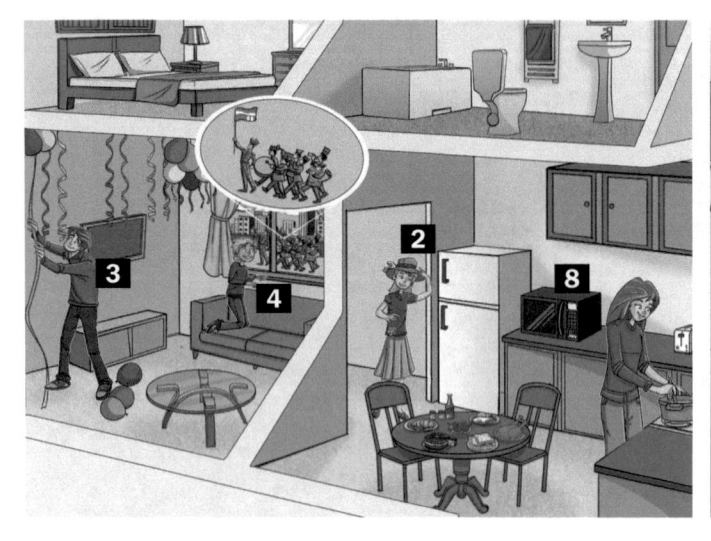

1. A L P Y C S U M I — *play music*
2. S R E S D P U — _____
3. T U P P U R E D O O N S I A C T — _____
4. C H A W T A A D E R P A — _____
5. E V H A A D O O G M I T E — _____
6. V E G I A T R E E N P S — _____
7. E S T F O F R O R K I W E S F — _____
8. P E A R R E P L I S P A C E O D O F — _____
9. D L H O A S T O N E C T — _____

2 Circle the correct answers.

1. Our neighbor **has a good time / puts up decorations** for nearly every holiday. People from all over town drive by his house to see them.

2. My favorite part of celebrating is when people **give a present / set off fireworks**. They look so pretty in the night sky.

3. My grandfather won't go with us anymore to **prepare special foods / watch the parade**. He said he doesn't like crowds.

4. Tino comes to every party. He really likes to **have a good time / hold a contest**.

5. Bridget likes to **dress up / play music** at parties, but she'll let you suggest songs.

6. I love costume parties! Especially when they **hold a contest / prepare special food**. I usually have creative ideas and win.

7. My boyfriend doesn't like going to weddings because he doesn't like to **dress up / watch a parade**.

8. My family always **plays music / prepares special food** for our celebrations. We've been making the same delicious dishes for years!

9. My brother likes to **give presents / hold contests**. He makes all his gifts by hand.

GRAMMAR Verb + -ing form (gerund) or infinitive

1 Circle the correct answers. If both answers are possible, circle both.

1. Tiffany hates **going / to go** to parties.
2. Michael learned **dancing / to dance** for his wedding.
3. They're considering **having / to have** a New Year's party.
4. We haven't forgotten **bringing / to bring** a dish to the party.
5. My uncle started **grilling / to grill** the chicken already.
6. My younger sister tried **staying up / to stay up** until midnight on New Year's Eve, but she fell asleep at 11 o'clock.

2 Correct the sentences with either the infinitive or -ing form. If the sentences are already correct, write *correct*.

1. What kind of music do you want ~~playing~~ at the party? *to play*
2. Do you remember to go a concert for the first time? _____
3. Some people don't like to dress up in costumes. _____
4. My sister doesn't enjoy to eat cake on her birthday. _____
5. My cousin plans having her graduation party at home. _____
6. Don't forget cleaning the house before the party. _____
7. Rachel and Tom discussed to have their wedding in Sonoma. _____
8. Heather loves to sing karaoke at parties. _____

3 Put the words in the correct order to make sentences. When necessary, change the verbs to the infinitive or the -ing form. More than one answer may be possible.

1. I / can't / a / was / remember / when / have / two / birthday party / I / .

   I can't remember having a birthday party when I was two.

2. Tracy / arrive / at / on time / our house / expects / .

   _____

3. try / the / eat / once / at / all / Don't / candy / .

   _____

4. The / the / start / teacher / game / party / prefers / with / a / .

   _____

5. Elliot / have / his / clowns / birthday / doesn't / party / at / enjoy / .

   _____

6. celebration / get / The / noisy / after / began / the / first fireworks / .

   _____

4 Write sentences that are true for you. Use the phrases *(not) enjoy, (not) want, love, hate,* and *(not) forget* with the infinitive or the -ing forms of the verbs.

1. ride a bike

   I love riding a bike.

2. dress up

   _____

3. give a present

   _____

4. prepare special food

   _____

5. put up decorations

   _____

6. set off fireworks

   _____

VOCABULARY — Descriptive adjectives

1 Circle nine more adjectives.

A	I	M	P	R	E	S	S	I	V	E	L
N	W	S	K	R	T	S	C	A	R	Y	I
I	E	T	S	Q	I	N	O	I	S	Y	V
A	Q	M	E	S	S	Y	V	H	R	E	E
T	R	A	D	I	T	I	O	N	A	L	L
H	Z	S	T	U	N	N	I	N	G	W	Y
P	E	A	C	E	F	U	L	V	W	A	N
L	A	V	P	J	P	Y	H	N	I	C	Q
A	W	M	G	C	R	O	W	D	E	D	H
S	Q	N	P	O	Q	H	T	K	O	E	S
E	Y	X	J	R	F	S	M	Z	C	J	Y
J	X	J	D	C	O	L	O	R	F	U	L

2 Circle the correct answers.

1. Yumi told me about the Japanese festival of *hanami*, or flower viewing. People have a picnic under the cherry blossoms in the spring. She said the women often wear a *kimono* during the *hanami* festival. A *kimono* is a kind of **crowded / lively / traditional** Japanese robe. *Hanami* sounded like a lovely, **crowded / noisy / peaceful** nature festival. But Yumi told me it was very **lively / stunning / traditional**, with lots of people singing and dancing.

2. On New Year's Eve, everyone in our city gathers downtown to wait for midnight. There are so many people! It's very **colorful / crowded / traditional**, but it feels safe and fun. When the clock strikes midnight, everyone cheers and it gets quite **colorful / messy / noisy**. My favorite part of New Year's is when the city sets off the fireworks. This year's fireworks display was particularly **peaceful / crowded / stunning**! I loved it. My younger brother didn't like the fireworks, though. He thought they were loud and **impressive / peaceful / scary**.

3. Ed went to a festival in India where people throw bright powder on each other. His photos are amazing. He has some beautiful shots of colored powder flying through the air. The powder is so **colorful / peaceful / traditional**. And it's **colorful / impressive / peaceful** that he didn't get powder all over his camera! He said the festival was wonderful, but it was very **crowded / messy / noisy**. He hasn't been able to wash the powder out of some of his clothing.

3 Write a paragraph describing a celebration, festival, or party using the words from Exercise 1 and your own information.

<u>We celebrated my grandparent's 40th anniversary recently. The dancing at their party was surprisingly lively! My uncle led off with a traditional song . . .</u>

GRAMMAR -ing form (gerund) as subject; by/for + -ing form

1 How is the *-ing* form used? Read the sentences and check (✓) the correct columns.

	As the subject	To show how to do something	To show the purpose or use of something
1. **Decorating** the house for parties is my favorite part of the holidays.	✓		
2. The annual parade is an occasion for **wearing** silly hats.			
3. Not **bringing** a gift to the party would be rude.			
4. **Watching** the fireworks by the river is stunning.			
5. We began the ceremony by **singing** a song.			
6. The rainy weather isn't good for **watching** the parade.			

2 Correct the mistakes.
  for having
  1. The park is perfect ~~by have~~ a picnic.
  2. They celebrated their anniversary for take a long cruise.
  3. One of Carrie's favorite things is for watches the leaves change color in the fall.
  4. He improved his test scores to study every day.
  5. My grandmother's kitchen is perfect by prepares food.
  6. I tell everyone that for go to the Art Festival was the highlight of my trip.

3 Complete the conversation with the gerund forms of the verbs in parentheses. Add *by* or *for*, if necessary.

Maria: What was that festival you went to in December?

Kevin: I went to the Chocolate Festival. It's the perfect festival ¹ *for learning* (learn) about different types of chocolate.

Maria: That must be helpful since you're in culinary school, right? ² _____ (go) to the festival, you're learning something new. It's like studying for you!

Kevin: It really is. You get a sense of the variety of chocolate ³ _____ (taste) a lot of different kinds.

Maria: Oh, yeah! ⁴ _____ (no eat) as many kinds as you can would be a mistake!

Kevin: And the festival is not just about flavor. ⁵ _____ (watch) how chocolates are made is important, too.

Maria: I've heard that ⁶ _____ (make) chocolates is difficult.

Kevin: It is. ⁷ _____ (take) photos of the demonstrations has been a great way to take notes on the process.

Maria: Well, I can't wait to see what you've learned!

4 Write two sentences for each gerund phrase: one using *by* and one using *for*. Use your own ideas.

1. watch a concert
   by: *I started my weekend by watching a concert on TV.*
   for: *The outdoor theater in the park is great for watching a concert.*

   by: _____
   for: _____

2. play music
   by: _____
   for: _____

3. have a party
   by: _____
   for: _____

4. go to a festival
   by: _____
   for: _____

CONVERSATION: Exclamations

1. Complete the conversation.

Great idea!	That'd be
How	That's such an
is so	~~What a~~

Josh: Hi, Lynn. I'm planning a birthday party for Glenn. I don't know what to do!

Lynn: ¹___What a___ nice thing to do! I'll help you. Does he know about the party or is it a surprise party?

Josh: Hey! A surprise party! ²_____ Let's do that.

Lynn: Why don't we have it at your place? That way it can be a surprise.

Josh: ³_____ smart of you to think of that! But I'm not sure about keeping it a surprise.

Lynn: Here's what you do: You pick him up to take him out for his birthday. Then you pretend to forget something at your house. Invite him in for a minute when you go back to get it. When he comes in, surprise!

Josh: ⁴_____ perfect! OK. What else do we need to do?

Lynn: He ⁵_____ into music. We'll need to make a really good playlist.

Josh: Very true. I can do that. Do we need to prepare food?

Lynn: Of course, and we'll need a cake.

Josh: Right! The cake! I almost forgot! ⁶_____ important part of a birthday!

Lynn: Totally. Oh, I have a great idea! We can get one of those cakes with a photograph on it, done in frosting!

Josh: He'd like that.

2 Circle the correct answers.

1. **A:** I think for our school dance this winter, we should get an ice sculpture!
   B: **Great idea!** / That'd be difficult. But won't it be expensive?

2. **A:** Let's take Mike to a concert instead of throwing him a party.
   B: **How / What a** great idea! It'll feel like a huge party.

3. **A:** Melanie's favorite color is green. We can serve all green foods and drinks at the party!
   B: **How / Is so** cool! Oh, as long as it's not all vegetables!

4. **A:** Instead of having music at the party, I thought we'd sing karaoke.
   B: **That'd be / Is so** a good idea, except that Chris doesn't like singing!

5. **A:** What can I do to help with the class trip?
   B: Well, the trip **how / is so** expensive. We need to come up with ideas to raise money for it.

6. **A:** We're renting go-karts for Belinda's birthday next month!
   B: **How / That's such** a fun idea.

READING TO WRITE

1 Jennifer started a company that plans parties. Complete Jennifer's email to her friend Craig. Write *so* or *too*.

To: CraigD@cup.net
From: JenniferLee@email.net
Subject: Too Fun!

Dear Craig,

I'm ¹*so* excited to tell you about how my party-planning company, Too Fun!, is doing. As you know, I started by planning my high school's graduation party. A lot of people think planning a party is a lot of work, but I don't. I love it. I like it when I have so much to do that I'm almost ² _____ busy to get it all done. We held the graduation in the school auditorium. We had an old-fashioned carnival theme, with games, prizes, and fun foods that people used to eat a long time ago. People took photos and had a great time.

Next, I planned my cousin's wedding reception. She paid me for it. It was ³ _____ luxurious! I rented a gorgeous inn along the coast. It was ⁴ _____ stunning. I hired a chef to prepare all of the couple's favorite foods. I planned for ⁵ _____ much food, though! We had a lot left over. But my cousin wasn't mad that I spent ⁶ _____ much on food. She was ⁷ _____ happy about her special day to care.

The next party I'm planning is a birthday party for our neighbor's daughter. I think I'm going to rent a pony! The pictures are going to be ⁸ _____ cute! I can just imagine it now.

How are things with you? Got any plans for your college graduation party? Let me know if you need any help!

Take care,

Jennifer

---

2 Read the email in Exercise 1 again. Answer the questions.

1. What two events did Jennifer plan?

   Event 1: *her high school's graduation party*

   Event 2: _____.

2. Where was each party held?

   Party 1: _____

   Party 2: _____

3. What did Jennifer have at each party?

   Party 1: _____

   Party 2: _____

4. What happened at each party?

   Party 1: _____

   Party 2: _____

5. What party is Jennifer planning next?

   _____

6. What will be special about the next party?

   _____

8 Mysteries and Secrets

VOCABULARY Adjectives with *un-*

1 Complete the puzzle.

Across

1. Something that you don't know is going to happen is _____.
3. Something that doesn't seem true is _____.
4. Something that doesn't happen most of the time is _____.
5. If you don't find an answer to a problem or mystery, it is _____.
6. Something that isn't recognized by most people is _____.
7. When bad things happen to you a lot, you are _____.

Down

1. Something that is not valuable or useful is _____.
2. Something that isn't needed is _____.
4. When something probably won't happen it is _____.

2 Complete the sentences with some of the words from Exercise 1. More than one answer may be correct.

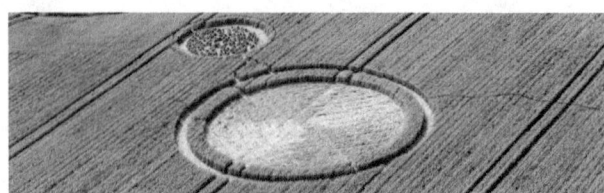

1. Mysterious crop circles appeared in the farmer's field. People came up with some pretty _____ explanations, like aliens caused the circles. But it turns out they were caused by an insect that makes an _____ pattern in the ground.

2. My brother is afraid he'll get bitten by a shark even though it's very _____. Very few people get bitten, so I think worrying about it is _____.

3. What happened to pilot Amelia Earhart is still an _____ mystery. But someone may have found a piece of her plane.

4. The reporter said that Banksy is a famous graffiti artist, but his real name and identity are _____. The reporter tried to discover the artist's true identity, but was _____ in his efforts to learn the truth.

5. A detective has to be careful when she looks for clues. A fingerprint or piece of hair that might seem small and _____ could turn out to be a big clue. And sometimes clues are found in _____ places, like on the backs of paintings or in the refrigerator!

3 Answer the questions with your own information.

1. Describe a time you felt unlucky.

   _____
   _____

2. Describe a time something unexpected happened to you or someone you know.

   _____
   _____

3. Describe something that you think is unbelievable.

   _____

4. Describe something that you think is unlikely to happen to you.

   _____

50 | Unit 8

GRAMMAR — Time clauses; present participle clauses

1 Use the chart to write sentences. Use the correct forms of the verbs. More than one answer may be possible.

Time clause	First event	Second event
1. before	Ben graduated.	He became a firefighter.
2. after	We had lived in the city for years.	We discovered our favorite restaurant.
3. when	They scored the final goal.	Helen arrived at the game.
4. when	I have enough money.	I will visit the Great Wall of China
5. before	It got dark out.	The fireworks started.

1. *Ben graduated before he became a firefighter.*
2. _____
3. _____
4. _____
5. _____

2 Complete the sentences about each pair of pictures with the correct time clauses. More than one answer may be possible.

1. She put on her helmet __*before*__ she went skateboarding.

2. Tina started taking photos _____ she got off the bus.

3. We saw dolphins in the river _____ our boat first left Iquitos, Peru.

4. We weren't scared _____ the bats came flying out of the cave!

3 Circle the correct answers.

1. Anna loved sushi **(as soon as)** / **until** she tried it.

2. José had booked his ticket to New Orleans **before** / **until** the hurricane hit. So he had to change his flight.

3. They will continue the space flight program **after** / **while** they have solved the problem.

4. Logan doesn't want to be in Chiang Mai **before** / **while** it's typhoon season.

5. The butterflies were arriving **after** / **when** the film crew was in Mexico, so they got great videos.

6. I had sore feet **before** / **after** I got my new running shoes. They are so much better than my old ones!

4 Write sentences that are true for you using time clauses. Use the words given.

1. since

   I've been interested in sharks since I was five.
   _____

2. before
   _____

3. when
   _____

4. after
   _____

VOCABULARY Reporting verbs

1 Circle the word that best replaces the underlined words.

1. Terry told me that there would be a surprise test on Tuesday. She did not explain how she knew that.
   a. agreed   b. (claimed)   c. recommended

2. By the way, when I spoke with him, Aaron said that he'd be studying at the library tonight.
   a. wrote   b. mentioned   c. insisted

3. My aunt finally answered my email asking about our family's history.
   a. replied to
   b. recommended to
   c. decided on

4. Charlotte liked my plan to start a book club. We're going to do it!
   a. recommended to
   b. admitted to
   c. agreed on

5. I wanted Chinese food and my sister wanted sushi, but my father said that we were going to get pizza for dinner.
   a. admitted   b. replied   c. decided

6. My friend told me to read Stephen King's novels. She thinks I'd like them.
   a. wrote   b. agreed   c. recommended

7. I knew my little brother drew on the wall, even though he wouldn't say that he did.
   a. admit it   b. recommend it   c. decide it

8. My mom said that I should clean the garage before watching TV.
   a. replied   b. claimed   c. insisted

9. The reporter said in the article that the mystery was solved. But the police chief didn't agree.
   a. admitted   b. agreed   c. wrote

2 Complete the sentences with the correct forms of the verbs.

admit	decide	recommend
agree	insist	reply
claim	~~mention~~	write

Alex: Hey, Bill. What's the matter?

Bill: What? Nothing! Did Haley ¹____mention____ something to you? She sent you over here, didn't she?

Alex: OK. I'll ²_____ it! She ³_____ that I find out what you're going to do.

Bill: I knew it! She ⁴_____ she doesn't mind if I run for student council against her. But I know she does mind.

Alex: I think you're right. It's just, she's upset because you ⁵_____ to run without talking to her first. It's weird to run against a close friend.

Bill: You know, I ⁶_____ it seems that way. I really do.

Alex: Well then, why did you do it?

Bill: Mr. Wells, my Political Science teacher, said it would help my college applications. He ⁷_____ that I do some extracurricular activities in school, like student council.

Alex: So, you'd ruin a friendship because you want a teacher to ⁸_____ a recommendation for you?

Bill: I hadn't really thought of it that way. But then again, if Haley is a good friend, she should understand. And, if she wants to work in politics, well, she'll have to get used to some friendly competition.

Alex: So, what should I tell her?

Bill: You don't have to talk to her about it. I'll ⁹_____ to her in person.

3 Answer the questions using your own information.

1. Explain something important that you decided recently.
   _____
2. What is something your parents insist that you do?
   _____
3. What book, movie, or TV show do you recommend to people the most?
   _____

GRAMMAR Reported speech

1 Match the quoted speech to the reported speech.

1. She said, "Yes, I hid it in the garage."
2. He said, "I heard a strange sound around midnight."
3. He said, "Go look in the attic."
4. She asked, "Did you see anything odd?"
5. She said, "We have to leave the light on at night."
6. He said, "I was at home the entire evening."

a. He said that he was at home the entire evening.
b. She asked me if I saw anything odd.
c. She admitted to hiding it in the garage.
d. He claimed to hear a strange sound around midnight.
e. He told me to look in the attic.
f. She insisted on leaving the light on at night.

2 Change the direct speech to reported speech. Use the subjects and verb forms in parentheses.

1. "Hide the new puppy in Damian's room." (Mom / say)

   Mom said to hide the new puppy in

   Damian's room.

2. "Pretend you didn't see anything." (she / recommend)
   _____

3. "We'll meet at the old clock." (we / agree)
   _____
4. "Where were you on the night of January 7?" (he / ask)
   _____
5. "Tim is hiding under the bed." (she / admit)
   _____
6. "I know who did it." (he / insist on)
   _____

Indirect questions

3 Read the indirect questions. Write the direct questions.

1. I wonder where the treasure is hidden.

   "Where is the treasure hidden?"

2. I don't know why he recommended telling her the secret.
   _____
3. Can you tell me why he said not to tell anyone?
   _____
4. I wonder if she asked why he did it.
   _____

4 Read the conversation. Rewrite the police officer's questions as indirect questions. Then rewrite the detective's answers as reported speech. Use the words in parentheses.

Detective: What was she doing when her bag was stolen?

Police officer: She was eating lunch.

Detective: Did she see anyone take it?

Police officer: No, she didn't.

Detective: Where was her bag sitting?

Police officer: It was hanging on the back of her chair.

1. **Detective:** *Can you tell me what she was doing*

   when her bag was stolen?

2. **Police officer:** _____ (said)
3. **Detective:** _____ (wonder)
4. **Police officer:** _____ (claimed)
5. **Detective:** _____ (tell)
6. **Police officer:** _____ (mention)

CONVERSATION — Confirming and denying

1. Put the words in the correct order to make sentences.

1. **A:** / is / invention / say / Richard Branson / that / people / interested in / Some / buying / your / !

   Some people say that Richard Branson is interested in buying your invention!

   B: absolutely / Yes, / !
   _____

3. **A:** / you / Is / were / attacked / true / by / a / it /shark / that / ?
   _____

   B: all / Not / at / !
   _____

5. **A:** your / profits / comment / on / you / Can / ?
   _____

   B: joking / must / You / be / !
   _____

2 Complete the conversation with the sentences from Exercise 1.

Dana: I'm interviewing Sam Logan. He invented a boat that you pedal and steer like a car. Sam, what was your inspiration for this invention?

Sam: I really like boats and bicycling. So I thought I'd put them together. I was surprised when it worked!

Dana: Sam has produced and sold about 125 of these so far. So, Sam, that seems like a lot to sell.
¹ _____

Sam: Well, Dana. They cost a lot to make, so really, I don't make much on each one. It's just fun for me.

Dana: ² _____ Is that true?

Sam: ³ _____
That's funny! I haven't heard from him. But if he does, I will make him a special one!

Dana: It seems like this could be dangerous.
⁴ _____

Sam: ⁵ _____
That's just a story someone made up! I've never seen any swimming out here. I think the vehicle is kind of large and would scare them.

Dana: Last question, can I take it for a spin?

Sam: ⁶ _____
Here, let me show you how to drive it . . .

READING TO WRITE

1 Complete the sentences with the correct phrases.

but I'd also   in order to   not only   so that

1. The thief had to be very quiet _____ not set off the alarms.

2. The thief lied _____ the detective wouldn't think he stole the jewelry.

3. "_____ did I know the thief was lying, _____ guessed where he hid the jewels," said the detective.

2 Complete the text with the phrases from Exercise 1.

MY SECRET

by Harry Sykes

I have a younger brother named Carl. When he was five and I was nine, we used to share the same bedroom. His bedtime was before mine. He would still sleep with his favorite teddy bear in those days. And every night, when I came to bed, I would place his other stuffed animals on his bed. ¹_____ would I put them in there, ²_____ dress them up in his clothing. I had to be very quiet ³_____ not wake him up.

Every morning, he'd wake up to find his stuffed animals wearing his clothing. He thought they got dressed during the night! Then I'd act surprised ⁴_____ he wouldn't suspect I did it. Finally, at breakfast, he'd tell my mother what clothes the toys were wearing. She thought he was making it all up! To this day, I've never admitted what I'd done.

3 Read the text again. Answer the questions.

1. What is the story about?

   _____

2. What is the background information?

   Who: _____

   Where: _____

   When: _____

3. What is the order of events?

   First: _____

   Next: _____

   Then: _____

   Last: _____

4. How does the story conclude?

   _____

REVIEW UNITS 7–8

1 Cross out the word that doesn't belong in each category.

1. **Preparing for a party:**
   ~~admit something~~   prepare special food
   dress up   put up decorations

2. **Celebrating:**
   write a report   have a good time
   hold a contest   set off fireworks

3. **Describing a party:**
   crowded   lively   reply   noisy

4. **Describing how people say things:**
   admit   claim   recommend   unsolved

2 Circle the correct words.

1. Juanita **admitted** / **claimed** to telling him about the surprise party.
2. Boris **mentioned** / **insisted** on driving us home after the celebration.
3. Luisa **agreed** / **wrote** to me that the party was a huge success.
4. Amy **agreed** / **told** to help me put up decorations before the party.
5. Ted **recommended** / **replied** to her question by email.

3 Write the quoted speech as reported speech. Use the words in parentheses.

1. Jill: "I told them about the contest." (claim)
   Jill claimed she told them about the contest.

2. Mark: "OK. I'll help you choose some music to play at the party." (agree)
   _____
   _____

3. Brandon: "You're coming to the party!" (insist)
   _____
   _____

4. Olga: "The food at the school festival was pretty good." (say)
   _____
   _____

5. Evan: "I saw them dancing at the party." (mention)
   _____
   _____

4 Complete the text with the correct words.

colorful	messy	~~traditional~~
crowded	noisy	unusual
lively	stunning	

Throw a Great Party!

We asked some teens for ideas on how to make your next party an event to remember. Here's what they said:

- **Alex:** ᵃFood is key to having a great event. Serve ¹ *traditional* foods, like sushi, but arrange them in an ² _____ way, for example, to look like a nature scene or a funny face the stranger the better! ᵇRemember to have napkins in case things get ³ _____!

- **Tracy:** ᶜPlay ⁴ _____ music to get people dancing! ᵈMove the furniture out of the way so the room doesn't feel ⁵ _____. You'll know everyone is having fun when it's so ⁶ _____ you have to talk loudly to be heard over the party!

- **Tom:** ᵉHold a contest! ᶠI really enjoy singing contests. Award a prize for the most ⁷ _____ performance. Or make it a costume party. Encourage people to get crazy with their costumes by offering a prize for the brightest and most ⁸ _____ costume.

5 Write the lettered sentences from the text in Activity 4 as reported speech.

a. Alex said *that food is key to having a great event.*
b. He also said that _____.
c. Tracy said to _____.
d. She also recommends _____.
e. Tom suggests _____.
f. He said that _____.

6 Complete the conversations. Use verb + *-ing* form or infinitive.

1. **A:** I don't know what to do for my birthday.
   B: I'd *consider having* (consider / have) a theme party.
2. **A:** I'm working on the invitation list for my wedding.
   B: Don't _____ (forget / send) them early.
3. **A:** I'm not sure where to have our company party.
   B: If you _____ (decide / have) the party at a restaurant, be sure to call early for a reservation.
4. **A:** I'm planning a karaoke party for my parents!
   B: Not everybody _____ (enjoy / sing) karaoke.
5. **A:** What did you get Jeff for his birthday?
   B: I _____ (try / get) him concert tickets, but they were sold out.

7 Correct the sentences.

1. Before ~~released~~ *releasing* the official report, the police wanted to make sure it was final.
2. When the detective will have all the facts, she'll reveal who committed the crime.
3. If you look at the map since you go, you won't get lost.
4. After to hide the prize money, the millionaire posted clues on his website so people could try to find it.
5. Jenna always reads the end of the mystery since she finishes the book.
6. Before they made the discovery, they shared their results with other scientists.

8 Complete the conversation.

am so	Not at all!	You must be joking!
Great idea!	That's such a	
~~Is it true that~~	Yes, absolutely!	

Erin: Hey, Russ. ¹ *Is it true that* you had a huge party last weekend?

Russ: ² _____
I was studying for my lifeguard test all weekend!

Erin: I was just kidding. But have you heard that I'm planning a big graduation party?

Russ: No way! ³ _____
How do you have time to plan a party with finals coming up?

Erin: I find the time because I want to do it! So get this, our whole class is invited. It'll be a three-day camping trip!

Russ: ⁴ _____
Camping is awesome.

Erin: I know. I
⁵ _____
excited. It's going to be at the lake. Can you be our lifeguard?

Russ: ⁶ _____.
I'd be happy to.
⁷ _____
great spot to camp.

Erin: Yeah!

Review 4 | **57**

9 Weird and Wonderful

VOCABULARY Story elements

1 Find seven more story element words.

O	X	W	G	Z	C	P	M	D	K	S	X	Q	T
B	Z	I	R	A	U	F	M	I	U	R	I	V	E
F	D	D	T	W	W	G	B	J	L	D	R	S	N
M	W	A	V	H	H	Q	V	C	F	S	J	E	D
R	F	O	G	V	L	G	O	F	W	E	I	X	I
M	A	I	N	C	H	A	R	A	C	T	E	R	N
P	Y	C	M	Z	V	Y	U	I	Z	T	T	C	G
E	B	Z	P	A	O	X	A	C	T	I	O	N	F
G	V	I	L	L	A	I	N	R	G	N	G	H	P
D	F	P	L	T	T	G	D	L	C	G	E	W	Q
B	H	G	K	X	Q	S	A	M	H	M	N	L	C
A	N	A	D	W	(P	L	O	T)	Y	B	I	D	K
L	U	O	E	H	E	R	O	M	G	I	Q	Q	R
H	L	W	S	U	S	P	E	N	S	E	K	C	B

2 Replace the underlined phrases with the words and phrases from Exercise 1. Some words will be used more than once.

1. Brenda thinks the *Harry Potter* movies do a good job of keeping the story the same and not changing the ~~things that happened~~. *plot*

2. The book series *Percy Jackson and the Olympians* is named after the <u>important person in the story</u>, Percy Jackson, so we know the books are about him.

3. When they made the movie *Jurassic Park*, they changed the <u>last part of the story</u> from how it was in the book.

4. Tim likes fantasy movies like *The Hobbit* because he likes the <u>place where and when the story happens</u>.

5. Darth Vader, President Coriolanus Snow, and the Joker, are all examples of the <u>bad person in a story</u>.

6. Luke Skywalker, Katniss Everdeen, and Batman are all examples of the <u>good person in a story</u>.

7. Angela wouldn't watch the movie *Jaws* because the <u>feeling of excitement when something is about to happen</u> was too much for her! She said it made her nervous.

8. *Indiana Jones and the Raiders of the Lost Ark* is one of Bill's favorite movies. He loves watching movies with a lot of <u>exciting things happening</u>.

3 Complete the sentences with your own information.

1. My favorite hero in a story is *Spider Man* because *I think it's cool the way he had to learn about power himself.*
   My favorite hero in a story is _____ because _____.

2. My favorite villain in a story is _____ because _____.

3. I don't like it when the main character is _____ because _____.

4. I liked the action in the story _____ because _____.

5. I think the story with the best setting is _____ because _____.

58 | Unit 9

GRAMMAR Third conditional

1 Write third conditional sentences with the information in the chart.

	Imaginary and untrue situation in the past	Impossible consequence
1.	Lesley / not save / the money	she / not buy / a car
2.	You / study	you / do better / on your test than me
3.	Carl / not hear / the noise	he / not lock / the door
4.	Karen and Cindy / not take / photos	no one / believe / their story
5.	Max / go / the beach	he / compete / the swimming contest
6.	I / be nice / to my coach	I / get / more help

1. *If Lesley hadn't saved the money, she wouldn't have bought a car.*

2. _____
3. _____
4. _____
5. _____
6. _____

2 Write the questions another way. Then answer the questions with your own information.

1. What would've happened if you had won a million dollars last year?

   Q: *If you had won a million dollars last year, what would've happened?*

   A: *I would have traveled around the world.*

2. What kind of movie would it have been if you had been in a movie?

   Q: _____
   A: _____

3. If you had helped a friend last year, who would you have helped?

   Q: _____
   A: _____

4. What celebrity would you have invited if you had had a big birthday party last year?

   Q: _____
   A: _____

5. If you had known what it would be like, what movie wouldn't you have watched?

   Q: _____
   A: _____

wish + past perfect

3 Put the words in the correct order to make sentences using *wish* + past perfect.

1. I / I / for / test / wish / studied / the / had / .

   I wish I had studied for the test.

2. gotten / I / sooner / had / wish / I / up / .

   _____

3. run / wishes / had / the / Mike / race / faster / he / in / .

   _____

4. gotten / Kim / had / she / wishes / concert / tickets / .

   _____

5. before / had / we / We / it / rained / left / wish / .

   _____

6. movie / hadn't / wish / heard / how / we / the / ended / We / .

   _____

VOCABULARY Linking phrases

1 Complete the sentences with a word or phrase from each box.

according	again
as a	course
in	fact
in	order to
of	result of
rather	than
so	that
then	to

1. Stephen King was signing books at the bookstore. _Of course_, I asked him to sign my copy of his book.
2. Jeanne moved to Hollywood _____ become a movie star.
3. Jonah thought it would be cool to see a ghost, but _____, maybe it wouldn't.
4. Leon could never get to the airport on time, so he bought his own plane _____ miss any more flights.
5. They held the wedding in secret _____ photographers wouldn't spoil their special day.
6. For a long time, Pluto was classified as a planet, when _____, it was really a "dwarf" planet.
7. _____ recent research, the Earth and Moon are 60 million years older than previously thought.
8. She's studied Chinese for years and _____ her studies, she speaks it very well now.

2 Put the words in the correct order to make sentences.

1. visit / most interesting / my friend Juan, / place / Macchu Picchu / According to / is / the / to / .
   According to my friend Juan, Macchu Picchu is the most interesting place to visit.

2. tomato / The / is considered a vegetable, / in / a fruit / fact, / it's / but / .
   _____.

3. formed / result / the hoodoos / of / As a / snow and rain, / were / .
   _____.

4. all / I / marine animals / love / . I / swim / with / Of / wouldn't / a shark / want to / course, / !
   _____
   _____

5. movie / video camera / in / to / make / order / John / is / buying / a / a / .
   _____

6. saved / she / money / could / that / Helen / go / college / to / so / .
   _____

7. than / we / a trip / Bryce Canyon, / Rather / took / there / about / just read / .
   _____

GRAMMAR Past modals of speculation

1 Read the sentences. Is the speaker sure or not sure? Check (✓) the correct columns.

	Sure	Not sure
1. Jorge must have been to Mexico City before.	✓	
2. His younger brother couldn't have learned to drive already.		
3. We may have been the first people to see the cave.		
4. Iris might have been at the dance last night.		
5. Henry must not have known that the show was canceled.		
6. They might not have seen this movie before.		

2 Match the statements with the correct speculations.

1. Liam wasn't home last night. __b__	a. He must have worked hard on it.
2. Tomás didn't go to the free concert last weekend. _____	b. He could have been at his grandmother's.
3. Albert didn't answer his phone. _____	c. He couldn't have completed all of the levels yet.
4. Erik's movie won the school video contest. _____	d. He might have turned it off.
5. Min-Jun got a new car. _____	e. He must not have known about it.
6. Eduard just got that new video game. _____	f. He must be so excited.

3 Complete the sentences. Use the modals in parentheses and *have* + past participle.

1. Anna was out in the rain. She _must not have brought_ (must not / bring) her umbrella.

2. Paul is tired today. He _____ (might / go) to bed late.

3. Joel didn't ride the roller coaster. He _____ (may / be) too scared.

4. Nicole's car has a flat tire. She _____ (could not / drive) to work today.

5. Alec didn't mention how his band's audition went. It _____ (may not / go) very well.

6. Jin-hee can't find her cat. But it _____ (might not / run) away.

4 Rewrite the sentences. Use the modals in parentheses and *have* + past participle.

1. Abby was worried about the test. (could)
   Abby could have been worried about the test.

2. They didn't eat dessert. (must not)
   _____

3. Greg went to the play by himself. (might)
   _____

4. We didn't get good seats in the theater. (could not)
   _____

5. Scientists know why the bees are dying. (must)
   _____

6. I lost my friend's necklace. (may)
   _____

CONVERSATION — Asking for more information

1. Put the words in the correct order to make sentences and questions.

1. about / Tell / me / it / .
   Tell me about it.

2. happened / What / next / ?
   _____

3. that / Why / was / ?
   _____

4. happened / what / So, / ?
   _____

5. what / next / brilliant / And / then / he / did / was / !
   _____

6. kind / of / what / business / Like / ?
   _____

2 Complete the conversation with the expressions from Exercise 1. More than one answer may be possible.

Jack: I read this really interesting story about Richard Branson last night.

Marnie: Richard Branson, the British businessman? The guy who started Virgin Airlines?
¹ *Tell me about it.*

Jack: Yeah, it's such an amazing story how he started an airline. He was in his late 20s and he had already started one business.

Marnie: ² _____

Jack: It was a business that sold records. He started it in 1972, and it was called Virgin Records. Anyway, one night, he was going to fly to the Virgin Islands in the Caribbean. But his flight was canceled. So he was stuck at the airport.

Marnie: ³ _____

Jack: Because there weren't any more flights that night. But he had to get to the Virgin Islands.

Marnie: ⁴ _____

Jack: He found a private plane that he could "charter," or rent. But he didn't have the money to charter it.

Marnie: ⁵ _____

Jack: He chartered the plane anyway!
⁶ _____
He made a sign that said "Virgin Airlines, $39." And he sold the other seats on the plane to the other passengers who would have been on his canceled flight. After that, he bought the plane!

READING TO WRITE

1 Complete Cesar's story with the adverbs in the box. Sometimes more than one answer is possible.

clearly	Luckily
~~Eventually~~	Obviously
finally	Suddenly
Finally	Unfortunately
fortunately	

The Robot Competition

by Cesar Guerrero

Last weekend, my friend Hiro and I entered a robot in my town's robot competition. We had worked on it for a year. [1] _Eventually_, it was ready to enter in the contest.

In the competition, each robot got a turn in front of the judges. You had to show what your robot could do. Hiro and I thought our robot was [2] _____ the best.

We waited and waited for our turn. The judges [3] _____ called our names. Hiro used the remote control to make our robot move. It walked, it spun, it punched. [4] _____, the robot did everything Hiro commanded it to do. Then I took the controls and made the robot dance. The robot [5] _____ did everything I wanted it to. [6] _____, we were very proud of our robot. When our turn was finished, Hiro and I thought we were going to win!

[7] _____, the judges couldn't decide! There was a tie between our robot and another robot. The judges made us perform one more time.

I took the controls and started to make the robot dance. [8] _____, the robot started to do different things. For several minutes, I tried to make it dance again, but it wouldn't respond to the controls. [9] _____, it rolled right off the table. Hiro and I lost the competition!

2 Read the story in Exercise 1 again. Look at the adverbs you wrote. Circle the words that show time, underline the words that show opinion, and put a box around the words that state a fact.

3 Read the story in Exercise 1 again. Circle the correct answers.

1. What happens first in the story?
   a. The boys enter their robot in a competition.
   b. The boys become judges.
   c. The boys learn how to make a robot.

2. When did the story happen?
   a. two years ago
   b. last month
   c. last weekend

3. Where did the story happen?
   a. at a robot competition
   b. at a robot club
   c. at a friend's house

4. What happened first?
   a. The robot suddenly stopped working.
   b. Cesar controlled the robot.
   c. The robot performed well.

5. What happened next?
   a. Cesar got mad at Hiro.
   b. Cesar broke the robot.
   c. The robot couldn't be controlled.

6. What happened at the end of the story?
   a. Cesar and Hiro won the competition.
   b. Cesar and Hiro lost the competition.
   c. Cesar and Hiro quit competing.

10 I Have To! I Can!

VOCABULARY Training and qualifications

1 Write the collocations. Use a word from each box.

application	course
application	degree
career	exam
college	experience
entrance	fees
training	form
work	path

1. You fill this out to get a job. **application form**

2. This program teaches you the skills you need to do a job. _____

3. You take this test to get into a college or university. _____

4. After you graduate from college, you earn one of these. _____

5. A summer job or internship to gain familiarity with the kind of career you want is this. _____

6. When you apply to get into colleges, you often have to pay these. _____

7. This is a series of steps leading to a desired job. _____

2 Write the phrases from Exercise 1 in the correct categories. Some may be used more than once.

1. **Things you needed to get into a college or university:**
   application form, _____, _____

2. **Things you might need to get a job:**
   _____, _____

3. **Things that can make up your career path:**
   _____, _____

3 Complete the sentences with some of the phrases from Exercise 1.

1. Miranda had to report all her grades and test scores as part of her _____.

2. Dean was surprised that he had to take an _____ for his local college.

3. Nadine knew that gaining _____ in local politics would look good on her résumé.

4. Kim decided not to pursue a _____ and instead started her own company. She wanted to follow a different _____ from her friends.

5. Genevieve was surprised that the _____ _____ required to become a veterinary technician was almost as long as getting a college degree.

6. Joel only applied to his top-three universities because he didn't want to pay any additional _____.

4 Answer the questions with your own information.

1. Do you want to get a college degree or go through a training course? Why?
   _____
   _____

2. What kind of work experience do you need for your career path?
   _____

3. What do you think of entrance exams?
   _____

4. Have you ever paid application fees?
   _____

GRAMMAR Past ability

1 Circle the correct words. Then match the questions with the correct responses.

1. **Could** / **Did** he **able to read** / **read** when he was three? _c_
2. **Was** / **Were** she **able to** / **managed to** take the entrance exam last weekend? ___
3. How **did** / **was** he **could** / **manage** to graduate from high school early? ___
4. What **could** / **managed** she **do** / **to do** at 12? ___
5. **Could** / **Did** he **able to** / **manage to** get the job? ___

a. He **could** / **managed to take** extra classes.
b. She **could** / **able to** speak Russian.
c. Yes, he **able to read** / **could read** simple books.
d. No, he **didn't** / **wasn't**. He didn't have enough work experience.
e. Yes, she **was** / **were**.

2 Put the words in the correct order to make sentences and questions.

1. college / you / summer / money / manage / to / enough / for / save / Did / this / ?

   Did you manage to save enough money for college this summer?

2. when / Karen / was / 18, / drive / couldn't / she / .

   _____

3. Cambridge / able / Yuri / to / How / get / accepted / to / was / ?

   _____

4. concert / didn't / manage / win / We / tickets / the / to / to / .

   _____

5. could / she / How / many / play / Nina / was / instruments / five / when / ?

   _____

6. the / they / to / at / able / conference / were / What / learn / ?

   _____

3 Look at Michael's activities. Complete questions about his past abilities using could (not), was/were able to, and managed to. Then answer the questions.

played music (five instruments)	at age 10
earned money by making digital music and DJing; bought a car	at age 16
played at a famous music festival	one summer while still in school
studied music at a local college; created a music app for smartphones in spare time	after graduating from high school

1. ___Could___ Michael ___play music___ when he was young?

   Yes, he could play five instruments.

2. How _____ he _____ buy a car at age 16?

   _____

3. What _____ he _____ one summer while he was still in school?

   _____

4. _____ he _____ study music after graduating from high school?

   _____

5. How _____ he _____ create a music app while studying music in college?

   _____

4 Answer the questions with your own information.

1. Could you drive when you were 10?

   _____

2. What could you do when you were nine?

   _____

3. Could you speak English very well last year?

   _____

4. What is the most difficult thing you've done? How did you manage to do it?

   _____

VOCABULARY Jobs

1 Look at the pictures and complete the crossword.

across
5.
7.
9.

down
1.
2.
3.
4.
6.
8.

2 Circle the correct answers.

1. Getting a law degree might be good for a career as **an athlete / a chef /(a politician.**
2. My cousin is interested in law. He thinks he wants to be a **babysitter / designer / police officer**.
3. Miho loves shopping and clothes. She should just get a job as a **babysitter / politician / salesperson**.
4. Andy has worked at many restaurants over the years. Eventually, he became the head **chef / designer / musician** at a fancy restaurant.
5. When my sister turns 13, she wants to start to work as a **babysitter / police officer / politician**.
6. Arun is creative and has great style. He wants to be **an athlete / a designer / a police officer**.
7. Nancy is great at skiing. She hopes to become a professional **athlete / artist / salesperson.**
8. Graham got a job with the symphony as a **babysitter / musician / politician**. Instead of an entrance exam, he had to perform a solo.
9. My friend is a successful **artist / chef / salesperson**. You can see her work in the museum.

3 Answer the questions with words from Exercise 1 and your own ideas.

1. Which jobs might active people enjoy?
   _____
   _____

2. Which jobs might creative people enjoy?
   _____

3. Which jobs might people who like to work with other people enjoy?
   _____

4. Name a famous person for four different jobs:

Job	Name
Athlete	Cristiano Ronaldo

66 | Unit 10

GRAMMAR Modal expressions for past and future

1 Match the questions with the answers.

1. Will you need a degree to be a politician? _e_	a. I'll need to take it by next November.
2. When will you need to take the entrance exam? ___	b. I had to talk to the manager and the owner of the company.
3. How often did you need to practice? ___	c. Yes, I will. But only for the first year.
4. Who did you have to talk to? ___	d. No, I didn't. But there was a fee to take the entrance exam.
5. Will you need to work on weekends? ___	e. No, I won't. But it would help.
6. Did you have to pay an application fee? ___	f. I needed to practice every day.

2 Circle the correct words.

Tara: Hi, Dan. Thanks for answering my questions about medical school. ¹**Did / Had** you ²**have to need / need to take** special classes in college before medical school?

Dan: Yes, I ³**did / had**. Everyone has to take pre-med. It's hard! It's a lot of chemistry, for one thing.

Tara: I've heard that. And what ⁴**did / would** you ⁵**have / have to do** to apply to medical school?

Dan: I ⁶**had to take / would take** the entrance exam. There's a special one for medical school. It's really hard.

Tara: Yeah? And what science classes ⁷**need / will** you ⁸**to take / have to take** when school starts in the fall?

Dan: I ⁹**will have to take / won't have to take** any!

Tara: What? Why?

Dan: Didn't my mom tell you? I got an offer from a soccer league! I can't turn that down! Looks like I ¹⁰**need to be / won't have to be** working on my soccer skills instead!

make and let

3 Complete the sentences with the correct form of _make_ or _let_.

1. Our English teacher ____made____ us give speeches so we would be comfortable talking to people.

2. I offered to help, but my parents won't _____ me work at their shop. They want me to spend my time doing homework instead.

3. Sometimes I _____ my friends influence my opinions too much.

4. Tim's school _____ everyone wear uniforms, except on Fridays, when the school _____ students wear what they want.

5. I can't believe Ian _____ you cut his hair! How did you talk him into it?

6. That news program didn't _____ me very happy.

4 Answer the questions with your own information.

1. What is something your teacher makes you do?
   My teacher makes me rewrite every paper.

2. What is something parents usually make their young children do?
   _____

3. What is something you have to make yourself do?
   _____

4. What do your friend's parents let him or her do?
   _____

5. What is something your parents will let you do when you're older?
   _____

6. What do you wish your school would let you do?
   _____

CONVERSATION: Making decisions

1 Match the phrases to make sentences.

1. How about _c_
2. Why ___
3. I've made up ___
4. That depends on ___
5. Ben might change his mind ___
6. Although, on second thought, ___

a. maybe we should make them see each other.
b. about coming on the hike.
c. going on a hike with him?
d. my mind.
e. the weather.
f. not?

2 Complete the conversation with the sentences from Exercise 1.

Doris: What should we do this weekend?

Frank: Ben is around this weekend. ¹ _How about going on a hike with him?_

Doris: ² _____
I heard it might rain. Also, I'm not sure about letting Ben coming with us.

Frank: ³ _____

Doris: Well, I told Sophia she could do something with us this weekend.

Frank: Oh, right. If Sophia's coming, ⁴ _____.

Doris: Yeah, he might. ⁵ _____ Then they'd have to get along.

Frank: I'm not sure that's a good idea.

Doris: You know what? ⁶ _____ I think we should have a big party. Then everyone will *have* to get along.

Frank: That might work.

Doris: Yeah, and if it doesn't, it might be interesting anyways!

68 | Unit 10

READING TO WRITE

1 Complete the sentences with *either . . . or* or *neither . . . nor*.

1. Jenny doesn't like peanut butter. And she doesn't like jelly.

   Jenny likes _____ peanut butter _____ jelly.

2. Misha wants to learn to play the violin. But if he can't play that, he'd be happy with piano.

   Misha wants to play _____ the violin _____ the piano.

2 Read the text. Then rewrite the underlined sentences using *either . . . or* or *neither . . . nor*.

Do you know Ella Marija Lani Yelich-O'Connor? Here's a hint: ¹She is not an actor. She is not a fashion designer. She's a singer. ²She is not from Australia. And she is not from the U.K. She's from New Zealand. She's under 25. Her stage name is one word. Guessed it yet?

If you guessed the pop singer Lorde, you're correct!

Lorde was interested in performing as a young girl. She was in drama school at the age of five. Her mother let her read all kinds of books as a child. When she was 13, her band won the school's talent show. When she was 15, she took singing lessons twice a week and also began writing songs. Eventually, she released a record, and the single "Royals" became a number-one hit in the United States in 2012, making Lorde the youngest singer to do that since 1988. Her debut album from 2013 was nominated for a Grammy Award. "Tennis Court" and "Glory and Gore" were hit songs from that album. She has also written songs for the *Hunger Games* movies soundtrack.

How does she sound? She doesn't play any instruments, so she uses her voice to carry the story of her songs. ³So you could call her voice intriguing. Some says it's mysterious. What type of music is it? ⁴I'd say her music is pop. Or it's electro. In 2013, *Time* magazine named her one of the most influential teenagers in the world. We can't wait to hear more from her!

1. _____
2. _____
3. _____
4. _____

3 Read the text again. Answer the questions.

1. What is Lorde's real name?

   _____

2. Where is she from?

   _____

3. What type of music does she play?

   _____

4. When and how did she start?

   _____

5. What are some of her hit songs?

   _____

6. What are some interesting facts about her?

   _____

REVIEW UNITS 9–10

1 Look at the pictures and complete the puzzle. Then use the words in grey to solve the riddle.

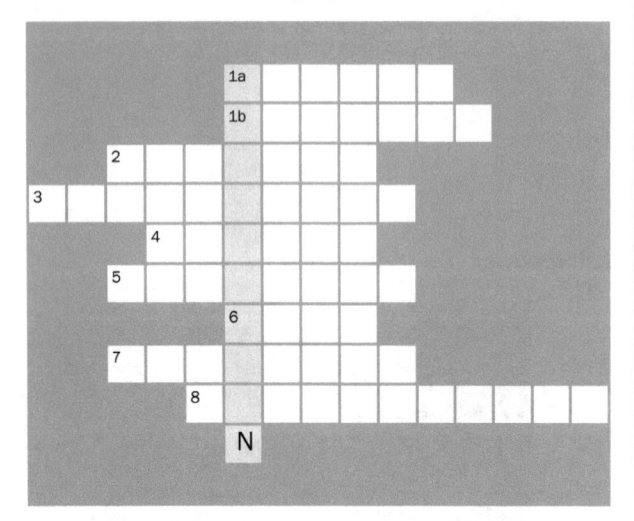

I am not an athlete, but I have to "run" for office. What job do I have?

1a. and 1b. (two words). _____

2. _____
3. _____
4. _____
5. _____
6. _____
7. _____
8. _____

2 Put the words in the correct order to make sentences.

1. have / Soren / to / entrance / take / Did / an / exam / ?

   _____

2. work / get / did / need / you / experience / to / What / ?

   _____

3. will / take / Jun Hee / When / training / to / have / the / course / ?

   _____

4. application / Kelly / had / forms / to / fill / seven / out / .

   _____

5. degree / have / college / to / Will / earn / a / Josh / ?

   _____

6. didn't / I / to / path / on / need / a / career / decide / .

   _____

3 Complete the sentences with the correct forms of *let* or *make*.

1. Our boss doesn't _____ us fill out time sheets.
2. That training course we took last month _____ us see police officers in a new way.
3. My parents won't _____ me drive until I'm 18!
4. My parents _____ me play computer games as often as I like, as long as my grades are good.

4 Complete the article with the correct words.

According to	In fact
~~as a result of~~	Rather than
in order to	so that

Hope LeVin

Who is Hope LeVin? She's a professional athlete. She grew up in the Turks and Caicos Islands in the Caribbean. She used to watch kiteboarders on the beach when she was growing up.

When she was 11, someone asked her if she'd like to learn how. She said yes, and ¹ *as a result* of that decision, she grew up to become a professional kiteboarder! ² _____ being an overnight success, Hope had to work hard for many years. She kited every day, but for the first couple of months, she could only ride in one direction. She kept practicing ³ _____, eventually, she could ride in both directions. ⁴ _____ Hope, you have to be really patient ⁵ _____ learn kiteboarding.

In 2013, she entered a kiteboarding competition in the Dominican Republic. She didn't expect to do well, but ⁶ _____, she managed to win second place! That was when she decided to turn pro.

When Hope isn't kiting, competing, or spreading the word of kiteboarding, she's studying for a long-distance degree in economics. That's Hope LeVin, flying high!

5 Circle the correct words.

Lois: Hi Emi! Did you hear what happened to Carl?

Emi: No, ¹(tell me about it) / like what?

Lois: He went to the city and tried out for that reality show for musicians.

Emi: That's great! ²**So, what happened? / In fact?**

Lois: Well, he wasn't going to audition at all. But his friend Dylan, who's in his band, got him to ³ **on second thought / change his mind**. So he went along with Dylan to the audition. He was thinking, ⁴"**Why was that / Why not** give it a try?" But then he said he almost didn't go through with it.

Emi: ⁵**On second thought. / Why was that?**

Lois: He said when they got there, there was only one spot left to audition. Dylan wanted it. And so did a bunch of other kids. They were all standing in line waiting to be chosen. So Carl ⁶**made up his mind / that depends on** that he'd let Dylan have the spot. And he went off to the side and just started listening to his headphones and dancing and singing to himself.

Emi: ⁷**And then what happened? / Like what?**

Lois: Well, one of the show's producers saw him dancing and singing to himself and she came over to him. She said, "⁸**How about / That depends on** if you take the last spot to audition?"

Emi: Oh my gosh! What did he do?

Lois: He said he looked over at Dylan and Dylan encouraged him, so he said yes! He's going to be on the show!

6 Read the conversation in Exercise 5 again. Imagine that Carl's audition was really a short story that Lois wrote. Answer the questions.

1. Who is the main character of the story?
   _____

2. What is the setting of the story?
   _____

3. In the story, was Dylan a hero, a villain, or neither? Why?
   _____

4. What was the plot of the story?
   _____
   _____

5. What happened at the end of the story?
   _____
   _____

7 Complete the sentences about Exercise 5. Use the words in parentheses to make the third conditional or past modals of speculation.

1. If Dylan hadn't invited him, Carl *wouldn't have gone to the audition*. (go /audition)

2. If Carl had stayed in line, _____. (might not / choose)

3. If Carl hadn't been singing and dancing on the side, the producer _____. (may not / notice)

4. But if Carl had stayed in line, he _____. (could not / be seen)

5. I bet Dylan _____ he _____ in line. (wish / had not / stay)

6. I wonder if Dylan _____ he _____ Carl to come to the audition! (wish / had not / ask)

Real or FAKE?

Unit 1 Video 1.1

BEFORE YOU WATCH

1 Answer these questions about how you use the Internet.

1. What websites do you use to get information? Name two. _____

2. Can you tell if a digital photo has been edited? How? _____

WHILE YOU WATCH

2 Watch the video. Are the sentences true (*T*) or false (*F*)? Correct the false sentences.

1. Until recently, people got most of their information from books. _____

2. In the past, it was easy to share visual information with a lot of people. _____

3. Today, anyone can claim to be an expert. _____

4. It's very easy now to manipulate visual information. _____

5. Only experts can decide if something is real or fake. _____

3 Watch the video again. Complete the sentences with the words you hear.

1. It used to take a lot of time and _____ to share information with a lot of people.

2. Books were usually _____ by _____.

3. But can you believe everything you _____ or _____?

4. They are controlling the _____ so you will _____ their product.

5. You just have to _____ attention and not _____ everything you see or read.

AFTER YOU WATCH

4 Work with a partner. Think about where you get your information. Do you trust what you read? Why or why not?

> I go on Wikipedia sometimes to research historical events. But I know that anyone can post on Wikipedia, so I always check another source.

Milan's FASHION WEEK

Unit 1 Video 1.3

BEFORE YOU WATCH

1 Look at the pictures and the sentences from the video. Complete the sentences with the correct words, then match the sentences to the pictures.

a.   b.   c.

make-up   patterns   photographers

1. Lots of _____ come to Milan for Fashion Week. _____

2. The designer Missoni is famous for his bold _____. _____

3. It takes hours to do each model's hair and _____! _____

WHILE YOU WATCH

2 Watch the video. Are the sentences true (*T*) or false (*F*)? Correct the false sentences.

1. The blogger got a chance to go to Milan recently. _____

2. Missoni often uses bright colors in his designs. _____

3. The blogger thinks it would be cool to be a model. _____

4. A lot of the models had long hair. _____

5. There was a big dinner after the show. _____

3 Watch the video again. Answer the questions.

1. What does the blogger call Milan? _____

2. Who is one of the blogger's favorite designers? _____

3. Why is there a lot of waiting around before the show? _____

4. What does the blogger not have patience for? _____

5. What do the models do at the end of the show? _____

AFTER YOU WATCH

4 Work in small groups. Discuss how fashions have changed in the past five years. What were styles you used to think were cool, but now you'd never wear?

> A few years ago, I used to wear really baggy jeans and big hats. I thought hoodies in really bright colors were cool – but not anymore!

Born to DIVE

Unit 2 Video 2.1

BEFORE YOU WATCH

1 Look at these pictures from the video of a free diver. Do you think the statements are true (*T*) or false (*F*)?

1. Free divers dive underwater on one breath of air. _____
2. Some professional free divers use equipment to help them breathe underwater. _____
3. Some free divers can stay underwater for three minutes or longer. _____

WHILE YOU WATCH

2 Watch the video. Circle the correct answers.

1. Which adjective best describes Michele?
   a. shy   b. determined   c. impatient
2. To become a professional diver, Michele must dive to a depth of more than _____ meters.
   a. 45   b. 50   c. 55
3. Michele's parents are _____ him.
   a. worried about   b. angry with   c. afraid of
4. Michele says his mother _____ what he does.
   a. is happy about   b. doesn't understand   c. doesn't like
5. Michele reaches _____ meters in the competition.
   a. 57   b. 67   c. 47

3 Watch the video again. Check (✓) the sentences you hear.

1. ❑ Fear is something you don't need.
2. ❑ I'm not scared because I know my limits.
3. ❑ On the day of the championship, there are big crowds.
4. ❑ He dives deep very fast.
5. ❑ His dream has finally come true!

AFTER YOU WATCH

4 Work with a partner. Discuss: Do you know anyone who has hurt themselves doing a sport? What happened?

> Well, my brother broke his leg skiing a few years ago. He was going down a hill, and he hit a tree.

Shanghai HEIGHTS

Unit 2 Video 2.3

BEFORE YOU WATCH

1 Look at this picture from the video. Answer the questions.

1. Where is this man and what is he doing? _____

2. Would you like to have his job? Why or why not? _____

WHILE YOU WATCH

2 Watch the video. Match the phrases to make true sentences.

1. Many people come to Shanghai _____
2. Sun Feng cleans the windows _____
3. He has not seen his family _____
4. He travels to his village _____
5. He is very happy _____

a. for months.
b. to hold his daughter.
c. by train.
d. to find jobs.
e. of tall buildings.

3 Watch the video again. Answer the questions.

1. Why did Sun Feng move to Shanghai? _____
2. What does he say is the worst thing about the job? _____
3. How did he feel the first time he did the job? _____
4. What does he bring home for everyone? _____
5. What does he give his father at dinner? _____

AFTER YOU WATCH

4 Work in small groups. Discuss: Would you ever take a job far from home? What kind of job would that be?

> Yes, I would. I would take a job that was really interesting and paid a lot of money. I'd also like to live in another country.

What A WASTE!

Unit 3 Video 3.1

BEFORE YOU WATCH

1 Look at these pictures from the video. Answer the questions.

1. What do you think is going to happen to these old computers? _____

2. The picture on the right is of a *landfill* – a large trash site. What do you think the people are doing there?
   _____

WHILE YOU WATCH

2 Watch the video. Answer the questions.

1. What is the first example of things we throw away each year? _____
2. How many cell phones do Americans throw away each day? _____
3. How many kilos of oil does it take to make one computer screen? _____
4. What could we do with our old computers? _____
5. What kind of phone is much cheaper than a new one? _____

3 Watch the video again. Circle the words you hear.

BILL NYE: What is e-waste?

MAN 1: Um, waste . . . **electricity / electric** that's wasted?

WOMAN 1: E-waste? **Ecology / Ecological** waste or something?

BILL NYE: Do you know what e-waste is?

WOMAN 2: Oh, maybe it's the **economic / economical** waste. Maybe like from the economy?

MAN 2: **Environment / Environmental** waste?

AFTER YOU WATCH

4 Work with a partner. Make a list of all your electronic devices. What will you do with them when they get old? Think of ways you could reduce your personal e-waste.

Device	To do
cell phone	donate to a charity
printer	return to manufacturer to recycle

76 | Unit 3

Mission: POSSIBLE?

Unit 3 Video 3.3

BEFORE YOU WATCH

1 Read the sentences. Write the letter of the correct definition of the underlined words.

1. Will <u>astronauts</u> ever travel to Mars? ____
2. Some people feel <u>motion sickness</u> when they try to read in a car. ____
3. Many emergency vehicles have <u>flashing</u> lights to warn people of danger. ____

a. something that appears quickly or suddenly
b. a person who travels in a spacecraft to outer space
c. a type of nausea

WHILE YOU WATCH

2 Watch the video. Are the sentences true (*T*) or false (*F*)? Correct the false sentences.

1. Scientists have mastered time travel. _____
2. Traveling in space makes some astronauts sick. _____
3. The professor invented special books for astronauts to read. _____
4. One woman wore normal, clear glasses. _____
5. The woman with the flashing glasses felt good. _____

3 Watch the video again. Answer the questions.

1. What do many astronauts suffer from? _____
2. What was unusual about the eyes of the one astronaut? _____
3. What was the difference between the glasses the two women wore?
   _____
4. What were the women doing in the car? _____
5. Which woman became sick? _____

AFTER YOU WATCH

4 Work in small groups. Discuss: Do you think humans will travel to other planets in your lifetime? Where will they go first? Would you want to travel in space?

> I think humans will go to Mars in my lifetime. Yes, I would want to travel in space, but it could be scary.

The ORIGIN OF ARGAN OIL

Unit 4 Video 4.1

BEFORE YOU WATCH

1 Look at the picture from the video. Answer the questions.

1. Where are these goats and what are they doing? _____

2. What are some foods we get from goats? _____

WHILE YOU WATCH

2 Watch the video. Answer the questions.

1. What is strange about the argan trees? _____

2. What are the goats doing? _____

3. What colors are the goats? _____

4. What do people make argan oil from? _____

5. What do people use argan oil for? _____

3 Watch the video again. Put the steps of making argan oil in order.

1. First, _____   a. women roast the argan seeds over a fire.

2. Then, _____   b. they make a paste from the seeds.

3. Then, _____   c. goats eat argan fruit from a tree.

4. Next, _____   d. the women make a delicate oil.

5. Finally, _____   e. the argan fruit passes through the goats' bodies.

AFTER YOU WATCH

4 Work with a partner. Make a list of at least three animals and what humans get from them.

Animal	Product
goat	milk
	cheese
	meat
	leather

Fruits of the SEA

Unit 4 Video 4.3

BEFORE YOU WATCH

1 **Look at these pictures from the video. Complete the sentences with the correct words.**

| good | islands | protein | seafood |

Japan is a group of [1]_____ surrounded by the sea. People here eat a lot of [2]_____.
Fish is very [3]_____ for you. It's full of [4]_____ and vitamins. Fishing is essential to life in these islands.

WHILE YOU WATCH

2 **Watch the video. Circle the correct words.**

1. In the first half of the video, most of the people are **young / old**.

2. Japanese people eat **10 percent / 10 tons** of all the fish caught in the world.

3. Fishermen catch squid **at night / in the morning**.

4. One of the most popular fish in Japan is the **abalone / bluefin tuna**.

5. Every day, over **40,000 / 400,000** buyers come to the Tokyo fish market.

3 **Watch the video again. Check (✔) the sentences you hear.**

1. ❑ Rich water. Water that is full of fish.

2. ❑ Life expectancy here is over 80 years old.

3. ❑ Further in, you can find squid.

4. ❑ Bluefin tuna swim in the deep waters of northern Japan.

5. ❑ There's no question of Japan's love for the sea.

AFTER YOU WATCH

4 **Work in small groups. Discuss: Do you eat a lot of seafood? What are your favorite types? If you don't eat seafood, what are other sources of protein in your diet?**

> I eat seafood about once a week. My favorite is shrimp. I also like fried fish.

A COOL EXPERIMENT

Unit 5 Video 5.1

BEFORE YOU WATCH

1 **Look at this graphic of global warming from the video. Do you think the sentences are true (T) or false (F)?**

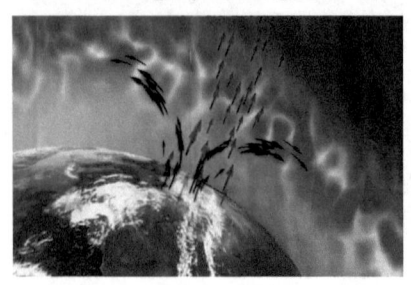

   1. Many scientists say temperatures around the world are rising. _____
   2. Greenhouse gases such as CO_2 and methane cool the Earth's environment. _____
   3. Humans produce greenhouse gases. _____

WHILE YOU WATCH

2 **Watch the video. Complete the sentences.**

   1. Eric is going to build _____ greenhouses, each with an _____ statue.
   2. He's going to fill _____ of the greenhouses with _____ air.
   3. Each box will receive the same _____ of _____.
   4. Computers will monitor the amount of _____ in the _____.
   5. Eric _____ to be part of the _____.

3 **Watch the video again. Circle any wrong words. Write the correct words on the lines.**

   Ex.: First, he looked at the (scientist) behind it. _____science_____

   1. Each box must be the same. _____
   2. He'll fill one box with CO_2, two with methane, and one with normal air. _____
   3. They'll need special machines to make the ice boxes. _____
   4. After four-and-a-half hours, the ice statues start to melt! _____
   5. Methane and CO_2 are major culprits for global warming. _____

AFTER YOU WATCH

4 **Work in small groups. Discuss: Do temperatures seem to be rising where you live? Are there more storms and floods where you live than there were several years ago?**

> I'm not sure. I think temperatures are a little warmer. We did have two big storms last year. My aunt's house was flooded.

Trendsetters

Unit 5 Video 5.3

BEFORE YOU WATCH

1. **Look at these pictures from the video and read the definition. Then answer the question.**

   Trendsetter /'trend' setər/ (noun)
   a person, organization, etc., that starts to do something that others then copy

   These girls are *trendsetters* in Japan. Think of a recent trend in your school. How and where did it start?
   _____

WHILE YOU WATCH

2. **Watch the video. Circle the correct adverbs.**

   1. In Japan, trends are **nearly / really** vital.
   2. The opinions of trendsetters are **slightly / extremely** important to companies.
   3. The girls are **absolutely / somewhat** impressed by the video booth.
   4. They think that the photo booth is **pretty / slightly** easier to use.
   5. The girls are **very / hardly** excited to meet their friends.

3. **Watch the video again. Answer the questions.**

   1. Where do the two girls live? _____
   2. What do companies in Japan want to know? _____
   3. What are the girls testing today? _____
   4. Which booth do the girls prefer? _____
   5. Why do companies care what Saeko and Yuko think about new products?
      _____

AFTER YOU WATCH

4. **Work with a partner. Make an advertisement for a new trend, such as a new style of shoes or a new smart device. Include graphics and text. Share your advertisement with the class.**

Survival OBJECTS

Unit 6 Video 6.1

BEFORE YOU WATCH

1 Look at the pictures from the video and read the sentences. Write the letter of the correct definition of each underlined word.

1. The man fills his <u>parachute</u> with snow so he doesn't fall down the mountains. _____
2. He sleeps in a <u>cave</u> in the snow. _____
3. There can be <u>cracks</u> in the ice beneath the deep snow that are very dangerous. _____

a. a piece of equipment that allows a person to fall slowly through the air when dropped from an aircraft
b. a very narrow break or opening in something
c. a large hole in the ground or in a hill

WHILE YOU WATCH

2 Watch the video. Answer the questions.

1. Why does Bear have to be careful in the beginning of the video? _____
2. How does he make his snow cave? _____
3. How does he get water to drink? _____
4. How does he stay warm at night? _____
5. What does he have to do in the morning to find food and keep warm?
_____

3 Watch the video again. Are the sentences true (*T*) or false (*F*)? Correct the false sentences.

1. Bear uses his backpack to dig in the snow. _____
2. During the night, Bear gets covered with water. _____
3. In the morning, there's nothing to eat. _____
4. In the trees, he finds fruit to eat. _____
5. The tea he makes has a lot of orange juice. _____

AFTER YOU WATCH

4 Work with a partner. Imagine that there is a fire in your home. You must leave in five minutes. What three things would you take with you?

> I'd definitely take my cat. And my phone . . . and my iPad!

The START OF THE WEB

Unit 6 Video 6.3

BEFORE YOU WATCH

1 Write sentences using at least three of the words below.

cell phone   message   network   text   web   wireless

1. _____
2. _____
3. _____

WHILE YOU WATCH

2 Watch the video. Answer the questions.

1. In the early days, where did most people use the Internet? _____

2. What did computers look like in the 1960s? _____

3. Who used computers in the 1960s? _____

4. When was the first email sent? _____

5. How did computers change in the 1980s and 1990s? _____

3 Watch the video again. Are the sentences true (*T*) or false (*F*)? Correct the false sentences.

1. Computers have always communicated with each other. _____

2. ARPANET was one of the first computer networks. _____

3. Computer networks have become smaller and cheaper. _____

4. Web pages and chat rooms became popular in the 1960s. _____

5. We can expect the Internet to continue growing. _____

AFTER YOU WATCH

4 Work in small groups. Complete the chart. Discuss: What websites did you like two years ago? What websites do you like now?

Websites I liked two years ago	Websites I like now
Facebook	*Tumblr*

Unit 6 | 83

Let's CELEBRATE

Unit 7 Video 7.1

BEFORE YOU WATCH

1 Look at the picture from the video. Answer the question.

This is a celebration in China. What festivals or holidays do people celebrate with fireworks in your country?
_____

WHILE YOU WATCH

2 Watch the video. Complete the phrases with the name of the correct country, then match them with phrases a–d to make true sentences.

1. People in ____China____ celebrate New Year's by ____
2. In winter, many people in _____ like to ____
3. In _____, spring is a time for ____
4. Autumn in _____ is when people celebrate ____

a. swim in outdoor pools.
b. Diwali.
c. watching cherry blossoms and picnicking.
d. lighting fireworks.

3 Watch the video again. Complete the sentences with the words you hear.

1. People all over the world enjoy celebrating the changing _____.
2. In China, _____ marks the beginning of a _____.
3. It's a time for visiting _____ and _____.
4. In Japan, _____ is the time of renewal.
5. In India, it's Diwali – the festival of _____ and the beginning of a _____ year.

AFTER YOU WATCH

4 Work in small groups. Discuss: How do you mark the changing of seasons? Do you wear different clothes, eat different foods, or do different things in each season?

> In the summer, I wear shorts and T-shirts and I go swimming almost every day. In the winter, I stay inside!

84 | Unit 7

Like FATHER, LIKE DAUGHTER

Unit 7 Video 7.3

BEFORE YOU WATCH

1 **Look at the picture from the video. Answer the questions.**

What is this person doing? Where do you think he is? _____

WHILE YOU WATCH

2 **Watch the video. Circle the correct words to complete the sentences.**

1. The first cliff divers were **fishermen / boaters**.

2. For nearly **88 / 80** years, only men were cliff divers.

3. José Luis is called "The Knife" because his dives are so **strong / precise**.

4. Iris's mother says that **diving / school** is first.

5. Before she dives, Iris feels **nervous / peaceful**.

3 **Watch the video again. Answer the questions.**

1. What is Acapulco famous for? _____

2. What did the fishermen challenge each other to do? _____

3. What tradition is Iris ready to change? _____

4. When does Iris practice diving? _____

5. How high is Iris's dive today? _____

AFTER YOU WATCH

4 **Work with a partner. Discuss: What sports used to be only for men, but now are for women, too? What sports still do not include women?**

> Soccer and basketball used to be only for men. I don't think there are any women playing football …

Unit 7 | 85

A LOST CIVILIZATION

Unit 8 Video 8.1

BEFORE YOU WATCH

1 **Look at the pictures from the video and read the definitions. Complete the sentences with the correct words.**

1. A worker removes a body from a _____ in the desert.

2. This _____ had been _____ for more than 700 years.

3. They found _____ such as this gold pitcher in the graves.

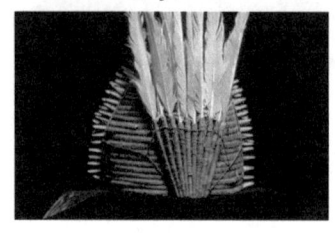

4. Some of the hats they found had the feathers of _____ birds.

artifacts: objects that were made by people long ago
grave: a place where a dead person is buried
mummy: a dead body that has been preserved
preserved: kept from decay; kept in its original condition
tropical: from the tropics (the hottest area on Earth)

WHILE YOU WATCH

2 **Watch the video. Circle the correct words.**

1. The Atacama Desert is next to the **Atlantic / Pacific** Ocean.
2. The bodies were preserved by the dry, **salty / heavy** sand.
3. Today there are **a few / no** buildings in the area.
4. Many graves had one or two **human / animal** heads.
5. The Amazon Forest is **near / far from** the Atacama Desert.

3 **Watch the video again. Answer the questions.**

1. What did workers discover in Peru about 15 years ago? _____
2. When did the Chiribaya live in the Ilo Valley? _____
3. How many people probably lived there? _____
4. Where did they get wool for their clothes? _____
5. Where might the tropical feathers have come from? _____

AFTER YOU WATCH

4 **What do you think life was like where you live 2,000 years ago? How many people lived there? What animals and plants lived there? Draw a picture, and then describe it to a partner.**

> So, 2,000 ago, about 1,000 people lived here. There were rabbits and bears and chickens. There were more trees and plants.

Mysteries OF THE BRAIN

Unit 8 Video 8.3

BEFORE YOU WATCH

1 Look at this picture from the video. Do you think the statements are true (*T*) or false (*F*)?

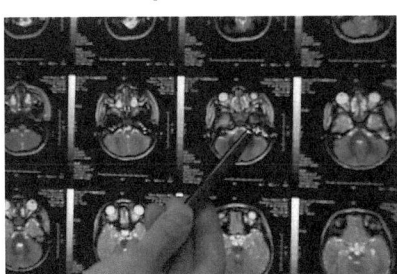

1. Scientists now understand how the brain works. _____
2. When something goes wrong with the brain, scientists can predict what will happen. _____
3. Each part of your brain has a different job. _____

WHILE YOU WATCH

2 Watch the video. Match the phrases to make true sentences.

1. When Michael was 10, he _____
2. A few years later, scientists _____
3. They found that not all parts of his brain _____
4. Dr. Jill Taylor's brain _____
5. After she was in the hospital, Jill _____

a. was damaged.
b. became interested in art.
c. were advanced.
d. graduated from college.
e. studied his brain.

3 Watch the video again. Correct the mistake in the sentences.

1. We can do amazing things when our mind and ~~hands~~ work together. _____ *body*
2. Michael does very well answering the doctors' questions about words and faces. _____
3. We know that the same parts of the brain control how we think and feel. _____
4. Dr. Jill Bolte Taylor was doing research on the human body. _____
5. We don't have many unanswered questions about the brain. _____

AFTER YOU WATCH

4 Work with a small group. Think about the different ways of learning. How do you prefer to learn something – by seeing, hearing, or doing?

> I like learning by seeing. I can remember things better if I can visualize the image in a book or the word on a page.

On THE RUN

Unit 9 Video 9.1

BEFORE YOU WATCH

1 Look at these pictures from the video. Circle the correct answers.

1. This man probably lives _____.
   a. with his family   b. by himself   c. with his friends

2. He probably _____.
   a. works in an office   b. goes to school   c. neither a. or b.

3. He probably has _____.
   a. cheated on a test   b. done something illegal   c. lied to his friend

WHILE YOU WATCH

2 Watch the video. Match the phrases to make true sentences.

1. First, Jamey stole _____   a. cars.
2. Then, he stole _____   b. police.
3. When he was 18, he began stealing _____   c. chickens.
4. Then, he hid from the _____   d. a horse.

3 Watch the video again. Answer the questions.

1. When did Jamey's crimes begin? _____
2. What did his best friend say about Jamey's actions? _____
3. Where did Jamey hide after he stole a car? _____
4. What did his mother tell him to do? _____
5. Where did the police find Jamey? _____
6. Where is Jamey now? _____

AFTER YOU WATCH

4 Complete this chart about Jamey. Then work with a partner. Compare what you wrote. Did you see and hear the same things?

Physical description	
What he thinks / says	
What he does	
What other people say about him	

Insectmobile

Unit 9 Video 9.3

BEFORE YOU WATCH

1 Look at the picture from the video. Answer the questions.

What do you think this object is? What is its function? _____

_____

WHILE YOU WATCH

2 Watch the video. Match the phrases to make true sentences.

1. The scientists get a flat tire and they _____   a. are really stable.

2. To learn more about insects, they _____   b. build a prototype.

3. They learn that insects with six legs _____   c. test the real vehicle.

4. Then, they _____   d. decide that legs may be better than wheels.

5. Finally, they _____   e. go to a university to talk to an expert.

3 Watch the video again. Circle the correct adverbs.

1. The scientists are driving when **finally / suddenly** they get a flat tire.

2. The broken wheel **actually / really** gives them some new ideas.

3. They decide that **clearly / slightly** there's a reason creatures have legs instead of wheels.

4. **Fortunately / Unfortunately**, they find an expert on insects at the university.

5. **Finally / Suddenly**, they build a vehicle and test it.

AFTER YOU WATCH

4 Work with a small group. Discuss: How would you improve an object you use every day, such as your phone or your car?

> Well, I'd make my phone do everything my computer can do. I'd make my car respond to voice commands. I'd also make the seats more comfortable.

Future DIRECTIONS

Unit 10 Video 10.1

BEFORE YOU WATCH

1 Look at these pictures from the video. Answer the questions.

1. What do you think this woman's job might be? _____

2. Like most people in China, she is an only child. How do you think being an only child affects her relationship with her parents? _____

WHILE YOU WATCH

2 Watch the video. Answer the questions.

1. How does Jolene start each day? _____

2. What does Jolene say about herself? _____

3. What are her two jobs? _____

4. What do her parents think of her career? _____

5. What does she sometimes worry about? _____

3 Watch the video again. Match the columns to make phrases from the video.

1. feel _____   a. as an equal

2. have _____   b. a different path in life

3. make _____   c. positive about

4. take _____   d. the guts to

5. treat _____   e. a contribution to

AFTER YOU WATCH

4 Work in a small group. Make a list of at least three jobs that used to be done only by men or only by women, but are now done by both sexes. Why were these jobs done only by men or by women? Discuss your lists.

> Well, soldiers used to be only men because it was a dangerous job. The leaders of many countries have usually been men, but today, it is more common for women to be in positions of power, too.

90 | Unit 10

The Young and the BRAVE

Unit 10 Video 10.3

BEFORE YOU WATCH

1 Look at the pictures from the video. Answer the questions.

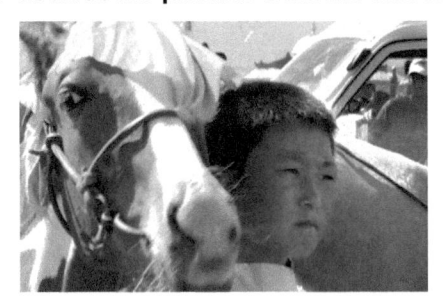

1. What do you think these children are doing and why? _____

2. What reward might they get for doing this? _____

WHILE YOU WATCH

2 Watch the video. Complete the sentences.

1. Inner Mongolia has thousands of kilometers of grasslands and _____.

2. They play the same games today that they played _____ ago.

3. The children had to train for the race for _____.

4. They ride their horses without _____.

5. When their horses get tired, the children _____ to them.

3 Watch the video again. Answer the questions.

1. What abilities are Mongols famous for? _____

2. When do many Mongol children learn how to ride horses? _____

3. How old are the children in the horse race? _____

4. How long is the race? _____

5. Who wins the race? _____

AFTER YOU WATCH

4 Work with a partner. Discuss: Are there certain things that children do better than adults? Why?

> Children are usually better with technology than adults are. I think children can learn things on a computer faster than adults because they're not afraid of technology.

Notes

Notes

Credits

The authors and publishers acknowledge the following sources of copyright material and are grateful for the permissions granted. While every effort has been made, it has not always been possible to identify the sources of all the material used, or to trace all copyright holders. If any omissions are brought to our notice, we will be happy to include the appropriate acknowledgements on reprinting.

p. 5 (BL): Alamy/©Jan Wlodarczyk; p. 7 (CL): Getty Images/Henrik Sorensen; p. 9 (BL): Getty Images/Zoranm; p. 15 (TL): Shutterstock/Testing; p. 16 (TL): Shutterstock/CandyBox Images; p. 17 (CL): Getty Images/M-imagephotography/iStockphoto; p. 18 (A): Getty Images/Hero Images; p. 18 (B): Shuttertstock/Jianghaistudio; p. 18 (C): Shutterstock/Halfpoint; p. 18 (D): Getty Images/Joel Eichler; p. 18 (E): Getty Images/Mark Bowden; p. 18 (F): Alamy/©Hero Images Inc.; p. 18 (G): Shutterstock/William Perugini; p. 18 (H): Shutterstock/Bikeriderlondon; p. 21 (CR): Shutterstock/Sean Locke Photography; p. 22 (1): Shutterstock/Yuriy Rudyy; p. 22 (2): Shutterstock/Photographee.eu; p. 22 (3): Shutterstock/Sergey Ryzhov; p. 22 (4): Shutterstock/Iakov Filimonov; p. 22 (5): Shutterstock/Photographee.eu; p. 22 (6): Shutterstock/ffolas; p. 22 (7): Shutterstock/Africa Studio; p. 22 (8): Getty Images/Ryerson Clark; p. 22 (9): Getty Images/Dennis Hoyne; p. 23 (TR): Shutterstock/Jacek Chabraszewski; p. 27 (CR): Shutterstock/Ulga; p. 30 (CL): Getty Images/PhotoAlto/Frederic Cirou; p. 31 (CL): Shutterstock/Konrad Mostert; p. 35 (C): Getty Images/DreamPictures; p. 36 (1): Shutterstock/Nickolay Khoroshkov; p. 36 (2): Shutterstock/R. MACKAY PHOTOGRAPHY, LLC; p. 36 (3): Shutterstock/Nikita Rogul; p. 36 (4): Getty Images/phanlop888/iStockphoto; p. 36 (5): Shutterstock/Maggee; p. 36 (6): Shutterstock/Africa Studio; p. 36 (7): Shutterstock/Mdblk1984; p. 36 (8): Shutterstock/Olga Kovalenko; p. 36 (9): Shutterstock/Olga Popova; p. 36 (10): Alamy/©Corbis Super; p. 41 (TR): Shutterstock/Igor Lateci; Shutterstock/sunlight77; p. 46 (CL): Shutterstock/PAUL ATKINSON; p. 47 (CR): Alamy/©Renato Granieri; p. 50 (TR): Alamy/©David Parker; p. 62 (CT): Getty Images/Andy Shaw/Bloomberg; p. 63 (CL): Alamy/©Paolo Patrizi; p. 69 (CR): Alamy/©ZUMA Press, Inc.; p. 70 (1): Alamy/©Gabe Palmer; p. 70 (2): Shutterstock/Valeriy Velikov; p. 70 (3): Getty Images/Steve Debenport; p. 70 (4): Shutterstock/Stasique; p. 70 (5): Alamy/©fStop Images GmbH; p. 70 (6): Shutterstock/Rido; p. 70 (7): Shutterstock/scyther5; p. 70 (8): Shutterstock/Andrey_Popov.

Front cover photography by Alamy/©Image Source Plus.

The publishers are grateful to the following illustrators:
Q2A Media Services, Inc.

All video stills by kind permission of Discovery Communications, LLC 2015.